# FAMILY COMMUNICATION

## A Guide to Emotional Health

by
Sven Wahlroos, Ph.D.

**A SIGNET BOOK**
**NEW AMERICAN LIBRARY**
TIMES MIRROR

*To my wife Eva*
*and to our children*
*Ingalill and Sven-Erik*

SIGNET TRADEMARK REG. U.S. PAT. OFF. AND FOREIGN COUNTRIES
REGISTERED TRADEMARK—MARCA REGISTRADA
HECHO EN CHICAGO, U.S.A.

SIGNET, SIGNET CLASSICS, MENTOR, PLUME AND MERIDIAN BOOKS
*are published by The New American Library, Inc.,*
*1301 Avenue of the Americas, New York, New York 10019*

First Signet Printing, July, 1976

1 2 3 4 5 6 7 8 9

PRINTED IN THE UNITED STATES OF AMERICA

# ACKNOWLEDGMENTS

I am grateful to several people for their help in making this book possible. The greatest boost came from my wife Eva who never failed in her support and understanding and who read the manuscript many times. Her remarks and suggestions were highly perceptive and led to many improvements.

My dear friend Dr. Helmut Würsten, Clinical Professor of Psychiatry (Child Psychology) at the University of Southern California and current President of the Los Angeles County Psychological Association, read the manuscript from the point of view of a clinical psychologist and made highly valuable suggestions.

Another long-time friend, Dr. Venustiano Pulido, our children's beloved pediatrician, read the manuscript from a pediatric point of view and provided me with much helpful advice. I am also indebted to him for many years of encouragement and support.

Dr. Rocco Motto, internationally recognized authority in the field of mental health and Director of the Reiss-Davis Child Study Center where I received the most important part of my training, read the manuscript from the point of view of a psychiatrist and psychoanalyst, and I remain profoundly grateful for his assistance. Dr. Edwin Sanford, President of Sanford Management Services, and Martin Strickler, M.S.W., Director of the Department of Social Work at the Los Angeles Psychiatric Services, provided me with both support and helpful suggestions.

I cannot individually name all the friends, colleagues, physicians, teachers, lawyers, and clergymen whose encouragement and suggestions over the years have contributed to the birth of this book, but I wish to assure each one of them of my deep appreciation.

Finally, a heartfelt thanks to all my patients, past and present, whose trust and cooperation have made me feel very fortunate in being a psychologist. And a bouquet of roses to my typists Betty Martin, Antonia Turman, and Dorothy Fialkoff, and to my indexer Roberta Goodwin, for a most conscientious and professional job.

# CONTENTS

# INTRODUCTION

The greatest happiness and the deepest satisfaction in life, the most intense enthusiasm and the most profound inner peace, all come from being a member of a loving family. Creative endeavor and spectacular adventures, pride in one's work and in personal improvement, helping others directly and indirectly, all have their satisfactions and moments of glory, but somehow remain incomplete or substitutelike if they are not combined with the daily secure happiness of harmonious family life. Perhaps only a deep, sincere, nonneurotic commitment to a religious faith can equal or surpass the wonderfulness of belonging to a close and loving family.

But why are there so many families which are disharmonious and in which love is hidden by chronic anger and resentment? Why is it that daily life in countless families means constant bickering and sourness and disappointment? Why is there so often strife and animosity between family members?

Surely it cannot be merely because of the wide prevalence of clinically manifest emotional illness. Even if we assume that ten or fifteen percent of the entire population is in need of professional help for emotional disturbance of one kind or another, this still would not explain why there are so many families in which none of the members can be considered emotionally disturbed in a clinical sense but in which, nevertheless, there is constant arguing and bickering or coldness and lack of affection.

Nor could the answer lie in a prevalence of meanness and hatred among human beings. The vast majority of people are well-meaning toward members of their family, at least, and when they consciously do something destructive it is mostly in anger, a feeling which they see as provoked by the other person! Nor could the reason for family strife be that so many families have abandoned the spiritual values of their forefathers, because the families of their forefathers had their own share of strife and bickering, and the present-day families of clergymen, for example, are not exempt from destructive interactions. Why then this prevalence of family discord and unhappiness?

The question sounds as if it demands a complicated answer, but I believe the answer is quite easily stated. In the vast majority of families troubled by conflict the main reason for the discord is simply that the consciously felt love and the good intentions harbored by the family members are not *communicated* in such a way that they are recognized. For example, a wife who consciously wishes to discuss a problem reasonably with her husband will often find herself "drawn into" a destructive argument and yet she had no desire to argue destructively or to hurt her husband when she brought up the problem for discussion! A father who is determined to have a calm and sensible discussion with his teen-ager about driving privileges may find himself engaged in a verbal battle in which mutual accusations and angry invectives are hurled back and forth, and when he thinks back, he does not really understand what happened to his determination to stay calm. He feels bad because he loves his boy and sincerely did not mean to go overboard like that.

This book provides a set of rules and guidelines intended to help family members put their consciously felt love and their positive conscious intentions into practice in such a manner that the good intentions *will* be recognized by the other members. Following the rules and precepts in the book will enable partners in communication to discuss problems without being "drawn into" a destructive argument. It will prevent nagging, whining, and bickering. It will "clear the emotional air" in the family and provide for sincerity, openness, and loving concern between family members. Thus, I hope this book will contribute significantly toward a satisfying and harmonious family life for the people who read it.

There are, of course, other emotions than love which must be communicated in a constructive rather than a destructive manner. Anger, for example, is an important, unavoidable, and not necessarily negative emotion; this book will show how anger can be communicated with constructive rather than destructive effects. In its scope, the book is sufficiently encompassing—and yet at the same time sufficiently specific—to serve as a test of whether or not professional help for existing intrafamily problems is needed: if following the rules given in this book leads to satisfying family living within a reasonable time, then the probability is that no psychotherapeutic intervention is needed. If family relationships are not improved through applying the rules and principles in this book, the likelihood is that significant psychopathology exists and professional help should be sought.

In my two decades of practice as a clinical psychologist I have become convinced that the key to improvement of family relationships—and thereby to emotional health in general—lies in *communication*. In the vast majority of families each member is filled with good intentions. No one consciously wants to argue in the destructive sense of the word; no one wants to nag or whine or to irritate another person; no one—with the rare exception of a sadist—wants to be mean or cruel or unfair. Yet the *effect* of much well-intentioned behavior is arguing or nagging or meanness or unfairness. An honest person will admit to the destructive effects of such behavior, but will add that he or she felt forced to it by the unreasonableness of the *other* person's behavior! The reason for these difficulties can only be that the consciously felt love and the good intentions were not communicated in such a way as to be perceived by the partner.

Psychology books have stressed the importance of love for more than half a century now. Has this helped family life? Certainly not to any observable extent. But why not? The reason is that most people do not need to be told the importance of love; they already have a conscious wish to show love toward their family members. It is just that unconscious factors as well as poor communication techniques interfere with their ability to do so. The existence of unconscious factors which influence behavior has been known since the beginning of the century. Sigmund Freud, in his *The Psychopathology of Everyday Life* (1901), showed the influence of unconscious factors on daily human behavior most vividly, but he gave no rules or precepts for counteracting the destructive interference of such factors in daily life. Thus, although his discoveries were important for the development of psychoanalysis and psychotherapy, relationships within families have not been improved significantly by these discoveries.

The fact is that consciously felt love must be communicated in such a way that it is *perceived* as love, and the rules for such communication have not heretofore been delineated specifically with examples taken from everyday life. It is also a fact that unconscious factors interfere with such communication in both the "sender" and the "receiver," and the role of these factors has not been specifically delineated either. This book will attempt to accomplish such delineation and thus give the family a set of guidelines to follow for improving the relationships between the members.

In this sense, I would like to see my book as a "psychopathology of everyday communication," a practical and useful description of what it is that interferes with the communication between one person and another, together with specific suggestions and rules concerning how to counteract such interference. Consider the following complaints which can be considered typical of the ones I hear every day in my office:

> "Communication is poor in our family." "My wife does not understand me." "My husband won't talk to me." "I can't get through to my teen-ager." "My daughter doesn't confide in me." "I can't stand this nagging and bickering and whining any longer." "I don't want to start an argument, so I don't say anything." "My parents are constantly hassling me and preaching to me."

In millions of families daily life is made unpleasant and frustrating by the destructive interactions which produce such complaints. Upon examination, these destructive interactions usually turn out to be the result of breaking certain rules of communication which, if followed, would make the destructive interactions almost impossible. The price paid for the breach of these rules is often terrible. As a matter of fact, most divorces and most cases of teen-agers running away from their homes, as well as many suicides and much of general psychopathology can be traced to poor communication.

There are other millions of families whose members "get along" on the surface, but only by avoiding open and sincere statements of feeling. The members of these families, because of such avoidance, can never really know each other and are thus unable to experience the wonderful sense of intimacy and "communion" which comes from open, sincere, and constructive communication. Even in many seemingly well-functioning families there are frequent—and needless—misunderstandings and hurts which interfere with the enjoyment and satisfaction of family life.

This book, then, is intended as a practical guide to help family members develop better communication and thus improve their own emotional health. Making a sincere attempt to follow its rules and principles will help a person significantly with his communication problems unless he is emotionally disturbed to a degree requiring psychotherapeutic intervention. If two or more partners in communication read the book and are sincere about applying its recommendations, the improvement is likely to be even more significant, again provided their relationship is not based on the gratification of destructive needs, in which case the parties concerned need to seek professional help.

I have found the principles laid down in this book of immense help in working with my patients. Especially if both spouses in a marriage will follow the rules of communication given in Part I and work toward the goals given in Part II, improvement in family relations is spectacular. It is, of course, impossible to cover *all* specific situations in any one book, so the members of a particular family may find it necessary to devise certain subrules of their own to fit their particular communication problem. However, the rules given are designed to be both general in scope and yet specifically applicable to everyday situations. The examples given cover most of the areas of communication which tend to give people difficulties in "getting through" to each other.

The emphasis in this book is on common sense, on practical everyday examples of communication, and on workable suggestions. The clinical examples are taken from my practice, which is primarily concerned with helping families and individuals with problems that are partly or wholly self-created (although the self-created aspect of the problem is often not apparent to the individual or family seeking help). The suggestions and rules incorporated in this book have been tried on a systematic basis for many years and are likely to be highly effective, provided there is at least a certain minimum of conscious motivation to try them out for an extended period of time and provided there is no significant psychopathology present.

The reader will find that frequent attention is paid in this book to how a person's self-concept influences and is influenced by communication. This is because of the extreme importance of the self-concept in guiding a person's actions. How a human being views himself will determine most of his actions and choices in life. Essentially he is going to choose what he feels he is worth. This holds true of his choice in friends, spouse, and career, as well as of less important choices. But what determines how he will view himself? How is his self-concept formed? The answer is: his self-concept is based largely on how he was treated by the significant people early in his life (mainly his parents). In other words, the parents' view of the child *as communicated through their actions in daily living* is the chief determinant of the child's self-concept.

There are limitations to what we as parents can do to help our children. But there are certain things we can do no matter what the external limitations may be. We can show our children that each one of them is a unique human being with essential worth as an individual and with a combination of qualities totally unlike that of any other person. We can help him develop the inner security of feeling loved which constitutes the foundation for his later ability to feel compassion and love for his fellow man. And, thirdly, we can see to it that his self-concept is positive, that he feels glad he is alive, glad that he is he. The outcome of our endeavors, however, depends on the quality of our daily communication in word and deed *as perceived by the child,* and in the improvement of this quality lies one of the contributions I hope this book will make.

Some topics which one might expect in a book on communication I have left out. Formal aspects, for example, seem to me to belong to a different type of book. There are excellent works on general semantics which deal with such formal aspects of communication, but I doubt that they will be of value in preventing an argument about why the dripping faucet has not yet been fixed or who is going to use the car next Friday night. Similarly, I have given no space to fitting the principles discussed into any old or new theoretical framework, or to constructing any conceptual models. Such attempts will not aid a mother in stopping the nagging of her son or a husband in showing more consideration in his behavior toward his wife. In other words, my intention in writing this book is simply to fill what I see as an urgent need for a common-sense guide to better communication in the family, not to write a treatise on communication in general.

In writing this book, I am also performing what I consider to be my duty as a human being and as a psychologist. During my twenty years of practice as a clinical psychologist I have seen my profession develop in directions which to me indicate irresponsibility, wantonness, and a proclivity toward sensationalism. An increasing number of workers in the mental health field are engaged in practices which attempt to "cure" emotional problems by such esoteric means as nude "encounters" in a swimming pool or contemplating the beauty of a flower or letting out a "primal scream"! Others delight in taking over the functions of the clergy and telling people what is right and what is wrong in a moral sense. Still others tell people how to vote on political issues and use clinical terminology ("paranoid," "psychopath") to lash out at politicians whose views they do not like.

An emotionally healthy individual with common sense instinctively perceives the silliness—and sometimes the outright danger—of such approaches and stays away from them. But an emotionally disturbed individual may be attracted to them, as he would be to anything which promises a magic cure or tells him, with an aura of authority, what choices to make in life. Thus, I feel it is the duty of those psychologists who are not drawn into these fads and who refuse to "play God" with people's lives, to call for a return to common sense, at the same time combining common sense with sound and well-established psychological principles.

Of course, there have always been fads in the field of psychology, as there have been in other sciences. Sigmund Freud's *The Interpretation of Dreams* and *The Psychopathology of Everyday Life* started a fad which lasted for more than half a century. But although these books were highly important for the development of psychoanalysis and psychotherapy, they never purported to help anyone directly with his everyday problems. The "helping quality" of these books was indirect and available only to patients in psychoanalysis. Moreover, psychoanalysis initially focussed its attention on inner conflicts and paid attention to neurotic interactions between individuals only to the extent that those interactions led to internalized conflicts. Thus psychoanalytic books did not offer much in the way of advice concerning how people should behave toward each other, and when such advice was offered or implied (as in the case of parent-child interactions) it was based either on scientifically demonstrable facts or on reasonable assumptions. Psychoanalytic books —even though they created a fad—were therefore in no way dangerous. True, a few individuals may have used psychoanalytic principles destructively by "mind-reading" their family members and friends, but on the whole the "Freudian fad" remained a parlor game more than anything else. As far as the therapeutic application of psychoanalytic principles, it was usually helpful to the patient. Even when psychoanalytic treatment failed, it was still in itself harmless and seldom dangerous, unless engaged in by untrained therapists.

A book which purports to help people directly must be based on common sense; otherwise it may become dangerous. If it is not based on common sense and creates a fad, it can exert a destructive influence on a great number of people. Today's fads in psychology are dangerous exactly because they combine a lack of common sense with being applicable to daily living. The irresponsible and extravagant claims made in books propagating current fads entice untold numbers of readers, desperate for help, to try out the authors' recommendations either in daily life or by seeking help from a professional who is an adherent of the particular approach advocated. Every month in my office I see casualties from the daily application of these approaches, as well as from "therapeutic" applications, ranging from victims of nude swimming pool "encounter therapy" to those who have responded to the extravagant claims made by fanatic believers in the latest fad.

One of the most widespread and at the same time one of the most destructive of all fads was "permissive education," from the bitter fruits of which we are still suffering today even if its die-hard adherents may attempt to disguise these fruits under the transparent cover of "youthful idealism." The destructiveness of an increasing minority of today's youth actually has nothing to do with idealism; it is a manifestation of their not having been taught controls in a reasonable and firm manner which would have communicated love and concern on the part of the parents rather than hunger for power. There are similarly dangerous fads springing up today under such euphemisms as "living in the here and now" (why should a person limit his life to only one dimension?), "groupmindedness," "social conscience," "encounter groups," occultism, astrology, and so on. If they are not counteracted by something enlightened and levelheaded, they could throw mankind into another Dark Age.

In writing this book I wish to contribute to a counterbalance against these fads. My book is essentially an appeal to common sense and reason—not sterile and limited reason which rests on game-rules such as logic, but reason in depth which takes into account the importance of feelings and attitudes as well as the likelihood of practical consequences.

I am well aware of the limitations of self-help. The efforts of a person to overcome psychological problems through reading tend to be successful only if he is relatively nondefensive and willing to look objectively at his own limitations and possible unconscious motivations. Highly defensive individuals ("innocent victims"), those suffering from compulsions and seemingly uncontrollable impulses, as well as persons suffering from other forms of psychopathology will need to combine reading this book with seeking professional psychological help.

In my practice as a psychologist I have always felt the need for a book which I could recommend to my patients and which could at the same time be used for preventive mental health purposes by the general public. But most of the books I see published in the field of psychology are either too general to contain specific information which can be used in everyday life or they are very specific and thus either too limited in scope or too technical. As a consequence of the irresponsible trend I referred to above, many books in the field of psychology and mental health seem to be published merely in order to create a sensation, with a total disregard for common sense. There is a clearly recognizable pattern to the publication of such books. It starts with a psychologist or psychiatrist or a journalist taking an old idea and giving it a new spectacular or catchy name. Or he may come up with a truly new but "weird" or outlandish idea instead. He then constructs a theory "around" this idea and describes a "therapy" based on it. He proceeds to write a book in which he claims that his approach is the solution to all human problems from nail-biting to international conflicts. At the same time, he attacks all other forms of psychotherapy (especially poor old Freud seems to be the whipping boy these days). Because of its sensationalistic approach, the book makes the best-seller list and is then followed by another book by someone else, touting a different sensational idea and a new therapy.

I hope I have avoided sensationalism in this book and that I have not made any extravagant claims. I have written it not to describe any cure-all or even any innovation, but rather as an attempt to combine common sense with what is best and most workable and practical in modern psychological practice. It is written for the purpose of aiding in the effort to prevent psychological disturbance and thus enhance emotional health and specifically for the purpose of helping families or individuals who find themselves involved in communication problems.

Thus, I have tried to approach problems from the point of view of what the individual and the family can reasonably *do* about them rather than from the point of view of any specific psychological theory or school. The rules and techniques suggested and the recommendations given follow from good sense and from experience based on clinical practice; they are not derived from any specific psychological theory. As a matter of fact, I am convinced that the main reason these rules and suggestions are so successful is that practically everyone to whom they are recommended recognizes them as making good sense.

An important purpose of this book is to help people with the often agonizing decision, "Shall I or shall I not seek professional help?" As a general rule we could say that if attempts to put the rules given in this book into effect do not help significantly in solving the problems in a family, then professional help is indicated. Throughout the book, however, I have made frequent reference to specific conditions when it is necessary to seek psychotherapeutic help. In making these references I have no particular "school" or "system" in mind; on the contrary, I feel it is best to go to a therapist who will tailor-make his treatment to the patient and not attempt to fit the patient into his own theoretical framework. Although my own orientation as a psychotherapist leans toward psychoanalytically-oriented psychotherapy, I would see myself as failing in my duty to the patient if I attempted to force him into such a therapeutic approach when another approach might work better in his case.

The recommendations to seek therapeutic help are not to be taken as an attempt on my part to describe psychotherapy as a panacea. There are times when psychotherapy fails or when the gains are disappointingly minor. The fact is, however, that if a patient gives reasonable cooperation in his treatment and his therapist uses tried and common-sense therapeutic approaches, specifically designed for the particular patient, the chances for significant improvement are good.

My hope is that this book will be recommended widely by physicians, psychologists, and teachers to families with young children because I feel that early identification and treatment of psychological problems is the main answer to the problem of emotional health. I also hope it will be recommended by clergymen to young people getting married and by lawyers to those seeking divorce. I have tried to make this book a practical and useful guide for dealing with specific problems concerning emotional health which occur in everyday life, and I hope my work will benefit as many people as possible.

In summary, this book is an attempt to help people *communicate* the love they feel, so that it will be perceived as love by the other person. It is an attempt to have the good conscious intentions which people fortunately possess to a high degree communicated *in action* and in such a manner that the effect will be as good as the intention itself. It has been said that the road to Hell is paved with the stones of good intentions. I hope that this book will enable people to use the same stones to construct a road to Heaven, if not on earth in general, then at least in their families.

# PART 1

---

# Rules of Communication

Communication is perhaps the most important of all topics in psychology. It is largely through communication that we become what we are; it is through communication that we learn what we know; it is largely through destructive communication that problems in human relationships are created, and it is through constructive communication that such problems are prevented or solved.

In this book we are going to concentrate on the last aspect: on how to prevent and solve problems in interpersonal relationships. We are going to show how people—usually without consciously meaning to—create problems through the use of destructive communication, and we are going to show how such problems can be prevented or solved by following a number of simple rules of communication.

As I mentioned in the introduction, we shall not deal with semantics in the strict sense of the term. We are going to deal with understanding communicative messages and with misunderstandings, but not with the type provided by the following example:

In the classified ad section of a small-town newspaper the following ad appeared on Monday:

FOR SALE: R. D. Jones has one sewing machine for sale. Phone 958 after 7 P.M. and ask for Mrs. Kelly who lives with him cheap.

On Tuesday—NOTICE: We regret having erred in R. D. Jones' ad yesterday. It should have read: One sewing machine for sale. Cheap. Phone 958 and ask for Mrs. Kelly who lives with him after 7 P.M.

On Wednesday—R. D. Jones has informed us that he has received several annoying telephone calls because of the error we made in his classified ad yesterday. His ad stands corrected as follows: FOR SALE: R. D. Jones has one sewing machine for sale. Cheap. Phone 958 after 7 P.M. and ask for Mrs. Kelly who loves with him.

3

Finally on Thursday—NOTICE: I, R. D. Jones, have no sewing machine for sale. I smashed it. Don't call 958 as the telephone has been taken out. I have not been carrying on with Mrs. Kelly. Until yesterday she was my housekeeper, but she quit.

Such misunderstandings are beyond the scope of this book, even though we do deal with inadvertent communicative messages and distortions of messages by the perceiver. The inadvertent messages and distorted perceptions we will analyze are of a different nature: they stem from unconscious destructive forces which reside in all of us and gain expression in our communication with others, usually without our consciously intending for that to happen.

Let us start by defining what we mean by *communication*. Some people think that communication refers only to talking and discussion or writing. Talking and discussion and writing are, indeed, important aspects of communication, but for the purpose of this book we will need a much broader definition. We will have to define communication as *any behavior that carries a message which is perceived by someone else.* The behavior can be verbal or nonverbal; it is still communication as long as it carries a message. The message may be intended or unintended, but if it is perceived it has, in fact, been communicated. The perception of the message may be conscious or unconscious, distorted or undistorted, but as soon as the message gets through on any level, we have communication.

Let us give some examples which should make the definition clear.

If you are walking alone in the forest and start whistling, there is no communication, unless you want to say that you are communicating with yourself. However, if somebody happens to be in the forest and hears you whistle, then there may or may not be communication involved: it depends on whether or not that other person consciously or unconsciously reads a message into your whistling. If he does read a meaning into it, there is communication. *Whether you are aware of it or not,* you have then communicated something like "I am here" or "I am happy" or "I can't carry a tune." In other words, you can communicate with another person without knowing that you have communicated anything! This is an important point to remember.

Now suppose you are at home with your wife and you are

whistling. In that situation again the whistling may or may not constitute communication; it depends on whether your wife perceives some meaning in it. The meaning may be "I feel happy" and if your wife perceives it this way, everything may be all right. (On the other hand, if you communicate "I am happy" right after giving her a bad time, the consequences may be disastrous!)

However, it may also be that your wife has told you in the past that she can't stand your whistling, that it "drives-her up the walls." In that case, *whether you know it or not,* the whistling may mean: "At this moment I don't give a hoot about what you like or don't like; I will do as I please!"

Some people think of communication only in the sense of good or pleasant or constructive communication. According to such a definition, if the husband whistles and the wife shows her anger by slamming the refrigerator door, the couple is not communicating at all. Using the definition of communication in this book, however, we would say that both husband and wife are communicating something destructive, albeit in an underhanded manner. The wife may slam the refrigerator door to communicate "I am mad at you but I am afraid to say anything because it will start an argument" and the husband may whistle to reply to her, "See if I care!"

Effective communication is not the same as good and constructive communication. The slamming of the refrigerator may communicate anger very effectively, but it is not constructive, problem-solving communication.

Communication, then, can be positive and constructive, but it can also be negative and destructive. And—unfortunately—*it can be consciously intended as positive while it is perceived as being negative.* Let us suppose, for example, that a man (the communicator) has said something which his wife (the perceiver) has taken to be hostile in nature, even though it was not consciously intended as such. We must take as a working principle that if the perceiver (the wife in this case) has lived with the communicator for some time, he (she) has become somewhat of an expert on the communicator and his behavior and therefore his (her) perception of the message as being negative is probably quite realistic (provided the perceiver is not psychotic). On the basis of the wife's (expert perceiver's) testimony, then, we can be reasonably sure that the husband's message was unconsciously intended to be negative even though the conscious intention was entirely positive. The degree of unconscious hostile intent we judge to have been present would, of course, be influenced by the wife's tendency to exaggerate or minimize, her special sensitivities, her tendency to find fault, etc.

If the wife of the whistling husband in our earlier example had in the past repeatedly pointed out to him that his whistling irritated her, we can be sure that he unconsciously knew what he was doing and either wanted—for neurotic reasons—to bother her or to show his power ("there is nothing you can do about it") or simply to deny the importance of her and of her wishes. These are, however, unconscious motivations and the husband cannot, or should not, be blamed for them. He certainly does not consciously say to himself: "Now I am going to irritate my wife by whistling"; this he would do only if he were a sadist and true sadists are actually not very numerous. What happens is that he does not give any conscious thought to her being irritated at all. He may become conscious of it when she slams the refrigerator door and may then stop. If he continues, however, it will be because of some rationalization or excuse, such as: "She is not my boss; I won't let her henpeck me like that," or "She must be premenstrual," or "I am not whistling that loud anyway; she is just being unreasonable." The husband, then, is likely to feel self-righteous: "How can my wife be so unreasonable and picky as to object to such a little thing as whistling? Especially when I didn't mean anything bad by doing it!"

The wife will likewise feel self-righteous and offended because she reasons like this: "I slave in this house from morning to night and do my best to take care of everybody, but nobody is concerned with what I like or don't like. I ask for so little, but even the smallest thing I ask for, such as my husband's stopping his horrible whistling, is denied! How unreasonable can a person be?"

So, both people in the conflict can feel self-righteous and indignant and offended by the other one. This is an example of negative and destructive communication (especially as it is used in destructive games; see Rule 20, below). On the following pages we will give a series of simple rules which must be followed if communication is to be constructive rather than problem-creating. The rules of communication are not arranged in order of importance for the simple reason that any one of the rules could be considered most important. They could, with equal usefulness, be arranged in any order. In my work with a patient, for example, I will often start with the rule which he is most likely to recognize himself as breaking. There is also considerable overlapping from one rule to another, and that is the way it should be. After all, these rules are merely different ways of stating what constitutes positive and constructive communication in the family.

In order to benefit from these rules you must be willing to apply them to *yourself*, rather than merely use them to point out your partner's deficiencies in communication. Under no circumstance should you use the rules to hit your partner over the head: "This is what I have been trying to tell you for years" or "You never believed me when I told you how harmful your conduct was; now will you believe it when you see it in print?" If you are a parent who is rigidly dependent on rules, you will have to be careful not to misuse the rules by constantly stressing them to your children. Use the rules in a spirit of calmness and tolerance and remember that example is the best teacher.

Some of the everyday illustrations given (such as "whistling" vs. "slamming refrigerator door") may seem like trivia. Make no mistake: the ruining of a relationship usually comes from seemingly minor everyday displays of inconsideration, hostility, and contempt, etc., not from major betrayals and disasters. Similarly, a good relationship is based on daily evidence of caring, concern, and openness, combined with tactfulness, rather than on ostentatious generosity and showers of attention.

A sincere conscious wish to improve your communication is a prerequisite, then, for benefiting from the rules that follow. If the sincere wish and determination are there and you slip once in a while and break some of the rules, don't worry: no one is perfect and we all break some of the rules occasionally. Just don't use the fact that no one is perfect as an excuse for frequent slipping!

# 1. "YOU ARE MAKING ME CONFUSED!"

*Rule 1: Remember that actions speak louder than words; nonverbal communication is more powerful than verbal communication.*

When a person's actions communicate the same message as his words there is no problem (unless the message is deliberately destructive). But when the messages are contradictory the result is almost always a multitude of problems. Such problems are difficult to solve when the family members are not used to seeing behavior as communicative. On the other hand, if the family members are made aware of the powerful meaning and impact of communication-through-behavior, then the contradictory messages can be pointed out, discussed, and resolved.

How is this done, specifically? Let us go through several examples to show how contradictory communication can be handled in daily life.

> A child's parents keep telling him to put away his toys after playing with them, yet he sees his father leaving parts of the newspaper scattered all over the living room.

In this example, the father must be made aware—perhaps by his wife (Rule Number 8 states that all family members are experts on each other and on each other's behavior) —that by leaving newspapers around he is *teaching his child to be messy!* He is saying—without being aware of it—"This is the way to behave as an adult, as a mature person. It is a good idea (or at least: "It is OK . . .") to be messy." A very small child may not be consciously aware of the contradiction involved but is likely to imitate the action rather than follow verbal admonitions. Soon, however, a child becomes aware of this double standard and—whether he verbalizes it or not—he will then feel that his parents are unfair and hypocritical.

There are a multitude of negative behaviors which parents* teach their children through example: impatience, rudeness, nagging (usually called "whining" when the child does it), excuses, etc. When the child has learned these behaviors, the parents often see the child as being "bad" rather than as being quick to learn. It should follow from this that the parents must help each other become aware of communicating contradictory messages to the child and see to it that the child is being taught the same lesson in action as he is taught in words.

> Johnny says that he is old enough to stay up later at night and that he does not need so much sleep. However, it is almost impossible to get him up in the morning in time to go to school.

In this example, many parents would say: "No, Johnny, you are tired and you need your sleep; you can't stay up later." This is usually futile because Johnny does not feel tired and he thinks he is a better expert than you on the question of whether he is tired or not and on how much sleep he needs. And certainly some children do need less sleep than their parents think. So when you say that you know better than he whether he is tired and needs more sleep, he will see you as an unreasonable adult who either likes to show his power and push little kids around 'or wants to get his child out of the way, or perhaps both. His indignant resistance may lead to your nagging him every evening. It may lead to a lot of unpleasantness, fighting, and unhappiness.

However, if you recognize that you are being given contradictory messages and point this out, the child cannot feel that you are being unreasonable. He may still *claim* that you are not fair, but secretly he will know that your point is well taken. What you can say to him, then, is something like this:

---

*Parents are, of course, not the only source of such undesirable learning. Other adults, older siblings, and playmates share in the responsibility. However, since the teaching done by parents is more powerful in its effects, it behooves them to see to it that they teach desirable behavior through example and not merely through words.

"Johnny, you make me confused! In the evening you tell me that you need less sleep, but *in the morning you tell me that you need more sleep.* Please make up your mind about what you really want and then we will discuss it again. If for two weeks you tell me both in the evening *and in the morning* that you need less sleep, then we will let you stay up half an hour longer." Johnny may well object to this arrangement and give you some "static" about it, but secretly he will know that it is fair and reasonable. Thus, you can listen to his objections to be sure that you have taken his ideas and feelings into account, but if he cannot come up with a reasonable point in favor of his position, you must be firm and insist on being given the same message in the morning as in the evening.

The general behavior of a teen-ager, glassy stares and incoherent speech, suspicious fragments of phone conversations ("Boy, I really freaked out last time," "I'd like to get some more of you-know-what"), and strange drawings on the writing pad, make his parents fear that he is involved with drugs. Yet when they question him concerning his activities and friends, he accuses them of being snoopy and paranoid, insisting that everything is all right and they have nothing to worry about.

Here the teen-ager must be asked why he is saying two opposite things. On the one hand, he says: "Don't worry, everything is all right, I'm not doing anything wrong." But through his behavior on the telephone, through the doodles he leaves around, and through the way he looks and behaves when he comes in at night, he is saying: "Please worry about me; there is something shady going on; I might be involved with drugs."

Obviously this is a problem which *must* be discussed and you, the parent, must not be deterred by your teen-ager's protestations and denials. If he says that you are just imagining the glassy stares, for example, you ask him if he feels he knows you well enough to say that you worry too much. He will say yes, that's what he has been saying all along. You can then point out to him that you have the same expertise: you know him well, too, and you know that he is not his usual self when he comes in at night. Then you tell him that you will stop your worrying, suspiciousness, and snooping *as soon as he asks you to stop* through his behavior. Further protective-preventive action may also be necessary when involvement with drugs is suspected.

If your teen-ager denies that you possess the ability to see differences in him, you must ask him for evidence. It is possible that he can furnish such evidence. You may be a chronic worrier; you may habitually make mountains out of molehills or jump to conclusions; you may be insensitive to his needs and his feelings. If he points out such liabilities to you, you must listen nondefensively and agree to examine your behavior and try to understand him and yourself better. However, you must also make clear to him that virtually all parents nowadays are worried about their children becoming involved with drugs and that you are no exception, especially since many studies have shown that this worry is realistic. Then you go on to tell him that you will stop worrying as soon as he asks you to stop through a change in his behavior.

> A child wants a new toy and keeps nagging his parents to buy it for him. However, he keeps his room messy and does not put away the toys he has.

By now it should be clear how to handle this type of situation. First you examine whether contradictory communication is involved. If it is, then you point it out and ask the other person to make up his mind and to give you messages that are not contradictory. If contradictory messages are not involved, you discuss the problem thoroughly with the other person, making sure that you listen and ask questions (Rule 19) and that you take his feelings and opinions and ideas into account (Rule 13); then you make your decision and state the reasons for the decision to the other person (Rule 4), taking care not to use excuses (Rule 16).

In the example above (where contradictory messages are clearly involved), you can say something like: "Son, I want to listen to you, but you make me confused; I don't know what I should listen to. You are telling me *in words* that you don't have enough toys, that you need one more. But in actions, *in what you do,* you are telling me that you have too many toys, that you can't handle what you have now and can't put it where it belongs. Now, when you have told me *by what you do* that you can handle more toys, then we will discuss the matter again."

It is very important to teach a child through such everyday examples that all people communicate not only by what they say but also, and especially, by what they do or do not do. Always stress that actions speak louder than words, that nonverbal communication is more powerful than verbal communication. But remember that you must live up to that rule yourself and set a good example for your child in noncontradictory communication.

Children communicate all kinds of important messages to their parents through their behavior rather than through words. For example, it would be an extremely rare child who would verbally tell his parents: "I would like you to help me control what I do, because I cannot yet control myself." But the child will unconsciously tell his parents about his need for more (or sometimes less) control *through his actions*. Sometimes the need is even conscious! More than once I have had the experience of a teen-ager telling me in my offfice how he (she) envies a friend who has strict but reasonable parents who make it clear what he (she) can and cannot do. But even when the need for stricter control is conscious it is not expressed verbally to the parent; rather, it is expressed through actions which ask the parent to impose tighter control.

> A wife says that she tries to do everything to please her husband, yet she will not fix him his favorite dessert, no matter how often he asks for it.

In this case, if the husband keeps feeling irritated or resentful because his wife will not make his favorite dessert, he must bring the issue up with his wife and contrast her behavior with her words. Unfortunately, many people will not do this because they are afraid of seeming picky or nagging or they are afraid of starting an argument. But in this case, if the husband feels significant resentment, *not* bringing up the issue for serious discussion would in itself be a way of being destructive (Rule 10), because the resentment is then allowed to build up over the weeks and months and may cause the husband—consciously or unconsciously—to "get back" at his wife either by doing something that she does not like or by refusing to do something that she especially likes, leading to the creation of a vicious circle, since the wife, as a consequence, will feel even less like doing something nice for her husband.

Thus, if the husband feels strongly about the issue, he must bring it up for discussion and ask his wife for a specific reason why she does not make his favorite dessert. If she accuses him of picking or nagging or starting an argument, he must ask her—in a friendly manner, without provocative challenge, defiance, or sarcasm—to show him *how* he could bring up the subject without irritating her. If she gives him a vague commitment ("I'll do it when I have the time" or "I'll do it when I get around to it"), he must request a specific commitment, asking her to apply Rule 4 (be clear and specific) if she protests.

The husband must also ask his wife if there is something he is doing or neglecting to do that makes her feel resentful toward him. If so, he will need to correct his behavior accordingly. But in his response to his wife he must beware of playing games (Rule 20), as he would be if he, for example, were to say: "I will do it (or "I'll stop doing it") as soon as you have made the dessert."

> A husband says that nothing is the matter, but through his nonverbal behavior (long face, pouting, sighing with eyes directed upward, shoulder shrugs, etc.) he indicates that he is terribly displeased.

The example above is actually illustrative of a type of crazy-making (see Unfair Technique 11-XI). The husband is transmitting two contradictory statements concerning reality, thus implying that his wife cannot trust her senses! The wife in this example must insist on responding to the language of the body (the behavior) rather than to the words, and demand that her husband verbalize his displeasure.

Failure to accept and apply the principle that behavior speaks louder than words is the cause of much interpersonal strife and conflict. It is, without a doubt, one of the main causes of divorce, for example. If the words of the spouses concerned say "I love you" but their deeds say "I don't give a hoot about your feelings and wishes," then their marriage is in serious trouble no matter how minor the act or omission may seem that carries the latter message. Obvious marital problems (adultery, physical fighting, sexual problems, disagreements over finances, in-law trouble, etc.) are either more spectacular examples of Rule 1 or expressions of selfishness, inconsideration, and disrespect.

Recent divorce laws have taken this into account in dispensing with the need for having a spectacular cause and a villain who has flagrantly abused the victim. "Incompatibility" and "mental cruelty" are now accepted as sufficient causes. These are, however, misleading terms. Very few people are consciously cruel and very few couples can be considered incompatible if they are willing to work on improving their marriage. What happens in most of the marriages that break up is that the spouses engage—unwittingly—in daily acts of commission or omission which in themselves seem very minor but which carry the powerful, rejecting message: "Your feelings and wishes are not important to me." Such daily, seemingly minor, rejecting actions or inactions actually amount to a type of Chinese water-drop torture. The acts or "drops" which comprise the torture may seen ridiculously minor to outsiders and often even to the participants themselves, but they are highly effective in destroying a relationship.

Suppose, for example, that a wife has asked her husband over and over to clean the washbowl after he shaves. He, however, forgets to do so almost every morning. This, in *effect*, carries the message: "Your wishes are not important to me," and the message is infinitely stronger than the words "I want to make you happy, darling." But most people, unfortunately, do not attach enough importance to the *effect* of their communication (Rule 12); instead, they stare themselves blind at their conscious intention. Accordingly, the husband will feel that his wife is picky and unreasonable if she keeps mentioning such a "minor matter." The wife, similarly, may stop mentioning it, since she does not want to appear a nagging wife. But she still gets the message and her resentment grows, causing her—often unwittingly—to retaliate by not doing things the way her husband would like to see them done, thus communicating to him, in return: "Your wishes are not important to me either."

There are often a multitude of such communications, usually in the form of some type of inconsideration: the cap is not put back on the toothpaste tube, the milk is not put into the refrigerator, the husband does not call when he is going to be late or does not say good-bye when he leaves in the morning, the wife does not pick up yesterday's potato chip that has fallen on the floor or does not have a clean shirt ready or keeps forgetting to sew on a button. All of these actions can communicate: "I will not give your wishes an important place in my thoughts." They do not *necessarily* communicate such a message, however; it all depends on what the partner reads into the message. If he reads a serious message into it he must speak up and insist that the behavior be changed so that the nonverbal message becomes the same as the verbal one.

When problems develop in a relationship, they can often be dealt with simply by analyzing the communication, verbal and nonverbal, transmitted from one partner to the other. Only when such analysis fails to produce a good relationship is individual psychotherapy with each partner clearly indicated. The method I follow is simple and I will give no name to it, nor will I claim that its use always works wonders; there are already too many "therapies" in the field presenting themselves as panaceas. The method usually does work well, however. It is simply a derivative of common sense and involves the following three steps:

1. The therapist confronts the partners in the relationship with the messages each is unwittingly transmitting to the other. Sometimes this is enough for significant and lasting improvement, especially with well motivated patients.
2. The therapist teaches the partners in the relationship constructive communication rules and techniques, such as the ones described in this book, for improving communication. There are many cases in my experience in which significant and lasting improvements have resulted from this step alone, making it unnecessary to go into a more analytic or uncovering therapy.
3. If confrontation and didactic measures fail to bring about the desired degree of improvement, an analysis of deeper and more unconscious motivation must be undertaken.

Sometimes it is enough merely to point out the contrast between the verbal and the nonverbal messages. This is easy to do when the contrast is obvious, such as when a wife says to her husband that she is not flirting with other men even though everyone observing her can see that she is. When the contradictory behavior is more subtle, however, confronting the person with the contrast becomes more difficult, as shown in the following example taken from my practice.

Ever since their courtship Larry and Brenda* had used subtle means of provoking each other. Now, after only six months of marriage Larry had become "insanely jealous," as Brenda put it. Invariably, after an evening out with friends, Larry would accuse Brenda of being interested in other men, Brenda would deny the accusation, and violent arguments would ensue.

What was Larry's "evidence"? "She treats other men nicer than me when we are out somewhere, she smiles at them but not at me, and she talks to them all the time and hardly says a word to me. She sits with her back half-turned against me and behaves as if she were not even in my company. And how do you explain this: every time we go out with another couple to a restaurant and sit down in a horseshoe booth, she puts her purse between herself and me, never between herself and the other man!" Larry added that he felt Brenda was "by nature" cold and rejecting.

Most husbands would probably not even notice where their wives put their purses in a restaurant. But Larry was quite insecure and hyper-alert to any sign of rejection. Brenda therefore felt that it was he who should be in psychotherapy, not she. What she did not realize consciously (unconsciously she must have) and what I therefore had to point out to her was that her action communicated to Larry: "I am putting a wall between you and me."

In the course of my seeing Larry and Brenda it turned out —as it usually does—that there was no culprit and no victim in this situation: *both* used subtle means to provoke each other. Brenda did indeed do what Larry had accused her of (she noticed that she did have an almost irresistible compulsion to put her purse between herself and Larry!), but Larry had his own repertoire of subtly destructive behavior: he tended to ignore what his wife said to him and when he did reply it was often with some sarcastic remark. He did not consciously realize that this communicated to Brenda: "Don't talk to me or include me in any way, because I will make it very unpleasant for you if you do!" He was quite startled when I "translated" his behavior in this way, but he saw the point.

In Larry's and Brenda's case it was sufficient to confront them with the messages they were unwittingly communicating through their behavior. Larry readily admitted to the destructiveness of his sarcasm and his ignoring Brenda's remarks. Brenda was at first reluctant to cooperate since she saw the whole problem as created by Larry's "pathological jealousy." She felt that he was picking on "little things" and she did

---

*All names used in examples in this book are fictitious.

not want to spend the rest of her life watching every little move she made.

She did not have to, nor would it have been a healthy way of living if she had had to watch herself constantly. But she had to realize what her behavior communicated to her husband and modify it long enough for him to feel convinced of her love and attention. When I reassured her on this point she promised to cooperate; with both spouses working on the problem it was resolved in less than half a year. This may seem like a long time to some, but the fact is that Brenda had fully expected that her husband would have to be in treatment at least a couple of years for his "pathological jealousy." Moreover, I happen to know (through Brenda's best girlfriend who is now my patient) that Brenda and Larry are continuing to have a good marriage relationship.

The procedure I followed in the case of Larry and Brenda can be criticized as being "symptomatic treatment." Such treatment is indeed worthless if there is no degree of conscious insight but merely a suppression of certain types of behavior. That, however, was not the case with Larry and Brenda. They did achieve insight: insight into what they were communicating to each other through their behavior. And this insight was sufficient to stop the destructive behavior. They did not need to spend a great deal of time and money to discover the basic underlying causes for their neurotic game (neurotic games are described in Rule 20). Admittedly, it often happens that insight into what one is communicating is not enough: the patient must enter individual uncovering psychotherapy and work on underlying causes. But perhaps just as often insight into what one is communicating *is* enough. Therefore, it is reasonable to find out first whether analysis of communication will be sufficient, before initiating a major psychotherapeutic treatment program.

For this "simple" approach to work, however, the cooperation of *both* parties is usually needed and even with such cooperation there is the possibility that "deeper" analytical therapeutic work will be necessary. But the confrontation of each party with the communicative nature of their behavior is a necessary step if a realistic view of an interaction is going to develop, and without such a realistic view so-called "therapeutic insights" into deeper motivation may not lead to any change of behavior. If Larry and Brenda had not been willing to look at the communicative aspects of their behavior, they might still harbor the distorted idea that Larry suffered from a specific disease called "pathological jealousy" or that Brenda was "by nature" cold and rejecting.

The presence or absence of a certain type of behavior can, as we have seen, be highly communicative. But sometimes the presence or absence of the behavior itself is of little significance compared with the *manner* in which the behavior is or is not carried out, as shown through the following example.

A husband says to his wife: "Would you please bring me a cup of coffee?" Provided his wife has heard his request, there are four main ways in which she can react, each communicating a different message (which the husband may or may not perceive):

1. She can bring him the coffee graciously, feeling positive and kindly or neutral about the situation.

2. She can refuse in a friendly and tactful manner with no conscious or unconscious attempt to hurt her husband. She can, for example, say something like: "Darling, I have been on my feet all day, so I would really appreciate it if you wouldn't mind getting the coffee yourself."

3. She can bring him the coffee feeling angry and resentful about it. The outward signs of resentment may range from slamming around in the kitchen and spilling the coffee over his trousers when serving it to a sour smile and a sarcastic "Is there anything else you would like, dear?" with a drawn-out contemptuous emphasis on "dear." Unless the wife is a brilliant actress or the husband extremely insensitive, he will notice the resentment from clues in his wife's behavior.

4. She can refuse in an angry and hostile or guilt-provoking manner: "Get it yourself, you lazy bum. You think I am your slave or something?" (See Unfair Technique 11-I and 11-X.) Or: "When do you ever do anything for me?" (See Unfair Technique 11-V and 11-VI.)

Reactions 1 and 2 are healthy and constructive; reactions 3 and 4 are unhealthy and destructive. There is a *positive* way to consent and to refuse and there is a *negative* way to consent and to refuse. Thus, whether the husband gets his cup of coffee or not is not nearly as important as *how* he gets it or does not get it.* In terms of psycho-pathology the worst reaction is number 3, where the messages are contradictory: the bringing of the coffee says that the request is reasonable and acceptable; the manner in which it is done says that the request is unreasonable and unacceptable.

Reaction number 4 clearly indicates pathology in the relationship but the resentment is open and can be dealt with constructively as soon as the unfair techniques are abandoned.

There are, of course, other possible reactions to the request, mainly involving mixed feelings:

5. The wife may be tired and feel like resting, but recognizing that she is usually not attentive enough to her husband—and wanting to improve the marriage relationship—she may bring him the coffee, feeling that this is one way of contributing to the improvement. Since the basic motivation involved is constructive, this would be classified as a healthy reaction, provided it does not add to lingering resentments.

6. The wife may feel that she should please her husband and may basically want to do so, but may refuse because she feels too resentful to do anything for him at the moment or because she feels he would be winning a game if she did. The degree of health or unhealth involved in this reaction would depend on the manner of refusal: is it open and honest; are excuses involved; is it a way of continuing a game? And so on.

If you are having problems in a relationship, it may be useful to examine your reactions to a request in terms of the "coffee cup paradigm" given above. Keep in mind that the reasonableness of the request depends on the situation, on the feelings of the partners involved, and on the history of the relationship. It does not depend merely on surface logic (see Unfair Technique 11-VI). Try to be particularly

---

*Do not make the mistake of thinking that this "coffee cup example" is trivial. If reactions 1 and 2 are typical of the relationship, the couple in question have created a "heaven on earth" right in their own home. If, on the other hand, reactions 3 and 4 are characteristic of the interactions between husband and wife, they are living in a self-created hell.

aware of your own tone of voice, facial expression, gestures, sighing, shoulder-shrugging, etc., and—since this is difficult —accept the information you get from your family members regarding your use of such nonverbal methods of communication (Rule 8).

Merely seeing to it that your actions agree with your words will go a long way toward improving your communication. Examining those nonverbal messages of which you are unaware but which your family members can perceive can give you a great deal of insight into yourself since consciously unintended behavior is usually prompted by unconscious needs and purposes.

As a conclusion to this section, let me give you a rule which might help you and the people around you all your life: *Express Your Positive Feelings in Both Actions and Words, But Express Your Negative Feelings Only in Words!* For a description of how to communicate your anger constructively rather than destructively, see Rules 10 and 11.

## 2. "YOU ARE PICKING ON ME AGAIN!"

*Rule 2: Define what is important and stress it; define what is unimportant and ignore it.*

This rule sounds as simple as the previous one but nevertheless an amazingly large number of people find it difficult to follow. And the tragic consequence of not following this rule is that daily life in the family becomes imbued with the same hell of Chinese water-drop torture to which we referred above in discussing the seemingly minor, repetitive actions (or inactions) which can lead to the breakup of a marriage, because they communicate "Your feelings and wishes are not important to me."

The people who break this rule most often—and most conspicuously—are a breed of petty tyrants known as *faultfinders*. Through their faultfinding they break several other communication rules, too, for example, 3, 5, 8, 12, 15, 17, and 19, but their main characteristic is that they cannot or will not distinguish between what is important and what is unimportant. They will, as a matter of fact, often refuse to define openly what to them is important and what is unimportant, mainly because they cannot find anything that falls in the latter category.

Let us consider this horrible and yet widespread practice called faultfinding. In my work as a psychologist I have daily opportunities to observe how destructive faultfinding is, how much damage it can do to human relationships, how it can ruin family life and drive couples to divorce, how it can make the children see the family as something to avoid rather than something to enjoy.

Criticism is a necessary and important part of helping another person grow as a human being. Without compassionate and helpful criticism from concerned and loving intimate associates (family members, friends) a person cannot really develop in a healthy manner, because he lives too close to himself to be capable of detecting all or even most of the flaws and areas in his personality that need improvement. However, such criticism must be discriminate and take into account the fact that no human being is perfect and that there are many matters which are so unimportant that they should be ignored rather than "rubbed in." When criticism becomes indiscriminate it is called faultfinding and it leads to most destructive consequences both in human interactions and in the development of a person, especially a child.

What are the factors which make faultfinding so destructive? They are to be sought both in the causes and the effects of faultfinding and it will be useful for us to list some of these factors in terms of their communication value.

1. Faultfinding is destructive because of its very definition. It is defined here in terms of communication as a way of saying: "I do not accept you as a human being because I will not recognize in practice and in daily living that human beings are imperfect." In other words, faultfinding expresses a lack of acceptance of people and a distorted view of reality.

2. Because of the basic lack of acceptance involved, fault-finding ruins human relationships, makes people feel hostile toward each other, sours the daily atmosphere of the home and makes it a place of misery rather than of happiness and satisfaction.

3. Faultfinding is destructive not only to the "victims" (many of whom are not as innocent as it may appear), but to the faultfinder himself or herself, as well. That is because fault-finding makes the other person either turn you off completely or counterattack or store up resentment against you. Even if the other person does not say anything, he is likely to think to himself: "Oh God, there he starts in again with his constant picking and criticizing, can't he ever get off my back?"

4. It follows that faultfinding is an ineffective method for changing the behavior of others. It may produce initial results, but if it is kept up it will lead to the other person not really hearing what you are saying; he may hear it in a mechanical sense but it will soon "go out through the other ear." Rest assured, however, that the lack of acceptance involved is received and understood.

5. Thus faultfinding can be dangerous, because when the time comes that you have a truly necessary and important criticism to make, you are powerless then, having diluted the effectiveness of your arguments in advance so that they no longer mean anything to the person being criticized. The danger is especially apparent in the case of children who—through faultfinding—have been taught to think: "Never mind, it's just that cranky old parent-faultfinder putting on his broken record again."

6. Faultfinding teaches unreasonableness and intolerance. Since it induces distaste it may lead the other party (spouse, child, employee, etc.) to become unreasonable in the other extreme by becoming especially careless and making an excessive number of mistakes, thus setting up a neurotic interaction (see p. 209).

7. Faultfinding is a consequence of reliance on certain destructive defense mechanisms. The typical faultfinder either projects his own shortcomings onto another person or displaces his anger toward one person (e.g., boss) onto another (e.g., wife). Most often faultfinding is an unconscious way of trying to hide one's own weaknesses by projecting them onto someone else. Thus, it could be described as an

unconscious strategy which involves constantly calling attention to the other person's shortcomings in the vain hope that he will then not notice your own shortcomings. The practice of faultfinding will consume all the energy that should be spent by the faultfinder in recognizing his own shortcomings and working to overcome them. When displacement is involved, the energy should be spent on working out the problem with the "real" object of the anger instead of letting someone else suffer for the faultfinder's sins.

8. The worst destructive effect of faultfinding is on the self-concept of a child. A child needs encouragement, to see himself as basically good and worthwhile, to develop confidence in his own ability to solve problems. A faultfinding parent (heaven forbid that the child should have two parents with the same "disease"!) will make him feel discouraged. The child will feel that there is nothing he can do right and that he is doomed to failure even before trying. His parent's telling him *in words* (under the guise of encouraging him) how much better he could do if only he tried will only add insult to injury. Faultfinding can do a great deal of damage to an adult, especially if his self-concept is already poor. Just think how much more damage it can do to a child who is in the process of developing his feelings about himself, feelings that may stay with him for the rest of his life, since they are notoriously difficult to change or modify later on.

One way to deal with a faultfinder is to sit down with him and discuss the issue of what is important and what is unimportant *to him*. Instead of getting into disagreements about what should be included on either list, just be sure that several items are mentioned on the list of *unimportant* matters and then get a firm commitment from the faultfinder, preferably in writing, that he will pay a certain sum, say one dollar, to the Cancer Fund or the Reiss-Davis Child Study Center, or any other charity whenever he mentions one of the items on the "unimportant list." Note that the money involved in the fine must leave the family; it cannot go toward a vacation fund or the children's education. If it does, there will be less incentive to stick to the agreement.

Faultfinders break Rule 2 by not defining what is unimportant or not being able to ignore it. They behave as if every little thing which is not to their liking were highly important and therefore in need of "correction." But there are also people who use a diametrically opposite way of breaking Rule 2. These are the people who behave as if everything were unimportant! Considering most matters unimportant is a type of behavior which can turn another person into a seeming faultfinder even though the reality is that he is merely conscientious and responsible. Certainly a careless person can keep a faultfinder feeling justified in his faultfinding.

Faultfinders and careless people often marry each other. One reason for this is that each will then feel more justified in his own behavior. The faultfinder will have plenty of opportunity to engage in finding faults and will have ample realistic cause to do so if his partner is inordinately careless. The careless partner, on the other hand, will realistically be able to say: "Well, there is no way my spouse can be pleased anyway, so why should I even try?" Thus, both will be engaged in a neurotic game in which the (unconscious) object is for each to be able to feel indignant and self-justified and to see the partner as being unreasonable.

The best way to handle a careless person is to use the same method used with faultfinders. You ask the careless person to specify what he considers important and what unimportant. Here you make a special point of seeing to it that several matters are mentioned on the *important list* and then you ask for a firm commitment that whenever one of those matters is neglected, the careless person is required to repair it, mend it, or attend to it in some effective way, since it has now been defined as important. "Fines" in a monetary sense will often not work with a careless person, since money may not mean much to him. Therefore, other methods have to be used, the best one being his having to perform a chore which he considers unimportant. For example, if the careless person has neglected to pay a bill (an item he has previously put down on the list of important matters), he can be required to wash the windows (an activity he had previously listed as unimportant).

A word of caution is called for here. "Methods" and "techniques" to deal with other people must be used in a spirit of compassion and with interest in the other person's feelings and thoughts. They are not to be used as ways to manipulate other people or to "use psychology" on them. The best way to apply any method given in this book is first to discuss it thoroughly with the partner and listen to his feelings concerning the method and what it is intended to accomplish. He must be given an opportunity to voice any reasonable objection he may have and to propose an alternate solution. He should also be asked if there are some behaviors he wishes *you* would stop engaging in and then the two of you can discuss methods which could be used to stop *your* negative behavior also. Such a procedure ensures that the approach is cooperative and fair rather than manipulative and pushy.

When one party refuses to agree on any methods for achieving improvement in the relationship or when the methods do not work, the partners in the relationship must seek professional psychological help. The same is true when one partner is so supersensitive to *any* criticism that the other partner is afraid to voice his or her feelings openly.

Finally we should mention that there are minor and subtle ways of finding fault which may not directly influence the partner's self-concept but which nevertheless interfere with constructive communication. Again, such faultfinding fails to discriminate between important and unimportant matters. Consider the following examples:

> *Child:* "I had a terrible nightmare, mother. I dreamed that those old curtains in my room rolled themselves up into a ball and became a terrible monster."

> *Faultfinding mother:* "But those are *new* curtains, dear."
>
> *Discerning mother:* "Tell me how you felt about it."

> *Mother* (trying to help solve a problem for her teen-age daughter): "I have an idea. Why don't you take a girlfriend along and go and see him [potential boyfriend] at that ice-cream parlor where he works?"

> *Faultfinding teen-ager:* "How many times do I have to tell you: he does not work in an ice-cream parlor; he works in a grocery store."
>
> *Discerning teen-ager:* "Say, that's an interesting idea. Maybe I could take Vicky along. By the way, he works in a grocery store."

> *Child:* "Dad, do you think I could have a BB-gun now that I'm twelve? I promise to be very careful. And Craig across the street is only eleven and he got one from his parents."

*Faultfinding father:* "Craig did not get his BB-gun from his parents; he got it from his uncle."

*Discerning father:* "Well, let's discuss it. I feel that . . ." or "No, son, you will have to wait until you are thirteen because . . ."

It can readily be seen from these examples that the fault-finding partner gets the communication away from the main issue, while the discerning partner picks out the main message and addresses himself (herself) to it. Corrections, if any, are made as "by-the-way" comments. In this way the communication stays on the subject and there is more chance for problem-solving or merely pleasant interchange to develop.

To sum up and amplify Rule 2: Make it clear verbally as well as in your behavior what you consider important and what you are willing to overlook because you accept your partner as a human being. Do not be afraid to criticize constructively and point out significant mistakes that must be corrected. But be sure that you do not waste and dilute your judgments on trivial matters, because if you do, you will create resentment, hurt other people's feelings, sometimes permanently, provoke the other person into the opposite behavior from that which you desire, and you will not be heard when it really counts. If you, on the other hand, are sparing in your criticisms and reasonable in your judgments, you will create goodwill, help improve the other person's self-image, and have a much better chance to be heard and understood and maybe even agreed with when something important comes up.

# 3. "HOW CAN I PRAISE IF THERE IS NOTHING TO PRAISE?"

*Rule 3: Make your communication as realistically positive as possible.*

By positive communication I mean any communication which shows regard for the other person's worth as a human being, encourages the development of his potentials, and tends to give him courage and self-confidence. This type of communication will be beneficial to the other person's self-concept, especially in the case of children.

The rule, MAKE YOUR COMMUNICATION AS REALISTICALLY POSITIVE AS POSSIBLE, has little or nothing to do with any so-called "power of positive thinking." The positive thinking approach is of limited value and can usually help only people with minor problems. The theory in such an approach is that if a person repeats positive thoughts often enough, they are going to "seep down" into his unconscious and bury or get rid of the negative thoughts. The potentials for all kinds of wonderful things which have hitherto lain dormant are then supposedly released in the person who engages in positive thinking. The theory is not borne out by clinical observation; on the contrary, it appears to be impossible to *consciously* influence one's unconscious. However, one's own satisfaction with, and the reactions of other people to, one's positive *actions* can have most beneficial effects on both conscious and unconscious levels of awareness. Therefore, apart from some value inherent in autosuggestion and self-reflection, the power of positive thinking is really limited to whether or not and to what degree the thoughts are accompanied by positive action.

What we are talking about here is positive *action* which

includes positive speech, but not necessarily positive thoughts. In a sense, Rule 3 sounds like an admonition directed to a faultfinder, and there is no doubt but that faultfinders constitute a large group of Rule 3 violators. However, the *first* step in dealing with a faultfinder is not to try to persuade him to "turn positive"; rather, as we made clear in the previous chapter, it is to get him to limit his faultfinding to important matters. You can be a negative person without being a faultfinder, as in this example:

> *Child:* "Mother, can I have a cookie?"

> *Negative mother:* "No you can't."

> *Positive mother:* "Yes, as soon as we have our snack time." Or: "Yes, together with your ice cream for dessert tonight." Or: "Yes, when you have finished such and such."

In the example above, both mothers may be faced with some whining from the child. However, whining is more likely as a response to a flat "no" because the child is "left in the air"; he does not know when his request will be granted. Also, the negative mother is more likely to have a child who will see her as automatically and unthinkingly saying "no" to *any* request. In other words, the child of the negative mother is likely to see her as unreasonable, with all the negative implications this has for the area of discipline. It is true that there are occasions when negative comments must be made and you certainly cannot run a family without making negative comments once in a while, but you must keep in mind the *proportion* between positive comments and negative comments and achieve a reasonable balance between the two.* Certainly, when a statement *can* be phrased positively it should not be stated in negative terms. Further examples:

> *Parent:* "I am sorry, but we cannot let you go that far on your bike."

> *Negative child:* "You never let me do anything."

> *Positive child:* "Could we please discuss exactly how far I can go?"

---

*For a discussion on how to bring up necessary negative comments, see Rules 10 and 14.

*Wife:* "Do you think we can afford a new refrigerator?"

*Negative husband:* "There you go again with your constant demands."    *Positive husband:* "Let's go over the budget together and see."

A positive approach to life is characterized by a recognition of, and a stress on, the creative opportunities inherent in a situation, whether they have to do with fulfillment of needs or encouraging good qualities or developing skills. Perhaps the most important earmarks of such a positive approach are recognition of value and praise of accomplishment.

Again, as we shall see in a later discussion of the development of a person's self-concept, it is of utmost importance that the parents in day-to-day living recognize the inherent value of the child as a person and reward his accomplishments with sincere praise. He must often have the experience of his parents' recognizing his good qualities rather than dwelling on the "bad" ones. The child should often have the experience of having achieved something good and praiseworthy and of being a success. He can develop these feelings only if his accomplishments are recognized by people whose judgment he respects.

To take good behavior for granted and comment only on negative behavior is grossly unreasonable. Good behavior, as defined by our society, is not "natural." On the contrary, it is the result of careful, conscientious, and loving upbringing. This is obvious when you consider the wild and usually destructive behavior of children who have grown up virtually without parental guidance. Good behavior needs to be reinforced or rewarded, in words as well as in deeds. Comments such as "You did a good job," "We are very proud of how well you behaved in the restaurant," "Boy, you certainly learned that quickly," etc., are effective rewards with most children. Some children respond well to just a warm smile or a gesture of pride and approval. Others may also need some material rewards at times. But all children need to have good—or improved—behavior recognized in some positive manner.

A typical negativistic person will say: "But how can I praise if there is no accomplishment to praise? I would be a hypocrite if I did that and the child would soon see that I don't mean what I say and that I am just trying to manipulate him or 'use psychology' on him. And furthermore, I don't want him to think he did something well if he didn't." These are statements which *sound* logical, but which do not hold up on closer examination. Furthermore, logic is a game that can be played many ways and can be used to achieve all kinds of conclusions, even opposite ones. Logic is therefore a favorite among those who are looking for excuses.

The answer to the negativist's "logic" is five-fold:

1. First of all, no child (and no adult either, as far as that goes) behaves equally badly every day. People fluctuate in their behavior and can therefore be praised whenever the behavior is desirable, *if you are looking for positive aspects*. It is easy to find mistakes, faults, and negative elements in any person's behavior. It is equally easy to find desirable and positive elements in the same person's behavior if you look for them and do not take them for granted. Which elements you find will depend largely on your own orientation. Luckily, a person can often change his orientation from negative to positive merely by conscious decision and determination, provided he recognizes the problem in himself and is willing to change. In those cases where a negativistic person cannot change by conscious decision, psychotherapy is indicated.

2. Secondly, you must use the other person's *past performance* as a yardstick. The recognition and praise must be based on *improvements* and not on the attainment of a preset standard. If you base your reactions on your own ideas of what the other person should be capable of, you may indeed feel that you have to criticize constantly. But—and this is especially true of children who are, in fact, constantly developing—if you use the other person's past performance as a criterion, you will find many opportunities to praise him and encourage him.

3. It is indeed true that children (and many adults) see through insincerity very quickly. But if you look for positive elements and improvements and adopt past performances as a yardstick, you will be able to praise the child sincerely and often and your praise will be realistic; there will be no hypocrisy involved. Furthermore the criticisms that are necessary will then have a much better effect, because the child will see you as fairminded and reasonable and worth listening to.

4. People tend—in the long run, at least—to respond positively to realistic praise and they tend to try to live up to the expectations others have of them, if the expectations are realistic.

5. The fear that a person will stop trying to improve if he is praised is almost always unfounded. Many parents, especially, fear that if you praise a child "too soon," he will think: "This is good enough, I don't need to do any better." Although such a reaction is theoretically possible, I have never known anyone to respond in that manner. On the contrary, recognition and praise tend to spur a person on to further achievement, whereas negative criticism—especially if it is chronic—or refusal to recognize improvement tends to elicit a "what's the use" reaction.

For those who like figures and something concrete to shoot for I would say: try to keep the praise-to-criticism ratio at eighty or ninety percent praise* to twenty or ten percent criticism. Even if you can keep the ratio to 60 to 40 percent, you will still probably do all right and your child's self-concept will have a good chance to develop positively. He will feel that he is capable of doing well and that his achievements are recognized and valued by others.

I am sad to say, however, in all too many families this ratio is reversed and we find eighty percent or more criticism and twenty percent or less praise. These are often families that are in need of professional help, but—perhaps because this problem is so widespread—many people seem to think that it is inevitable and will use the fact that the problem is widespread as an excuse for not seeking help from a psychologist. Or—equally often—they will attribute the fault-finding to some kind of inborn and unchangeable "nature" or "personality" of the faultfinder, and will therefore not seek help.

The tragic result is that in these families the children are likely to develop a poor self-concept, which will severely affect their future life and make it miserable. And a poor self-concept can ruin a person's life, because each individual *tends to choose what he feels he is worth*. This is true of the choice of friends and associates as well as of the choice of

---

*Since no one is perfect, one hundred percent praise would indicate lack of realism or some blind spot in whoever is doing the praising.

marriage partner and career, etc. More immediately, a poor self-concept can lead to the aforementioned "what's-the-use" attitude, which may reflect itself in poor performance in school and can lead to a vicious circle in which the child fails more and more and therefore gets more and more criticism which further undermines his self-concept, leading to more failure and criticism, until he gives up altogether.

A family in which there is more criticism than encouragement and praise must therefore seek professional help if the faultfinder (or faultfinders) involved cannot himself (themselves) effect a sufficient change.

An important point to keep in mind in praising a child is that, as a rule, it is *specific* acts, accomplishments, and improvements that should be praised. General characteristics such as intelligence should be praised sparingly, if at all. The well-meant statement, "You are such a bright boy" or "You are a very intelligent girl," may backfire for the following reasons:

1. The child may not feel that he is intelligent and, if so, he may get the idea that you simply do not understand him. In such a case, he may start doing worse in school to prove to you what he thinks he is really like.

2. The child may feel that you are biased in his favor, simply because you are his parent. Any praise which is not specific and based on a demonstrable act will then be discounted by the child as an expression of this bias. Similarly, any criticism will be more devastating in its effect on the child's self-concept, because if a positively biased person finds a fault, it must really be a serious one.

3. The child may feel that you view him in a distorted light because your own personal pride would be hurt if your child were not intelligent. This feeling is quite often realistic. The violent anger (rather than constructive concern and helpfulness) that many parents show when their child brings home a poor report card shows that such parents indeed are *personally hurt* rather than being primarily concerned with the welfare of their child. If the child senses that your personal self-image is dependent on his performance, he will, naturally, resent the burden of devoting his life to your vanity and need for support, and he may then study even less in spite of all disciplinary measures.

4. The child may feel that his pleasure in succeeding is re-moved if he is praised for a general characteristic. The reasoning would be as follows: "If you think I am really as intelligent as all that, then A's are nothing to be happy about, they should be expected as a matter of course. And B's are an outright failure." Some children reason this way consciously. A great many more may feel this way on an unconscious level and may again start doing poorly just to get the parent to stop the general praise which removes the child's pleasure in accomplishment.

For these reasons, it is best to *let the child draw his own conclusions* from your recognition of his specific accomplishments. He himself knows when he has done well but he needs your recognition and praise in order to confirm it. With each confirmation his self-confidence grows. When you show enthusiastic recognition of his realistic accomplishments, then he *himself* will draw the conclusion that he is intelligent or good or skillful or whatever positive quality is involved. And it is his *own* conclusion that counts in the long run, not yours.

Even necessary criticism can be made positively and with-out belittling or humiliating the child. The criticism should be specific and should be accompanied by a friendly demon-stration of what the desirable behavior should have been. Thus, when a child has made a mistake, the parent is not to say: "For God's sake, what is the matter with you? How stupid can one be!" (Unfair Technique 11-X: Humiliating the partner), but rather: "That was not right, I'll show you how it should be done."

In commenting on Rule 3, I have dealt mostly with the negative effects on children if the rule is not followed. The negative effect on adults is, of course, also important but usually is not decisive for personal development, since in an adult the self-concept is already formed. In the case of an adult with a poor self-concept, however, the effects of con-stantly negative communication can be disastrous. Even when an adult has a positive self-concept, it may take positive communication from others to "bring out the best" in him.

# 4. "I KNOW I HAVE MY FAULTS, TOO, BUT . . ."

## Rule 4: Be clear and specific in your communication.

Among the formal requirements of effective communication one of the foremost is that communication should be clear and specific. This is of especial importance when communication is used for problem solving. Yet a large number of people have a tendency to be vague in their statements, not realizing that a problem stated vaguely is much less likely to be solved than a problem which is stated clearly. An even greater number of people have an unfortunate tendency to digress and to bring up a multitude of problems all at once, again not realizing that the more problems that are talked about at the same time the less the likelihood is that any one of them will be solved.

An infinite variety of problems and misunderstandings can arise from unclear and vague communication. It is unnecessary, and probably impossible, to attempt to give examples of all possible consequences. Innumerable tragedies, and perhaps just as many comical situations, have originated in unclear communication, and examples are readily found in daily life, literature, and drama. In this section, therefore, we are going to describe only the three aspects or corollaries of this rule which are most frequently violated in daily communication between family members.

The first corollary to this rule is: *Define and clarify the terms and expressions you use and ask your partner to define and clarify his terms and expressions. Avoid vagueness.*

The clarity and specificity for which you should strive in your communication must, of course, include the vocabulary you use. Precise vocabulary and clearly defined terms are especially important when you state your expectations and wishes, because your partner in communication may otherwise make assumptions which can later lead to unnecessary conflict between the two of you.

It is particularly important for parents to define their criteria for performance, the limits they wish to impose on their child's behavior, and the behavior which they expect from the child. Do not, for example, say: "I want you to come home early today." The child's conception of "early" may be vastly different from yours and his interpretation of what you mean is likely to be influenced by his own needs (to have fun, to be with his friends). Instead, tell your child: "Today I must ask you to be home by 5:30 sharp, because. . . ."

Just as it is important that you be clear and specific in your statements, it is equally important that you *do not accept the use of vague words by your communication partner.* Such acceptance can lead to a great deal of trouble.

If a mother, for example, asks a child to do a chore and accepts the answer "I'll do it later," she is actually creating a nagging problem (Rule 17). The term "later" must be defined or pinned down ("I will do it by five o'clock"), otherwise the child will feel no commitment to do the chore soon, since "later" can always be stretched without breaking a promise.

It should be obvious that accepting a nonspecific commitment ("I'll take care of it one of these days," "I'll do it when I get around to it," "Yes, I guess," etc.) leads to future problems. But if it is so obvious, why do some people (such as Betty in the example on p. 84, Rule 10) accept such actual noncommitments over and over again? The answer can only be that despite the obvious disadvantages (things not getting done, being irritated, feeling rejected by the other person's lack of consideration, etc.), there are hidden neurotic values in taking the other person at his word: getting him in trouble, "rubbing his face in it," portraying him as unreasonable, recreating a nagging-parent vs. uncooperative-child situation, etc.

The commitment "I'll try" or "I'll try harder next time" is laudable and well-intentioned. It is, however, of little value unless "trying" is defined in specific terms, because of two reasons: (1) most people feel they are trying, as it is, and

(2) what is seen as trying by one person may not be accepted as trying by another. The commitment must therefore be put specifically, such as:

"I will get up at seven-thirty from now on."

"I will call you if I am going to be more than half-an-hour late."

"I will clean the garage tomorrow morning right after breakfast."

"I will give twenty dollars to the Cancer Fund each time I swear or use foul language in front of the children."

"I will make a list of everything that needs to be done and go over it each morning."

"I will do my homework every day starting twenty minutes after I come home from school."

You must be specific in your commitments and you must insist that others be specific in their commitments. The word "commitment" should be taken broadly here and should include promises and threats, rewards and punishments. A promise is not very valuable if it is not specific; a vague expectation of some unspecified reward does not spur one to the same effort as the certain knowledge of a specific reward. Vague threats induce anxiety which can interfere with performance and with healthy personality development, and a vague expectation of some untoward consequence does not lead to the same effectiveness in impulse control as the knowledge of a specific punishment. The failure to be specific encourages the other party to make assumptions which are based on wishful thinking rather than on reality, it leads to accusations of unfairness, disappointments, frustrations, and anxiety, in short, to all kinds of unnecessary problems in human interrelationships.

Even failing to define a single word can lead to problems, sometimes to tragic consequences. This is often true, for example, if the word which remains undefined is used for the purpose of finding an excuse. To illustrate: it often happens that people postpone psychotherapeutic help for themselves or their children because they feel the problem is actually quite "normal." By the time the person comes in for psychotherapeutic help, the problem may, as a result of the postponement, have reached such a degree of chronicity and severity that it may be very difficult to treat. What happens in this case is that many people fail to define the word "normal" and thus confuse the use of the word "normal $=$ occurring frequently in the population" with the use of the word "normal = functioning in a healthy manner." Immature and irresponsible behavior, for example, may be very frequent and in that sense normal (witness the saying "boys will be boys"), but it is usually destructive in its consequences and therefore abnormal, in the sense of being unhealthy. To postpone psychotherapy because a symptom or disturbing behavior is "normal," meaning frequent in its occurrence, is dangerous exactly because it neglects the fact that the symptom or disturbing behavior is abnormal, in the sense of being unhealthy. Unclear terminology facilitates the use of excuses, as seen from the fact that the same person who postpones psychotherapy because a serious psychological problem is frequent-normal is *not* likely to postpone treatment for a serious medical problem such as appendicitis or lung cancer even though the medical problem may also be frequent-normal. One reason for this double standard is, of course, that in the case of a psychological problem the connection "ill health" does not come to mind as easily as in the case of a physical disease.

Married couples with problems will sometimes consult a psychologist to see "who is right." It comes as a shock to them to discover that the question is meaningless unless it is defined and specified, such as: "Is it psychologically healthy for our relationship that I spend so much time on my hobbies" or "Is it psychologically healthy for the children that my husband starts arguments in front of them?" Even these questions are not specific enough to be answered with a categorical yes or no, but they are more meaningful than they would be if they employed the terms "right" or "wrong."

Vagueness in vocabulary and definition is particularly prevalent among the teen-agers of today. The use of a vague vocabulary gives the teen-agers a feeling of general understanding among each other which is often false and unrealistic. This is especially true of the subgroup referred to as "hippies."* Hippies claim to have better communication among each other than "Establishment" people, but the fact is that the "rapping" they do with each other is terribly egocentric and noncommunicative. Due to the vagueness of the

---

*Since very few think of themselves as "hippies," I will define a hippie pragmatically as a person who would be called a hippie by more than fifty percent of a random sample of the population who would have a chance to meet him.

vocabulary they use (and probably to personality problems as well), there are even more communication problems and misunderstandings among hippies than among users of conventional vocabulary. At least that is the observation I have made in doing psychotherapy with hippies.

The second corollary to Rule 4 is: *Explain the reasons for all your decisions.*

In order for a child to develop proper impulse control, judicious parental authority has to be exercised whether or not the child fully understands or accepts the reasons for it. Especially in the earliest years when the child has a very hazy idea of cause and effect there may be many occasions when he will have to obey rules, follow directives, and abide by decisions without any meaningful understanding of their purpose. But this fact does not excuse the parent from *trying* to help the child understand the reasons for a rule or directive or helping him grasp the basis for the parent's decision, whatever it may be. As a matter of fact, the very attempt to explain reasons to a child will help him develop his ability to perceive cause and effect in addition to giving him an example of consideration and courtesy. Therefore, after the child has reached the age of two or so, the rule should be: at least try to explain the reasons for all your decisions, rules, or directives. It should go without saying that breaking this rule with a school-age child or an adult is simply rudeness.

This rule is broken especially often by parents who— whether they admit it or not—like to show their power. These are parents who say: "I don't have the time to stand and argue with you; just do as I say," or "I don't have to explain anything to you; you just do as you are told." These parents are in for a great deal of trouble.

There are two main reasons why they are going to have trouble. One is that no person can incorporate or accept a rule he does not like if he does not know the reason for it. A child may obey his parents' decision or rule superficially and at the moment, but if he does not understand the reason for it he will not accept it, and sooner or later the parents will have a rebellion on their hands. In any case, the child will not develop self-discipline, since he cannot accept the rules.

The other reason why parents who demand unquestioning obedience will have trouble is that the child will see them as unreasonable and he will have realistic cause for this view. And one of the main causes of interpersonal conflict is unreasonableness. It is also one of the main deterrents to constructive communication. Chances are that when a child does not communicate constructively with his parents, it is at least partly because the latter are unreasonable in some way.

On the other hand, if a child understands the reasons for a rule or for your decision to say yes or no, then he is much more likely to accept the rule or to make the same decision on his own when you are absent. He is also much more likely to see you as a reasonable person to whom he can come and talk over his problems. It may take some extra time for you to explain your reasons, but it is a good investment for the future.

Most parents would agree that what we want for our children is not that they should blindly follow our rules without thinking; if that were the case, what would our children do later on in life when we are not around? Instead, we want our children to know and accept the basic principles on which we base our rules and decisions, so that they will come to the same conclusions themselves. Then they will develop what will help them most in life: an *inner discipline* which will guide their actions even when we are not there to tell them what to do and what not to do. And that, in turn, will eventually lead to our being able to *trust* our children when we are away from them.

The child should be given a reason even when you suspect that the child actually knows the reason and is just trying to upset you or manipulate you. If you yell: "I have told you the reason a thousand times, I am not going to repeat it," the child has led you into a trap. First of all, if the child's (unconscious) purpose was to upset you, he has succeeded. Secondly, he can accuse you of being unfair and exaggerating or lying, because you cannot prove that he knows or remembers the reason or that you have actually stated it one thousand times! Thirdly, he can accuse you of being illogical and using excuses, because if you have truly said something one thousand times, what possible harm could it do to say it once more? Fourthly, he may then accuse you of not really having any good reason for your decision. In any case, you have walked into a trap.

On the other hand, if you tell him the reason calmly and matter-of-factly, he has failed in his attempt to manipulate you and cannot accuse you of being unfair. In addition, you have given him an excellent practical lesson on how to be reasonable, courteous, and patient in the face of provocation.

Both in connection with counseling at my office and in the course of my lecturing on these subjects, parents have asked me, "Don't I have a right not to give a reason?" My answer is that perhaps a parent has such a right, but if so, it would still be both silly and destructive to exercise that right in view of the many problems that are likely to follow as a consequence.

In the case of any child old enough to grasp what the words "why" and "because" mean, the phrase, "Do it because I say so," should be used only under one or two circumstances. The first is when your house is on fire, the second is when your boat is sinking. Perhaps you can think of other emergencies, but I fervently hope that you will never have to use that phrase at all.

The third corollary to Rule 4 is: *Be specific about your own part in creating a problem.*

"We don't talk about our defects—other people do that," says Hans Christian Andersen in "The Teapot." Yet most people consciously want to be fair, reasonable, and open about their mistakes. You may often hear the statement: "He does not admit his mistakes," but I doubt that you have ever heard anyone say: "I do not admit my mistakes," unless you are a psychotherapist and even then it would be a rare patient who would make such a statement. People like to see themselves as being reasonable enough to admit their mistakes and shortcomings, but many people can admit them only in terms of a vague generality. These latter individuals find it most difficult to be open, frank, and honest in discussing *specifically* what they did to help create a problem or to make it worse.

What these people will do instead is *pay lip-service* to recognizing their faults and shortcomings, usually in the context of either attacking someone else's specific shortcomings or listing their own assets. We have all met the kind of person who says:

"I know I have faults, too, but . . ." and then he follows up with a long list of the specific crimes that the *other* person has committed or with a description of his own wonderful deeds. Or, he may say something like:

"I know I am not perfect, but . . ." or "Of course, no one is perfect and I am willing to admit to my mistakes, too, but

. . . ," and then comes the list of the other person's specific imperfections or his own excellent features.

How do you handle a person like that?

It will usually not pay for you to start defending yourself with respect to the list of specific crimes you are being charged with. Even if you can remember them all and successfully defend yourself, more crimes will be added to the list when you are through with your defense. So don't even try. It may, however, be a good idea to take notes on the "crimes" and keep them for future reference as valuable information about you, since they have been observed by a person (spouse, child, parent, sibling, friend) who knows you well (Rule 8).

Another poor way of reacting to this type of person would be to start yelling back at him about the things *he* has done that you feel are destructive (see Unfair Technique 11-III). Such competitions in "who can heap more accusations on the other" are futile and serve merely to release more adrenalin into the bloodstream.

The best way to handle the multibarreled attack preceded by "I have faults, too, but . . ." is the following. You wait until your partner is through with his list of specific crimes, then say to him: "Listen, I am interested in the first thing you mentioned when you started talking, the part where you said that you, too, have faults. I wonder if you could please elaborate on that point and give specific examples of what you meant. Then we can look both at what I can do about my shortcomings and what you can do about yours." (Care must be taken here that you don't use a sarcastic tone of voice; see Unfair Technique 11-XIII.) °

You will find that the person who hides behind a general admission of imperfection usually becomes highly uncomfortable when asked to be specific about his own shortcomings. The reason it is so difficult for him to give examples is that he *himself* is afraid of looking at what he does *specifically* to contribute to the problems. He tries to fool himself and you into thinking that he is reasonable, objective, and willing to admit his own mistakes. It is as if he would say: "Look how fair I am, I admit my own faults first, so now I have permission to tear into you." Actually, of course, it is *unfair* to be general about one's own mistakes and specific about those the other person has made.

If you follow the recommendation given here and say,

"Please give me some examples of *your* faults," the other person, due to his fear of seeing or admitting his own specific shortcomings, may be unable (read: unconsciously unwilling) to give you such examples. You can then ask him if he feels it is fair for him to pretend that he admits his faults when, in fact, he can give no examples of what they are.

Often unable to find a single specific fault in himself, the attacker will resort to a "fault" which, far from being the result of honest self-scrutiny, merely constitutes a renewal of the attack, such as:

"Well, my main fault is that I have treated you too nicely," or "My main fault is that I let you get away with too much," or even "My fault is that I married you in the first place!" In other words, the attacker continues to pretend that he is willing to admit to his own faults, but the "faults" he mentions are backhanded ways of keeping up or escalating the attack. This must be pointed out to the attacker. If he recognizes the validity of the point, a step has been taken toward better communication between the partners.

If the attacker does not recognize—or claims not to recognize—the fact that the "admission" of his own faults actually constitutes a renewed attack, then what he claims to be his faults must be written down. The attacker must then be asked what he thinks would happen if the "faults" were shown to a third person whom he trusts and who would be asked: "Are these statements honest admissions of shortcomings?" If the attacker says that an unbiased third party would answer "yes," then he is either consciously dishonest or he distorts emotional reality to such an extent that he is in definite need of professional help.

If the attacker responds to the challenge with sarcasm, such as by saying: "Well, I am sure you can name a long list, so why should I bother?" then he is to be called on the fact that sarcasm is an unfair technique. If he denies having been sarcastic, you ask him to repeat his statement (which usually has the effect of either removing the sarcastic aspect or making it more obvious), or you point out that the issue is not whether *you* can see his faults, but whether *he* can. (Beware of hostility in tone of voice here!)

A good communication exercise for both parties is to reverse the phraseology and say "I know *you* have faults, too, but I . . ." and then list one's *own* shortcomings, provocations, inconsiderations, etc. If done in good faith, this exercise can be highly valuable, mainly because it prevents each party from playing the innocent victim (Rule 20).

# 5. "WHY DO YOU NEVER DO YOUR HOMEWORK BEFORE WATCHING TV?"

## Rule 5: Be realistic and reasonable in your statements.

Many people have a tendency, when they tell someone about something they have experienced, to amplify the story with colorful adjectives, exaggerations, and phrases that "sound good" and are intended to make the story more interesting. The desire, in other words, is not to give an objective account of what happened, but rather, to make a point, stress unusual aspects, or give the story stronger impact. In this there is, of course, usually no harm. On the contrary, literature would be hopelessly drab and could not exist as an art form if the tendency to make something "sound good" did not exist.

However, in communication between people there are occasions when this "amplifying tendency" can be destructive. This is especially true when accusations are made.

There is nothing inherently destructive about accusations. As a matter of fact, accusations are necessary and unavoidable in a truly intimate and caring relationship where both parties wish to improve and help each other improve. Accusations are a way of confronting another person with behavior that is, in the opinion of the accuser, unacceptable or destructive.

Accusations, however, can easily become destructive through such added factors as tone of voice (e.g., contempt or belittling), frequency (e.g., picking and nagging), and exaggerations. In this chapter we shall focus on the use of exaggeration (and its counterpart, which we shall call "minimization") to make a story carry stronger impact.

Accusations are potentially valuable to *both* parties in an intimate relationship. The accuser holds up a mirror to the accused and says: this is how I see you, please change such and such. If the picture is recognizable to the accused and if he wishes to work on improving himself and the relationship, he will then attempt to change the "faults" observed. This will earn him increased respect and goodwill from the accuser, provided the accuser is a person of reasonable emotional health who has not made the accusation for neurotic or destructive purposes. The accuser will also benefit, partly from the improvement in the relationship, partly from the open and sincere and nondestructive release of his feelings, and partly from the knowledge that he has contributed to the personal growth of his partner.

However, if the picture painted by the accuser is so exaggerated and distorted that it is not recognizable, the accused party will not change; on the contrary, he will feel resentment and anger and therefore will be less likely to work on improving the relationship. Equally destructive or futile effects of accusations will ensue if the accused is neurotically hypersensitive to criticism, even when it is constructive and given in a helpful spirit.

There are five reasons why accusations which employ exaggeration tend to backfire:

1. If your accusation distorts reality (or what the other person sees as reality) significantly, the accused will not only reject the image you are painting, he will actually direct his attention and energy to the *opposite* of what you want him to consider. Let us take some examples.

    a. If you say to a child: "Why do you never do your homework before watching TV?" the word "never" will probably distort the picture you are painting enough to make the child resentful and angry. He will, as a consequence, direct all his attention and energy to trying to remember those times when he *did* do his homework first! He will then, in turn, probably exaggerate this frequency and minimize the number of times he watched TV first. The two of you are then deadlocked and a power struggle may ensue in which each party accuses the other of not telling the "truth." Or you may have to back down and admit that you were exaggerating, which will weaken your position in the discussion because the child is by now more preoccupied with having proved you wrong than willing to listen to your revised accusation. In other words, by employing the exaggeration "never" to amplify your point, you have actually lost your point even before you start the discussion.

It is, of course, a good idea to admit when you are wrong. It is the morally right and the reasonable thing to do and it gives your child a good example to follow. But why set up a situation in advance in which you have to "back down" because you started the discussion by making an unreasonable statement?

If you had said, instead: "I think it happens too often that you watch TV before you do your homework," then at least your child cannot deny what you are saying without himself being unreasonable. And even if he does deny your accusation, he will at least secretly know that you are correct, and that is sometimes enough to effect a change.

The best way, of course, is to discuss the setting of a rule to cover the time of homework and to spell out the consequences resulting from breaking that rule.

b. If you say to your husband: "Why do you always have to come home late?" or "Why do you never call me when you are going to be late?" he may search his mind for those times when he did not come home late or for the one time that he did call you and you gave him a bad time on the phone. You will then either be deadlocked in a power struggle or you will have to back down and rephrase your accusation. The effectiveness of the rephrasing will then depend primarily on how much resentment was engendered by the original exaggeration and on how reasonable your husband is.

c. Suppose your teen-ager has to be home by twelve-thirty on Saturday night and actually shows up at one-fifteen. The next day, if you say: "We can't have this kind of irresponsibility and inconsideration around here, you were a whole hour late in coming home last night," the most likely result is that your teen-ager will say: "But dad, I was only a half-hour late," and you may find yourself haggling about minutes instead of discussing responsibility, consideration, and other important issues.

d. An especially provocative thing to say is the rhetorical phrase often used by parents who are ineffective communicators: "Haven't I always been fair with you?" Unless the relationship with the child is unusually good, which it hardly would be in the case of parents who communicate ineffectively, this phrase will only direct the child's attention to all the times that the parent has been unfair. Not that there is anything the matter with your hearing about the times when you have been unfair. That is valuable information and should help you improve as a person and as a parent. But the time to hear about it is not when you are trying to get a point across to another person.

Usually, the most you could hope to get out of a rhetorical question such as "Haven't I always been fair with you?" is a sullen acknowledgment. And what have you gained by that?

2. Another reason why accusations which employ exaggeration tend to backfire is that they are, by definition, unfair. If you frequently make such accusations, the other person will build up an image of you as an unfair and unreasonable person, one with whom one cannot discuss matters objectively.

3. A third reason is that the very unfairness involved may give the other person an excuse to stop trying to improve. He may think: "Boy, if my mother (or father or spouse) forgets all the good things I do and only remembers the bad things, then why should I bother to try at all?"

Statements such as "You never do anything right" or "You have always been that way" have the effect of making the other person feel hopeless and thus more likely to give up altogether. They should, of course, be replaced with statements that are realistic and constructive, such as "The way to do this is. . . ." and "It happens much too often that you. . . ." Even if the person addressed does not respond positively to these latter statements, at least no further damage has been done.

4. A fourth reason is that any exaggeration makes you vulnerable to the counteraccusation that you are *lying*. And even though you may convince the other that you were not really lying, you were only stretching the truth a little, your point is still lost and you are forced to be on the defensive.

5. Finally, exaggerated accusations backfire or, at best, are useless, because the other person may think your point must be pretty weak if you have to employ exaggeration to bolster it up.

The rule that you must be realistic and reasonable in

your statements applies not only to accusations but also to confessions. If you minimize your own shortcomings (as when a person with frequent temper-outbursts says: "I guess I have lost my temper a couple of times"), you will give the impression that you are dishonest, afraid to face yourself realistically, unreasonable, and unlikely to improve, since you do not see the magnitude of your problem.

It goes without saying that the same arguments hold for minimizing the other person's good characteristics and accomplishments, and exaggerating your own good qualities.

In reacting to another person's exaggerations, it is a good idea not to deny them indignantly, but instead to correct them reasonably and tactfully by replying as if the other person had also been reasonable. Let us conclude the discussion of Rule 5 with an example contrasting a destructive with a constructive way of replying to an exaggeration.

> *Husband:* "How come you can never keep clean socks for me in the drawer?"
>
> *Wife* (breaking against sound rules of communication): "How dare you come with those ridiculous accusations again? I can't stand your constant exaggerations. It has only happened once before and you know it. Anyway, what do you expect? You never put your clothes in the hamper. You think I am your slave, don't you? Well, we'll see about that. You'll be sorry one of these days."
>
> *Wife* (following sound rules of communication and tactfully correcting her husband's exaggeration): "I know you feel it happens too often and it makes you angry. I will do my best to see that it doesn't happen again. You will help me, won't you, by remembering to put your clothes in the hamper?"

Realism and reasonableness in your statements may not always lead to results in terms of directly influencing your partner to become more realistic or reasonable. Your partner may have certain neurotic needs which are incompatible with mature give-and-take interaction, and for which he may need psychotherapeutic attention. But you are not to use this possibility as an excuse for being unrealistic and unreasonable yourself. If you stay realistic and reasonable, tactful and compassionate, constructive rather than destructive, you will have the satisfaction of knowing that, even though a problem exists between you and your partner, you are at least not contributing to making it worse.

# 6. "I DIDN'T THINK YOU WOULD MIND."

*Rule 6: Test all your assumptions verbally. Get your partner's ok before you act.*

The importance of testing assumptions cannot be overemphasized, because a large proportion of human conflicts, destructive arguments, ill feeling, and sometimes tragic consequences are due to assumptions not having been tested, consultations not having been made, clarifications not having been asked for. The person who goes ahead with decisions without consulting his partner in communication is usually in for serious trouble, especially if this is a chronically recurring pattern. The partner who was not consulted will often become indignant and angry *even if* he would probably have agreed to the decision anyway, had he been asked. The lack of consultation, the failure to test the assumption, is rude and insulting and can be condoned only in an emergency.

The "victim" may suppress his feelings and not say a word about it. This may eventually lead to severe problems connected with "bottling up" feelings. But even if the "victim" shows the anger, his indignant reproaches are often met by such phrases as "Well, I didn't think you would mind" or "How was I to know that you would object?" Perhaps there are occasions when such replies would be legitimate, but I cannot think of any at the time of writing. Most such replies, perhaps all of them, are excuses. Assumptions are safe only after they have been tested by asking the partner what his wishes are and then, of course, they are no longer assumptions. When you know a person well, you are likely to have tested several assumptions with him and you are therefore likely to know what his preferences are, so you cannot use lack of knowledge as an excuse. If, on the other hand, you are not sure, you can always ask. In case you feel you do not know a person well even though he is a family member, there is certainly no excuse for not asking what his preference is. Let us examine a few examples that illustrate the destructiveness that can be the result of not testing assumptions.

I remember a very sad case of a fifteen-year-old girl, Diane, who had run away from home to stay with a man who was in his late twenties. After her parents had found her and brought her home they contacted me for help. I agreed to see the girl on the condition that the parents would also come in and explore their part in the problem.

In my first session with Diane I asked her what it was that had triggered her decision to run away from home, and she told me the following incident:

Diane had for a long time had a large box in her room. In the box were old toys, books, dolls, and trinkets from her earlier childhood. The box contributed to the messiness of her room, about which her mother nagged her daily. Diane did not touch the things in the old box, but neither did she put it in the closet or do anything else than the barest minimum to keep her room tidied up.

There was intense hatred on Diane's face and anger in her voice when she told me that one day when she returned from sleeping over at a girlfriend's house, she found the box gone. Her parents had put it out with the trash cans and it had been taken away. After a horrible scene Diane—who had never before been violent—forced her mother *at knife-point* to drive to the city dump and help her look for the box. Their efforts were in vain. Seething with anger, Diane returned to the house with her mother for more arguments and fights. Her mother kept saying, "We thought you weren't interested in that old junk," and "Why didn't you tell us you wanted to keep it." Diane screamed back that they weren't interested in what she had to say anyway unless it was something that they wanted to hear. By the time Diane's father came home, she had run away.

Diane was essentially correct in her accusation. Her parents complained bitterly that Diane constantly rejected them and did not take their feelings into account; yet it was clear that they themselves seldom listened seriously to her; they really did not consider anything she had to say important and they dealt with her many grievances in a most offhanded and self-justifying manner. They took the attitude that, being older, they always knew better than she did what was best for her. Instead of admitting their unfairness they used excuses to cover it up. The mother, for example, said: "We just felt we had to throw it out because the room was so messy." This is an excuse, because there was no need to throw out the box without warning. Diane could have been told: "You must get your room straightened out by Monday; otherwise we will have to do it ourselves and then we might throw things away that you might want to keep." This would have constituted fair warning and Diane would have known that she herself had caused her things to be thrown away, had she not heeded the warning.

If the incident with the thrown away box had been an isolated and atypical event, or if it had been preceded by adequate warning, Diane would probably have forgiven her parents some time after expressing her anger. She would have realized that anyone can make a mistake and she would certainly not have done anything drastic. As it was, however, the incident was typical of her parents' lack of consideration in dealing with her and to Diane it was final proof that she could never achieve a satisfactory relationship with them. Her decision was made on this basis: "Since I and everything that makes me what I am doesn't make any difference to my parents anyway, I may as well run away and find someone to whom I mean something."

The shock of Diane's running away and moving in with a much older man made the parents quite cooperative in psychotherapy. Diane, too, came to realize that by keeping her room messy and by other provocations and inconsiderations she had virtually "teased" her parents into doing what they did. Through each member working on his own contributions to the problems, the family finally was able to establish good and warm relationships among its members, which in turn benefited Diane's younger brother and sister, who had already started to show signs of developing emotional problems both at home and in school.

Dr. T. was a man many would envy. His success as a physician had brought him professional recognition and respect as well as wealth. He had a beautiful wife, four fine children, and a home that had been featured in architectural magazines. However, he felt most unhappy in his relationship with his wife. It was his second marriage to a woman who made him feel henpecked. He had divorced his first wife primarily because he felt she constantly bossed him around. He had been attracted to his present wife because she had seemed to be very sweet, compliant, and willing to follow him in his decisions. During the courtship she had loved to surprise him with little attentions which he had enjoyed immensely, little knowing (consciously, that is) that they would play a most destructive part in his marriage to her.

Dr. T.'s second wife prided herself on knowing exactly what he liked and set out to decorate the new house they had bought without consulting her husband. In the beginning he humored her and pretended he was happy with her choices, but it soon developed that they had most dissimilar tastes and he got tired of coming home to a new "surprise" practically every night. Dr. T. got angrier with each incident and started accusing his wife of deliberately doing things behind his back, with the purpose of upsetting him (see Unfair Technique 11-II). There were other problems in the new marriage, too, due partly to his "short temper" and partly to his wife's unpredictability. As a consequence, he retreated more and more to his dark, oak-paneled study which he loved and which he himself had decorated to look somewhat like a cozy British club for gentlemen.

Finally, the tensions in the marriage became so pronounced and Dr. T.'s depression and withdrawal grew so acute that he contacted me for help. I had only had a few appointments with Dr. and Mrs. T. when one night, right after I had gone to bed, I received an emergency call from the local airport. It was Dr. T., calling me to let me know that the engine of his private plane was running and that he planned to crash it into the mountainside near his house! All he wanted me to do was to notify his wife so that she could watch! I had to take his threat seriously; he had a history of impulsive acting out. It took me more than two hours to "talk him out" of his scheme and get him to agree to come to the office and talk about it. Since he refused to come in that night, I saw him early the following morning. He told me the following story:

On the evening of the phone call, Dr. T. had returned home to loving kisses from his wife who had his cocktail ready and showed that certain expectant look on her face that told him that a new surprise was in store. After a pleasant dinner he retreated into his study as usual to do some reading. But when he opened the door he got a shock which made him feel so dizzy he had to support himself against the doorpost. The darkly stained expensive oak paneling that he loved so much had been covered with a white wallpaper with small blue flowers on it! The heavy green draperies had been replaced by light blue ones with a pattern of small white flowers. Instead of the solid Turkish smoking table of black-stained wood and polished brass there was a "spinky" table of Danish design with a glass top. Where his old bookcase had been, containing rare editions of the classics, stood a magazine rack with an assortment of current issues, including fashion and housekeeping magazines. Where the old converted kerosene lamp had been was another "spinky" creation of walnut with a white shade on which there was a pattern of more small blue flowers. The elephant carved out of black teak with real ivory tusks, his favorite souvenir from his travels, had been replaced by a Swedish glass vase with fresh flowers and—oh no!—there were little blue flowers set into the glass also!

Dr. T. did not even step into what used to be his study. He quietly closed the door, went to the bedroom, and began to pack. His wife came in and was startled by his reaction. This time he did not need to say anything; she knew what was the matter, but she had *meant* so well! She felt the study was altogether too dark and gloomy; she had just wanted to make it feel more cheerful, especially since her husband had seemed so depressed of late! She felt they needed more togetherness in their marriage so she had planned to use his study for sewing while he did his reading. She was sure he would like the Danish modern design if he would just give himself a chance to get used to it. As for the blue flowers, she felt they were a perfect combination, blue for him and flowers for her! How could he be so unappreciative when she had thought he would be very happy and grateful?!

But this time, instead of flying off the handle as usual, with outward calmness Dr. T. packed his things and left the house despite his wife's crying pleas. He checked in at a motel, where he threw himself on the bed and began to brood. That was when he decided to commit suicide. He paid for his room, went to the airport, and started the engine of his plane. At the last moment, however, he got the idea that his wife should see him crash, but he did not want to speak with her directly, so he called me instead (the unconscious purpose for this probably was that he wanted to be prevented from taking his life).

As in the previous case, the shock this incident gave his wife ensured her cooperation in therapy. She had to face the fact that behind her sweet and compliant facade she was really a domineering tyrant who was actually rebelling against her own father, who had controlled her and her mother with an iron hand for the first two decades of her life. She had to achieve control over her own need to dominate, which expressed itself in her doing whatever she pleased without consulting her husband. In the early part of the marriage she had been able to hide this tendency behind the pretext—in which she herself had believed—that she knew what her husband would like and that she just wanted to give him nice surprises. However, her response to his later outbursts of anger (which reminded her of her father's tyranny) showed that she lived with a constant fear of being dominated and thus she needed to dominate. When her husband would flare up and accuse her of just wanting to hurt him, she would in turn accuse him of wanting her to be his slave!

In psychotherapy Mrs. T. had to learn to listen, actively listen, to her husband in order to understand his wishes and feelings. She had to face the fact that her "surprises," although consciously well meant, actually constituted a type of tyranny over her husband; she had to learn to test her assumptions with him before acting on them. Dr. T., on the other hand, had to face the fact that his irritability and "short temper" were indications of a fear of closeness and a reluctance to accept his wife as more than just an extension of himself. As these and other problems were solved in psychotherapy, he and his wife developed a satisfying and deeply rewarding marriage relationship.

The common element in the examples above is action without previous verbal testing of assumptions. Although the consequences are seldom as drastic as in the two cases described, they can still be severe enough to ruin a relationship, sometimes for life.

There are other ways of breaking Rule 6. There are people who make their lives miserable by "reading the worst" into what others say and do. If a statement could possibly be interpreted in more than one way, these people will choose the worst meaning. Examples:

Husband says, contentedly: "Boy, that was a good dinner!"

Wife says (or, worse, thinks): "I take it yesterday's dinner was not good enough."

Son: "This sweater looks fine on me."

Mother (who gave him two sweaters): "Why don't you like the other one?"

Employer: "You have done a good job."

Employee (thinking): "Why didn't he say excellent?"

These people are often narcissists with a poor self-concept and a cynical-gloomy-contemptuous-unrealistic view of the world and of other people. They unconsciously love playing martyr and collecting injustices. They seem to demand that others (1) read their minds, and then (2) tailor-make their words and actions exactly to fit what they have read. Narcissists, martyrs, and injustice collectors are not easy to treat in psychotherapy. Individual therapy alone is often not sufficient to overcome such deep-seated personality problems. I therefore recommend that such patients enter group psychotherapy, in which the emotional confrontations with other group members have a better chance of producing insights and consequent change of behavior.

To counteract any tendency to act on untested assumptions, it is important to ask one's partner frequently such questions as: "Do you mean that . . . ?" or "Let me see if I understand you correctly; you want to . . . ?" or "I want to see if I can state your position fairly; please correct me if I misunderstood you on some point." This technique is referred to as "feedback" and is often used as an exercise in marriage counseling. It must be pointed out, however, that in asking these questions and attempting to restate the partner's positions one must be extra careful not to use exaggerations or sarcastic distortions.

Especially when the partner accuses and/or makes demands for a change, it is very important to check whether one has understood the accusation or demand correctly. The demand for change may *sound* unreasonable at first, but if it is explored in detail rather than immediately denied, it may be found to be reasonable after all. If the accused sees the demand as unreasonable even after it has been fully detailed, he must say so, but he must state *specifically* what it is about the demand that is unreasonable and what he would be willing to offer instead. Again, the temptation to distort the partner's demand sarcastically ("I can see you just want me to be at your beck and call all the time," or "I thought so, you don't want me to ever go out with the boys," or "Well, would your majesty mind if I at least get five hours' sleep?") is to be suppressed completely. If there are negative feelings about the demand, they must be voiced constructively: "I get angry if I have to . . . (no exaggeration here!)," or "In the long run I think that would make me very resentful; couldn't we instead agree that . . . ," or "I really don't like that idea, but let's see if we could work it so that . . .(specific proposal)."

Before leaving the subject of assumptions we should point out that there are certain people, most of them notorious intellectualizers, who make it very difficult for others to check assumptions with them. Such a person insists that his wish cannot be rephrased without changing its meaning. And since the wish cannot be rephrased, it is virtually impossible to check whether one has understood it correctly. Let us take an example.

Mrs. N. called me one day to tell me that she had a marriage problem and would like to know how soon I could see her and her husband for an interview. I gave her the information and she said she would call back to set an appointment, which she did a few days later. It was decided that I would start by seeing Mrs. N. alone.

In my initial interview with Mrs. N. she described the difficulties she was having in her marriage. It seemed that, although the marriage was beset by a multitude of problems and dissatisfactions, most of the arguments she and her husband had were concerned with misunderstandings and, morever, it was always Mrs. N. who misunderstood her husband. She gave me a recent, typical example. Mrs. N. wanted to have her kitchen remodeled and her husband had agreed, whereupon they obtained three estimates of the cost involved from different contractors. They discussed the matter and decided that contractor X seemed to be the most reliable, even though his estimate was not the lowest. In order to be sure that she would not again "misunderstand," Mrs. N. ended the discussion by checking with her husband: "Are you agreed, then, that I should call Mr. X.?" The husband said yes. When the contractor showed up a week later to do the work, Mr. N. flew into a rage and accused his wife of having arranged the matter without consulting him about it!

Bewildered, Mrs. N. reminded him of the discussion they had had and asked him whether he remembered having said that he, too, felt that Mr. X. seemed to be the most reliable. He said yes, he remembered. Mrs. N. then asked him if he remembered having agreed to her calling Mr. X. The husband again said yes. Mrs. N. asked: "Then why are you angry?" Mr. N.'s reply: "I just said that you could call him; I didn't say that you could tell him to do the work!"

Flabbergasted and staring at her husband in disbelief, Mrs. N. asked: "Then for what possible other reason would I have called Mr. X.?" To this her husband merely shrugged his shoulders and said: "I don't know; it was your idea to call. I just said that you could call him."

Mrs. N. went on to tell me that their whole marriage was filled with such "misunderstandings" and that no matter how hard she tried to check decisions with her husband to be sure that she understood him correctly, the same thing happened again and again. After we had discussed other aspects of her marriage and I had obtained a history of Mrs. N.'s life, we ended the interview, the understanding being that Mr. N. would call me to make an appointment for himself.

The same evening I got a call from a frantic Mrs. N.: it had happened again! The husband had told her it was all right with him if she called me but he had not specifically agreed to her setting an appointment with me! True enough, but what other possible reason could she have had for calling me again? The same shoulder-shrug was the husband's response to this question. Nevertheless, Mrs. N. said that she was determined to have this problem solved and set an appointment for the two of them to come in to see me together.

In the joint session Mr. N. defended his position. He was a stickler for precision. His hobby, moreover, was semantics and he insisted that any rephrasing would give a message a different meaning than the one intended, therefore he kept insisting that what he said was all he meant and that his wife had better learn that fact if she wished to avoid misunderstandings in the future. Three of my questions, however, succeeded in his being forced to change his position.

1. My first question was: "How, then, would your wife be able to check whether she has understood you correctly? Would it not develop into a situation where she would have to cover all possibilities of interpretation as carefully as a lawyer, and would this not take all the spontaneity and joy out of your relationship?" Mr. N. said he would need to think about it; the point was worth considering.

2. My second question was whether Mr. N. thought that he was blame-free in the question of how the misunderstandings arose. Could he not, for example, have put his hobby of semantics into practical use by adding the phrase "but don't ask him to do the work" in the case of the contractor and the phrase "but don't set an appointment" in my case. Again, he thoughtfully nodded and said that he could have done so, but saw no need to at the time. Then was the same not true of his wife? She could have added: "to do the work" or "to set an appointment" but she saw no need to at the time! Now Mr. N. was beginning to see the point and for the first time said definitely

yes, he could see that they had both been breaking semantic rules.

3. My third question clinched it. I asked Mr. N. whether he lived by his own rules. Suppose he had planned a vacation with his wife and had asked her whether she would like to go to Hawaii, and suppose her answer had been yes. Suppose further that he had asked her whether she would like to go on the first of July and that she again had said yes. Suppose further that he had asked her whether he should call the travel bureau then, and she had again said yes. Would he then not assume that it would be all right for him to buy the tickets? Mr. N. nodded. "Then what would you say if your wife told you: 'I said I would *like* to go but I didn't say I *would* go!' "

With an embarrassed smile, Mr. N. said he got the point. Even better than that: he said that he could now see the value of going to a third party to discuss such problems and that he would be happy to continue coming in with his wife to work out their marriage problems!

It would seem from this example that Mrs. N. was an innocent victim of her husband's unwillingness to cooperate in efforts to make decisions and understandings specific and clear. This would perhaps be so if the situation is viewed out of the context of the rest of the marriage. However, a closer look at the marriage revealed that whenever anything went wrong, Mrs. N. would blame her husband for it. She would even blame him for decisions to which she herself had agreed, saying that he "talked her into" them, as if she did not have a mind of her own. The husband's unwillingness to make specific decisions was in part a way of retaliating against his wife and of avoiding responsibility for the consequences of decisions made. Thus, both spouses in this case were crazy-makers (see Unfair Technique 11-XI), the wife using crazy-making technique number 5 (p. 147) and the husband number 7 (p. 148).

The main lesson we can learn from the case of Mr. and Mrs. N. is that the partners in communication *share* the responsibility for making wishes and preferences clear as well as decisions. Therefore, if chronic misunderstandings occur which the partners are unable to prevent through their own efforts (for example, by reading this book and attempting to put its precepts into practice), *both* partners should seek the help of a third, professionally trained, party in order to get at the source of the misunderstandings and work out a program for their prevention.

# 7. "HOW CAN YOU SAY SOMETHING LIKE THAT?"

*Rule 7: Recognize that each event can be seen from different points of view.*

When you ask some people why they get angry with each other so often and get into so many destructive arguments and fights, they often reply: "That's because we disagree about so many things." In other words, they see a disagreement as inevitably leading to an argument. The fact is, however, that differences of opinion can lead to very interesting and rewarding discussions; they do not have to lead to arguments at all.

Some parents, for example, are threatened when their children disagree with them and see such disagreement as "talking back" or "being sassy," even though the children are not being disrespectful in their choice of words or tone of voice. Instead of welcoming a discussion of views, such parents get angry with their children for expressing a different opinion. In scolding the children for voicing dissent, parents do a great deal of damage:

1. They discourage the development of independent and creative ideas and opinions in their children.

2. They establish a dictator/subject relationship rather than an interested-parent/thinking-child relationship, thus inviting later rebellion.

3. They deprive the child of the rewarding experience of stimulating his mind through a thought-provoking discussion and exchange of ideas.

Of course, the parents must insist on their children's disagreement being voiced in a respectful manner, in choice of words as well as tone of voice (Rule 14). It would hurt not only the parents but the children themselves if the latter are allowed to get away with being disrespectful. The rule must be that all disagreements are welcome and will be thoroughly considered and discussed, but only if they are brought forth respectfully. (It should go without saying that the Fourth Commandment in the Old Testament, "Honor thy father and thy mother," must be expanded with the reciprocal "and respect thy child as a human being"; furthermore, not only should children respect their parents but the parents must also try their best to be worthy of such respect.)

Actually, there is good reason to welcome opportunities to discuss objections and differences of opinion, as long as the parties involved are respectful of one another. It is a good idea, especially in larger families, to *create* opportunities for the family members to voice their feelings. This can be done particularly well in a Family Council, the meetings of which are scheduled in advance and in which each family member can present his ideas, opinions, and grievances and have them fully discussed.

Let us show through examples how a difference of opinion should and should not be handled.

A. If a child says to his parent: "I think you are unfair," there are many ways in which the parent can react. Unfortunately there are parents who are defensive and easily threatened and who would accuse the child of being sassy, if he said he thought they were unfair. He might then even be punished for voicing his opinion, which certainly constitutes gross injustice.

But there is a larger group of parents who would counter the statement "I think you are unfair" with a sermon expressing outrage, starting with "How can you say something like that? Just think how hard I work . . . etc., etc." and ending with ". . . so I don't want to ever hear nonsense like that from you again." The sermon is designed to steamroll over the child's opinion, belittle it, and imply that it is a stupid opinion to have in view of all the "facts." The "facts" are that the parents have always been fair and reasonable; everything they have done has always been for the good of the child and it hurts them to hear such ungrateful and rude accusations from him.

This type of sermon is destructive for several reasons:

1. It violates at least four of our Rules of Communication:
   a. The rule under discussion which states that there is more than one way to view a situation and that this fact must be recognized.
   b. Rule 8, which states that your family members are experts on your behavior.
   c. Rule 15, which states "Thou shalt not preach."
   d. Rule 19, which encourages you to listen and ask more questions in order to understand the feelings of the other person and how these feelings came about.

2. The outright denial of the child's point of view shows contempt and implies that he is stupid to hold such a view in the first place and, consequently, that his opinions are worthless. This is likely to lower the self-concept of the child, with all the serious consequences ensuing therefrom.

3. No one likes to sit and listen to another person bragging about how wonderful he is. The child is likely to feel: "Oh no, there he (or she) goes again with that old sermon" and may tune out the parent entirely.

4. The child may feel that you are unable or unwilling ever to understand him and his feelings.

5. As a consequence, he may give up trying to communicate with you at all in any positive sense of the word. He may start shrugging his shoulders instead, which is a way of communicating, of course, but a destructive one (see Unfair Technique 11-XIV).

6. By using only selected evidence in "proving" fairness, the sermon actually confirms the original accusation of unfairness.

So, when the child says "I think you are unfair" or voices any other opinion regarding you or any topic, it is a good investment to take the time to discuss his opinion thoroughly. If there is no chance to do so at the moment, you may suggest that the topic be discussed later, perhaps at the next meeting of the Family Council or, if he prefers, just between the two of you. Then, if he forgets to bring it up, you must remember to bring it up yourself; his feeling that you are unfair is too important a topic to let go undiscussed.

In the course of the discussion, if you cannot see how you

have been unfair, you must *ask him to present evidence:* "Show me how I am unfair." This will lead to positive results no matter what the outcome of the discussion is, for the following reasons.

1. If the child is able to demonstrate your unfairness, you have learned something very important about yourself. You can thank him for calling it to your attention, apologize, and promise to mend your ways in the future. (This presupposes maturity, common sense, and lack of defensiveness on your part.) It will increase your child's respect for you. It will not, as some parents fear, detract from your authority. It will also increase the child's respect for himself, because you have shown that you attach importance to his opinions and that you are willing to change your own thinking if he can present evidence for his point of view.

2. On the other hand, if the child can give you no evidence to show that you have been unfair, then you can ask him if he thinks *he* is really being fair in making an accusation which he cannot back up with examples. Whether he responds to this question or not, you have still given him a chance to present his case, and you have set the stage for him to *think through* this problem rather than just engaging in bickering and squabbling with you.

3. Or suppose you find out that you and your child have quite different ideas of what is fair and what is unfair. This, too, is valuable knowledge and can be the subject of interesting discussions (not sermons from you!). If his ideas of fairness seem distorted to you, you can discuss with him—preferably through questions designed to make him think—what his ideas would lead to if they were put into practice.

So, no matter how the discussion turns out, you have shown—through your interest in the child's opinion—that you are a reasonable person who tries to be fair and you have given him a good lesson in communication. The results have all been constructive, at least potentially. Moreover, even if there are no noticeable and immediate positive consequences, at least you have prevented negative or destructive consequences from developing.

B. Here is another example. A teen-age girl who is not old enough to drive herself says to her mother: "You never take me anywhere. Every time I ask if you can take me some-where you say that you are busy."

Let us analyze the statement from the standpoint of com-munication. The girl is most probably exaggerating and thereby breaking Rule 5, which states that you should be realistic and reasonable in your statements. She may also un-consciously be laying a trap for her mother to engage in a sermon, so that the girl can say to herself—or to her mother —that she is preaching again. A mother who does not follow sound rules of communication and who falls into the girl's trap would react as follows:

> *Daughter:* "You never take me anywhere. Every time I ask you to take me somewhere, you say you are busy."
>
> *Mother:* "How can you say something so ridiculous? What do you mean I never take you anywhere? All I do around here is chauffeur you kids around all day. I constantly have to drop everything and be at your beck and call. It's time you stopped ordering me around and you'd better remember I'm not going to stand for it any longer. Last week alone I must have taken you to a dozen places and you did not even thank me for it! I am not going to stand here and listen to your sassing me around. Anyway, when are you going to stop biting your nails? Look how ugly they are. (Etc., etc., a tirade like this can go on for a long time.)

This mother breaks several rules of communication, includ-ing Rule 5 ("constantly at your beck and call") and Unfair Technique 11-III (using counteraccusations). However, here we are concerned only with her unwillingness to see that the situation can be viewed differently from someone else's stand-point. This can only lead to negative results, as shown in Ex-ample A above.

Now let us listen to a mother who follows sound rules of communication.

> *Daughter:* "You never take me anywhere. Every time I ask you to take me somewhere, you say you are busy."
>
> *Mother* (subtly correcting daughter's exaggeration): "I know you feel I say 'No' too often, and maybe I do. I usually think I have good reasons for saying 'No,' but maybe you feel they are excuses. Give me some examples and let's go over them together."

This mother has followed Rule 5 (be realistic and reasonable) and the rule we are discussing (each event can be seen from a different point of view). She has not denied her daughter's statement but she has made it clear that she sees matters differently. She has indicated her willingness to understand her daughter's point of view and asked her for specific evidence. The burden of presenting evidence now rests on the daughter, as it should, since it was she who made the accusation. Best of all, this mother has given her daughter a valuable lesson in good communication.

C. An excerpt from a case history of one of my patients will serve to further stress the importance of recognizing that events can be viewed differently by different people.

> Janet, seventeen years old, was referred to my office because her mother considered her incorrigible. She was failing in school, stayed out late at night, ran around with "the wrong crowd," and had recently started attending parties where drugs were used.
>
> Janet had lived alone with her mother all her life and had never known her father, who had deserted the family when she was born. Her mother had devoted her entire life to giving Janet a good upbringing and to preparing her for the dangers she would face in life as she grew up, especially from men.
>
> One of the mother's main complaints was that Janet never opened up to her, never came to her with a problem, and never talked about her feelings. Since I had already had an interview with Janet in which some very strong feelings against her mother came out, I asked her mother: "Are you prepared to accept these feelings from your daughter if we can get to a point in therapy where she will open up to you and tell you about them?" The mother said: "Yes, of course, I would give anything if she would just come to me and discuss her feelings. I know I must have faults, too, and if she tells me about them I will do everything I can to correct them."
>
> Janet did well in her psychotherapy and the time came when she did go to her mother to talk about her feelings. What she said was: "Mother, I have some weird feelings to tell you about. I have not talked with you about them before, because I was afraid to hurt you, but you say you want me to be honest, so here goes. The truth is that I love you as a mother, but I also hate you at times. I don't know all the reasons yet for my hating you, but I think it has a lot to do with your always saying bad things about my dad and about

all men. I feel that no matter what my dad did, he was still my dad and you have no right to drag him down without mentioning the things you did that he didn't like. I feel it is terrible that you, because of what happened between you and my dad, have tried to make me fear and hate and despise all men. And I also feel that you yourself never tried to open up to me and be honest about your own feelings. You never tried to understand my way of seeing things and most of the time I feel you are unreasonable about what I can and cannot do."

At this Janet's mother flew into a horrible rage and screamed: "How dare you come and accuse me like that? You have no reason to say those terrible things about me and if you are so ungrateful for everything that I have done for you, you don't need to stay one minute more in my house."

Janet left and came to my office intending never to go back to her mother but to join a hippie commune instead. I got the mother on the phone and asked her to come to the office. By this time she had quieted down considerably and when I reminded her of what she had said in the first session about being willing to face any feelings that her daughter might express, she realized that she had bungled a wonderful opportunity to communicate meaningfully with her daughter. Janet and her mother made up and one of the results of their first "real" discussion was that the mother herself entered psychotherapy to work on her part in contributing to the problems!

At the time of writing, Janet is twenty-one and still lets me know from time to time how she is doing. She is engaged to be married and—wonder of wonders—so is her mother! Both like each other's choice and the relationship continues to improve.

So here we have a somewhat drastic—but in no way unique —example of what can happen if parents are not willing to recognize that the way they view a situation is not the only way it can reasonably be viewed. Make no mistake, Janet's mother harbored no conscious ill will toward her daughter; she thought she was helping Janet when she talked about men in general and she thought the rules she set were for Janet's own good. Parents who harbor conscious ill will toward their children are rare and would not, as a rule, even consider bringing their child to a psychotherapist. The worst obstacle in the relationship between Janet and her mother was the mother's refusal to attempt to see that there were important reasons for Janet's feelings toward her and that these reasons needed to be discussed reasonably and with mutual respect. Once this obstacle was overcome, it was clear sailing in psychotherapy and both Janet and her mother did well in improving their relationship and in their development and growth as individuals.

When anyone sees a situation differently, he is worth listening to. If he is an expert, however, he is worth listening to even more closely. This leads us to Rule 8 which is, in a sense, an amplification of Rule 7. The examples we gave above will therefore all apply to Rule 8.

# 8. "I AM NOT ANGRY, DAMN IT!"

*Rule 8: Recognize that your family members are experts on you and your behavior.*

This rule is similar to and in some ways a more specific example of Rule 7, but it is so important that it deserves a chapter of its own.

People with family problems often come to a psychologist to find out "what is wrong." The fact is, however, that if they would only listen closely to the diagnoses which other family members offer concerning what is wrong and accept their suggested remedies, they would often not need to seek professional help at all.

Many people are curiously reluctant to listen to and take advice from members of their own family. And yet the people you live with, your family members, have observed your behavior for a long time, know you intimately, can hear things in your voice and in your choice of words that you can't hear, and can see feelings reflected in your facial expressions that you yourself may not be aware of. As a matter of fact, in one sense your family members will always know *more* about you than any psychologist will and that is in how you "come off" to other members of your family. It is true that a psychologist may eventually know many things about you that other family members would not even suspect, but in the case of what you communicate through your daily behavior each family member is an outstanding expert on you.

Therefore, whatever a family member says about you must be taken very seriously and must be seen as valuable information. There are four main reasons why such valuable information is often scoffed at by the recipient:

1. One reason is that when an unpleasant truth is told in a family, it is often in anger, in the heat of an argument, and the truth is then often exaggerated to such an extent that it becomes a caricature and the recipient is therefore not willing to accept it as having any value at all.

2. Another reason is that the person telling the unpleasant truths has his own problems, sensitivities, and tendencies to distort and these are known to the recipient, who then uses the fact that the "truth-teller" is biased as an excuse to dismiss the charge entirely.

3. A third reason has to do with the unconscious power struggle which often goes on among family members and which may be perfectly obvious to outsiders but not to the participants themselves. In these power struggles the individuals often feel (unconsciously) that the "truth-teller" would achieve a victory if any validity were acknowledged to characterize his statements.

4. A person with a poor self-concept may find any derogatory statement concerning himself unacceptable, especially when it comes from a person to whom he consciously or unconsciously feels inferior.

However, such conscious and unconscious resistances can be broken through if a person will consciously decide to constantly keep Rule 8 in mind and thus, in effect, define his family members as experts on himself and on how he "comes off" (in contrast to what his conscious intentions are). He will have to allow for whatever exaggerations, biases, or distortions the family members may use to color their observations, and then consider the remaining kernel of truth and work on its elimination. He will be helped in this task if he faces the fact that zero cannot be multiplied; if something is exaggerated it must be there! Only a hallucinating psychotic can make something out of nothing and even a psychotic hallucination is not always unrelated to fact.

Let us take some examples.

A. Suppose that your wife breaks Rule 5 (which has to do with being realistic and reasonable in one's statements) and yells at you that she is getting fed up with your always using television as an escape from talking with her. You may be tempted to yell back that she doesn't know what she is talking about, that you don't watch TV that often or that she watches TV more than you or that you wouldn't be surprised if you did, the way she always yells at you. DON'T SAY ANY OF THESE THINGS. You may honestly feel this way, but neither truth nor honesty is an excuse for using destructive communication (see p. 174). Anger can be expressed constructively rather than destructively (see the introduction to Rule 11), but it is certainly not expressed constructively through the use of counteraccusations (see Unfair Technique 11-III).

Thus, when your wife yells at you that she is fed up with your always using television to escape from talking with her, allow *silently* for the exaggeration involved and recognize that she would not feel so strongly about the subject if it were not important to her and if you had not—at least in her judgment—gone too far. Tell her therefore that she has a good point and that you will mend your ways. At a later time, when she is less upset, you should bring up the topic yourself and at that time you can also tactfully mention her part in creating the problem. If you find yourself resentful over having given up some of your television time, you must tell her about your resentment and indicate your willingness to work out a reasonable compromise which both could live with.

An important rule of thumb in this connection is: NEVER DENY SOMETHING THAT YOU CANNOT BE SURE ABOUT. In this category would fall your tone of voice, your facial expressions, your gestures, and—by definition—your unconscious motivations. Let us take an example.

B. Suppose your husband says that your voice is sarcastic and that you look conceited. You may be unaware of any sarcasm and you may feel humble rather than conceited. But since you have little or no knowledge of how your voice sounds to others or of how others "really" see you, do not make the mistake of denying your husband's allegation. Simply tell him that you were not aware of it but that you appreciate his telling you about it (beware of sarcasm here!) and that you will try to overcome that problem with his help. Do not come back with the common but silly counterargument that no one else ever told you that you are sarcastic or conceited. First of all, such things are not often said socially and, secondly, no one else may have had as good an opportunity to observe you as your husband.

In this connection we should also mention a fact that is not generally known or thought of: a person can have feelings of which he is not aware but which other people can see most readily.

C. I once had in group psychotherapy a young woman, Linda, who had a very expressive face. Consciously she was not very defensive as patients go and she was most cooperative in her psychotherapy. However, after only a few group meetings we noticed that whenever a group member confronted Linda with something she had said or asked her a potentially embarrassing question, her face would show a definite grimace of disgust. When this was pointed out to her she was incredulous and dumbfounded. She even suspected that this was some kind of trick to get her to admit to feelings that were foreign to her conscious mind!

Linda had felt no conscious disgust or embarrassment about the statements and questions directed to her. She asked us to call to her attention the next time she made such a grimace, which we did. The very next time it happened we pointed it out to her while her face was still contorted in disgust and—she became aware of it! It was an important moment in Linda's psychotherapy, because it demonstrated very forcibly to her that she had feelings of which she was unaware. The grimaces did not disappear suddenly; as a matter of fact it took months for the last traces of them to go away. Especially on the subject of sex the grimace of disgust tended to come back even after it had disappeared in connection with other subjects. But finally it was gone completely, coinciding with significant progress in Linda's psychotherapy.

D. In another psychotherapy group I once had a male patient, Sam, who saw himself as being a jovial, kindly, and accepting person. Sam would never have come in for psychotherapy if it had not been for the fact that people seemed to shun him. He was living apart from his third wife, all three wives having complained that he was constantly angry. Despite being very skilled at his profession he had difficulties keeping a job, because his co-workers, as well as his superiors and subordinates, reacted negatively to him. He had no close friends at all. Sam could not understand why this should be, since he felt kindly toward everyone and harbored no conscious anger or ill will.

The very first group psychotherapy session with Sam proved crucial and changed his life from that point on. When he had talked for a while about his problems, one group member asked him what he was so angry about. Sam replied that he was not angry. The rest of the group mentioned that their impression, too, was that he seemed very angry about something. Sam ridiculed the idea and repeated that he felt no anger and that he had nothing to feel angry about. His denials became louder and more vehement. Finally, with a fire-red face and with foaming mouth, Sam slammed his fist down, screaming at the top of his lungs: "God damn it, won't you understand: I AM NOT ANGRY!" There followed a deadly silence, all the group members staring at Sam. Suddenly the insight came to him, his eyes widened with fright and astonishment and he whispered "My God!" Tears began to fill his eyes and he buried his head in his hands, sobbing softly. Psychotherapy from then on was easy in his case, although it took him some time to recognize his anger in different situations, control it, and live down his reputation with his estranged wife, potential friends, and co-workers. When he was finally able to identify the sources of his anger in early childhood, his "recovery" became complete, he went back to his wife and found himself making good friends both in and away from his work situation. Now he was truly what he had seen himself as before: jovial, kindly, and accepting of other people.

The lesson from these examples is: never deny the way you "come off" to other people. Nor would it be reasonable for you to deny what others have to say about your unconscious motivations. By definition you cannot be *directly* aware of unconscious motivation; if you could, it would not be called unconscious! However, you can indirectly become aware of what your unconscious motivation is through: the things you do that you do not consciously intend to do, the important things you forget, "slips of the tongue," dreams, so-called "free association" (letting your thoughts freely wander from subject to subject), and projective psychological testing. Unconscious motivation can never be denied; the most you could say against a specific charge such as "You unconsciously are afraid of success" is: "It does not fit the facts." But if it fits observable facts, no unconscious motivation can be definitely denied or definitely confirmed (although insights and sudden "eye-openers" may corroborate or fail to corroborate it). Let us take an example.

E. If your husband uses Unfair Technique 11-II (mind-reading) and yells at you that what you really want unconsciously is a slave and not a husband, or if your wife screams that you are unconsciously trying to get back at your mother by punishing *her* (your wife), there is no way you can disprove these statements. All you can say is that these are not conscious thoughts of yours, but that was already implied in the allegations. The best and safest thing to say is that you will think about that possibility. But you must mean it and actually THINK ABOUT IT.

By the way, how *do* you know if such statements are true? The answer is that without professional help you cannot be sure. But one thing is certain: the more such an explanation (which seems absurd to you) fits the facts, the more likely it is to be a valid explanation. In any case, it is futile and silly to deny something you do not know anything about.

Labeling, which is often used for the purpose of manufacturing excuses (Rule 16), is also used destructively to avoid looking at the truth of what someone else has to say about one's self: "That's a stupid thing to say," or "That's so ridiculous that I won't even comment on it," or "I have never heard anything as asinine as that," are merely attempts to cover up an unwillingness to come to terms with a problem which has been presented, perhaps in an exaggerated form. Such labels are clearly destructive to communication and must be replaced with comments such as:

"I really don't see it that way at all, but since you do, I have to think about it some more," or

"Tell me what I did that made you come to that conclusion," or

"I feel hurt by your phrasing it that way, but I know I hurt you, too, so I will think about it and see if I can't change."

A particularly insidious way of avoiding a challenge is "exaggerated agreement," with or without sarcastic overtones such as: "Yes, yes, I know I am no good," or "I can't see why you married a stupid idiot like me in the first place," or

"Since I seem to hurt you no matter what I do, why don't you just divorce me and get it over with!"

Such sneaky ways of avoiding a challenge can only be met by continued frank confrontation: "Come on, you are avoiding the specific issue we are discussing."

In summary, do not ever deny the validity of what another person, especially a family member, says about what impression you give or how you "come off." Instead, ask for *how* you give the impression, so that you can become aware of your unconscious communications. This will give you a deeper understanding of yourself and will improve your chances of having all your communicative messages correspond to your conscious intentions.

# 9. "IT WAS YOU WHO STARTED!"

## *Rule 9: Learn how to disagree without destructive arguments.*

A discussion can be defined as a communicative interaction in which there is an exchange of ideas and feelings and where the object is to reach more understanding or to solve a problem—or simply to enjoy each other's company. A discussion of problems between intimates, especially, requires that the other person's self-concept, feelings, desires, and goals be viewed with compassion and understanding by each participant and that such variables be seen as important elements in the discussion.

An argument, on the other hand, is a communicative interchange in which there is an expression of ideas and feelings, but where the partial or total, conscious or unconscious, purpose is to hurt the partner. Arguments are often accompanied by irritated and angry or whining and complaining tones of voice. The term "destructive argument" is therefore redundant but I am going to keep using it nevertheless in order to avoid misunderstandings, since there are many people who would say, "I enjoy a good argument" (meaning an "animated discussion" or a "vigorous debate"), while very few would say, "I enjoy a destructive argument."

Admittedly, discussions do not always lead to positive results. The degree of selfishness in each participant will certainly influence the possibility of coming to an agreement. And even when an agreement is made, a selfish person might still do as he pleases no matter how nicely he has discussed a problem and no matter what the agreements were at the end of the discussion. Discussions and agreements will also be influenced by the degree to which a person has control over his impulses. If effective control does not exist, discussions may be fruitless until the person in question has improved the control of his impulses through psychotherapy. Even when discussions do not lead to positive results, however, they are still preferable to destructive arguments in which the individuals subject each other to humiliations, sarcasms, and unfair attacks.

Fortunately, the vast majority of people are not ruthlessly selfish and do have reasonable impulse control. Similarly, the vast majority do want to work out problems through discussions rather than through hurtful arguments. Very few people consciously want to hurt other family members, except in moments of anger. Destructive words and actions are common, but conscious motivation involving ill will is rarer than people realize. Angry or destructive thoughts, statements, and deeds occur mostly with a conscious feeling of having a "just cause" or of having been provoked or, in the case of many crimes, with an absence of consideration or compassion for the feelings of a victim rather than hatred for the victim.

Unconsciously, however, there may be some sadism in all of us, as evidenced not only by our dreams and slips of the tongue, but by the fact that we hurt others without consciously meaning to. One manifestation of hurting others consists of the negative words and antagonistic tone of voice we use when we find ourselves embroiled in an argument. I say "find ourselves" because very few people consciously have a desire for a destructive argument. On the contrary, people feel "drawn into" an argument and they have a tendency to feel that the hurtful words they use are only uttered in defense against the other party's attack.

One often hears the statement "I don't like to argue." Such a statement is a symptom of a communication problem. If a communication problem did not exist in the case of the person making that statement, he would feel no need to let it come through his lips in the first place!

The statement "I don't like to argue" is suspicious on at least two counts:

1. Since almost no one consciously likes to argue, why would anyone ever find it necessary to say it at all? It is similar to saying, "I don't like it when I get heart-attacks!" Who does? If a person makes such a statement, he must be trying to convince someone, most probably himself, that he does not want to argue. And why would there be any need to convince anyone at all, unless there were, indeed, an unconscious enjoyment in hurting the other person? The very attempt to convince oneself or someone else is suspicious. "The lady doth protest too much, methinks," as Shakespeare has the queen say in *Hamlet*.

2. Suppose you have an inkblot on a piece of paper, a blob that really does not look like anything unless you use your imagination. Suppose further that you show this inkblot to another person and ask him what he thinks it looks like. And suppose he says: "Well, I don't think it looks like an elephant." What can you be sure of? You can be sure that he did see an elephant on that card, but then did not accept the idea! The same is the case with "I don't want to hurt my partner." The idea of hurting the partner is there somewhere on an unconscious or preconscious level of awareness, but it is not acceptable and is therefore denied consciously.

People use the phrase "I don't like to argue" for one of at least three purposes:

A. The basic purpose is common but almost always unconscious and involves a mild form of the defense mechanism called denial of feeling. It appears to be an almost universal human tendency to wish to deny the existence of an alter ego. Rare is the person who admits that there is a "devil" within him (and those who do admit it usually do it for the purpose of excusing their destructive actions). Yet:

> "Zwei Seelen wohnen, ach! in meiner Brust,
> die eine will sich von der andern trennen,"*

says Faust in Goethe's drama. All of us have a good or kind and a bad or evil part of our personality and we do not readily admit to the presence of the latter.

The unconscious purpose, then, of saying "I don't want to argue" in the face of evidence to the contrary, is to deny the presence of destructive motivation.

B. Another purpose, very common and often conscious, is to convince yourself and the world not only that you are innocent and lily white, but that it is the *other* person who *forces* you to be destructive when the discussion turns into an argument. The processes involved are blaming (conscious) and projection (unconscious). The statement "I don't want to argue" implies *"but you do"* and thus involves the pretense "I am the innocent victim of my communication partner's cruelty."

The person who says "I don't want to argue" is also like the pharisee in the Bible who beats his chest and says: "Thank God, I am not like that sinner over there." It is an attempt to defraud and deceive others—and often also yourself—into accepting your innocence and attributing negative motivation solely to other persons.

C. A third purpose, also very common and sometimes conscious, is to avoid a discussion. The reason for such avoidance is usually some fear, perhaps of embarrassment, of being found out, of losing, etc. The avoidance may be conscious or it may involve various degrees of the unconscious defense mechanism avoidance.

Observe, for example, *at what point* the other person says "I don't want to argue with you." It is often said at a point where you have made a remark or a statement which is difficult for the other person to refute. So, instead of saying, "Hey, you've got a good point there, maybe I should revise my thinking about this," he escapes the confrontation by saying, "I don't want to argue with you about it any further."

The objective and demonstrable fact is that no one can

*Bayard Taylor (Goethe: *Faust* [New York: Random House, 1950]) translates these lines as follows:
> "Two souls, alas! reside within my breast,
> And each withdraws from, and repels, its brother."
The second line is more literally, albeit less poetically, translated as:
> "And one wants to separate itself from the other."

*force* a person to be destructive, unless he points a loaded pistol at him or something equally drastic. Therefore, anyone entering into an argument must enjoy it on *some* level of his personality, usually unconscious, as we said. It is this part of us that makes us provoke an argument or jump into it with both feet when the opportunity presents itself.

No one can start an argument without the full cooperation of the partner. The fact that another person is ranting and raving certainly does not mean that *you* must rant and rave. Thus the accusation "it was you who started" cannot be used legitimately to excuse destructive communication on your part. Nor can you legitimately use the other person's behavior as an excuse for sarcasm (Unfair Technique 11-XIII) or for being silent which, by the way, can be one of the cruelest ways of fighting (Unfair Technique 11-XIV).

Statements such as "I don't want to argue" and "It was you who started" are earmarks of highly defensive persons. Especially a person who relies heavily on rationalization as a defense will often betray this reliance by becoming highly upset when his motives are questioned, even when it is made clear that the questioned motives are unconscious and inferable only from his behavior, verbal or nonverbal. A nondefensive person would consider the possible presence of such—consciously absurd—motives with interest and a desire for more self-understanding. A person who relies heavily on rationalization (or, actually, on *any* unconscious defense) would therefore be particularly susceptible to be "drawn into" a destructive argument involving mutual indignation.

What are the possible unconscious purposes and "benefits" of arguing? It would be impossible to list them all, since many are specific to the person(s) engaging in the argument, but the most common purposes of arguing are:

1. To express a destructive need: the need to hurt another person (and thereby usually also oneself).

2. To hide one's own shortcomings under a cloak of indignation (the indignation resulting from the other person's destructiveness during the argument).

3. To avoid anxiety-producing situations. Arguments are often engaged in, for example, to avoid sex or to avoid serious and meaningful discussions on certain disturbing topics.

4. To have an excuse for failure. Example: "I would have passed that test if you had not kept arguing all night."

5. To avoid an intimate relationship. Fear of intimacy (often due to destructive experience with intimate relationships in childhood) is a common problem and can, as a rule, only be solved in psychotherapy.

Destructive arguments stand in the way of solving problems and of achieving a trusting and intimate relationship with another person. Therefore arguments must be prevented or counteracted.

How, then, do you prevent a discussion from turning into a destructive argument? It is simpler than you may think. I know of a rule that works almost perfectly, if you follow it consistently. The rule is simply this: When the other person says something you consider insulting, provoking, unfair, or outrageous, CONSIDER IT *AN INVITATION TO ARGUE* AND THEN DECLINE THE INVITATION by reacting in a reasonable, concerned, and tactful manner. (To "decline" it in so many words by accusing the other person of wanting to start an argument is just another destructive and unfair technique, see Unfair Technique 11-X.)

For example, if what the other person says insults you, tell him calmly and with sincere concern that you felt insulted but that you realize he feels strongly about it and that you may have done something to hurt him which you want to correct. Then you continue the conversation without retaliating. (It should go without saying that you are not to take the other person's use of destructive techniques as an excuse for employing them yourself.)

One of the standard excuses of a rationalizer for retaliating is: "I am not going to let him (her) walk all over me like that!" The statement is actually not relevant, since reasonable, sincere, and constructive replies to whatever insults have been proffered do not in any way involve permission for the other party to "walk all over" anybody. Such an excuse makes sense only if the other person is viewed as an actual enemy, and even then the reasoning involved is questionable. However, if the other person is viewed as someone who has used a poor or destructive communication technique, the proper thing to do, of course, is to use a constructive technique when replying. Naturally, care must be taken that the "constructive" party does not "rub in" the destructiveness of the other party. Usually any such tendency is best counteracted by reasonably admitting the kernel of truth in or justification for the other person's attack.

To repeat: Invitations to argue are to be declined by reasonable, compassionate, and tactful replies. This is a very good rule to teach to your children, also. If you can help your children adopt the rule in their own behavior toward each other, you will certainly prevent a great deal of destructive sibling rivalry and unnecessary fighting. Children often justify hitting another child, for example, by mentioning some kind of insult the other child has hurled at them. Whenever that happens, tell your child that you will not recognize such an excuse; the other child was inviting him to a fight and he had no business accepting the invitation and then blaming the other child. You tell him that next time someone insults him all he needs to say is: "I'm sorry you feel that way" and let it go at that. Such a statement will usually take the other child by surprise and will stop the interaction. But even if it doesn't stop the other child from continuing the insults, it is still a good exercise in self-control.

Let us take a number of examples of potential invitations to argue and see how they can be handled destructively by being accepted or constructively by being declined. In discussing these examples it is not necessary to go into a discussion of whether or not, or to what extent, there actually is an unconscious motivation to extend an invitation to argue. The response does not *need* to depend on perceived motivation; it can be based, instead, on a determination not to escalate the issue into an argument and still discuss the topic openly and frankly.

| Potential Invitation | Accepted | Declined |
| --- | --- | --- |
| Child spills something on father's trousers. | "You goddamn clumsy idiot! Can't you do anything right?" | "You should be more careful. Go to the kitchen and ask mother for a wet rag." |
| Your spouse reads something sinister or hostile into your perfectly legitimate question or comment. | "God, there you go again reading things into what I say. Can't you ever accept anything the way it is meant?" | "Gee, I am sorry that it seemed as if I—.What I meant was that—." |

| Potential Invitation | Accepted | Declined |
|---|---|---|
| Wife to husband: "I wish you could at least learn not to throw your clothes on the floor!" | "Who are you to talk? Just look at the mess you constantly have in the kitchen!" | "You are right, it is a bad habit of mine and I'll make a conscious effort to work on it." |
| Child to parent: "You are a liar." | "No child of mine is going to talk to me that way. This time you'll get a whipping so you can't sit for days." | "It hurts me when you call me a liar. Anyway, how did you get that idea? Why is it not possible that I simply have a different memory of what happened?"* |
| Husband to wife: "I have changed my mind; we are not going to the mountains on our vacation." | "What kind of damned dictator are you anyway? I am through slaving for you, hear? I'll have the divorce papers served on you right in your office and then you'll see who calls the tune around here!" | "I want to talk to you about what kind of marriage we want. I do not want the kind of marriage where we tell the other one what to do without discussing it first." |
| Parent to teen-ager: "No, you can't go." | "I knew it! You always say no. Boy, will you be sorry when I am eighteen." | "Dad (Mom), I feel I am entitled to a reason. Please tell me why I can't go." |
| Brother to sister: "You are a dirty rat-fink." | "And you are a yellow-bellied punk. Drop dead." | "Did I do something that made you upset" Or: "Sorry you feel that way" (said sincerely). |

*It is also a good idea to make sure the child understands how serious the accusation is and to explore with him the differences between lying and being mistaken. This would be a good opportunity to teach him how to express his doubt of someone else's word tactfully.

| Potential Invitation | Accepted | Declined |
|---|---|---|
| *Parent to child:* "You always forget to turn off the light in the bathroom." | "That's not true; I almost always remember. It is you who always pick on me whatever I do." | "I'm sorry, I do forget too often and I'll work on that. But I also feel that you pick on me too often and I'd like you to stop doing that." |
| *Anyone to anyone:* "I don't agree." | "You just want to start an argument again." Or: "I knew it, you find fault with everything and never agree with anything reasonable." | "Please tell me what your objections are." |

In lecturing on this topic I often hear the question: "To what extent should a child be allowed to argue with his parents?" The answer, of course, is that it is the parents who should never be allowed to argue (destructively) with their child. The parents must insist on respect from the child, but they must also earn this respect by not entering into destructive arguments with their children. The parents' point of view must be given calmly (not coldly) and reasonably, no matter how much the child invites the parent to argue destructively (by whining, repeating, silliness, or unfair accusations).

Another factor which can be of great help in preventing discussions from turning into destructive arguments is a good-natured sense of humor. Many tensions have been eased and many crises prevented by a friendly and "disarming" humorous remark. The use of humor, however, is tricky and can be most disastrous if not applied tactfully and with sincere consideration for the other person's feelings. We will have more to say about the use of humor in the discussion of Rule 18.

So-called "constructive fighting" or "creative fighting" can sometimes be dangerous and is to be recommended only if both partners agree that it is a good idea and that they are achieving results in terms of greater intimacy and trust from such "fighting." The fact is, however, that when "fighting" produces good results (other than merely "clearing the air"), it usually turns out not to have been fighting at all but just good give-and-take communication, which is what we are recommending here.

The neurotic need to feel indignant (or offended, insulted, or outraged) and its role in producing destructive arguments will be discussed in connection with Rule 20 (beware of playing destructive games). Suffice it to say at this point that partners often unconsciously agree to give each other cause to feel indignant (offended, insulted, outraged) for the purpose of fighting about safer issues than the ones that are really behind the disturbance in the relationship.

It should be clear from what we have said above that disagreements and divergences of opinion in themselves could never cause a destructive argument. As we pointed out in discussing Rule 7 (each event can be seen from different points of view), disagreements can lead to highly rewarding and interesting discussions as well as to arguments, depending upon how the disagreements are used by the partners. Disagreements are therefore to be solved by following all the rules of communication outlined in this book. In the event that no agreement can be reached, the partners can either "agree to disagree" or throw a coin to see whose view will be followed.

Once an agreement has been reached, however, it is useful to keep in mind that agreements are sometimes perceived and/or remembered quite differently by the parties to the agreement. Thus, arguments can arise as to what the agreement actually was. If this happens frequently, it is best to start an "agreement book" into which agreements are entered and initialed by each party. Many agreements should, in any case, be time-limited and renegotiable, and the book would then serve as a useful reminder of when such renegotiations are due.

Finally, a few words about the wonderful art of conversation. In this book we are concentrating on discussion as a means of solving problems, primarily because that is its most essential function. But discussion can also be enjoyed for its own sake, for the enrichment it can bring to relationships when opinions are listened to with interest and respect, and for the personal development and growth which is likely to be the outcome of frequent meaningful conversations.

Dinner time is an excellent opportunity to teach the art of good conversation, especially since it is not a particularly good time to engage in problem solving. Families whose members cannot take their meals together are most unfortunate because the children especially in these families miss out on the most wonderful opportunity to learn good conversation (parents who cannot converse well themselves would do well to take some courses on the subject). Almost unforgivable is the tendency in some modern families habitually to eat with the television set turned on.

All members of the family should be encouraged (not forced, cajoled, or nagged) to take part in the conversation, express opinions and ideas, and relate experiences. The children should be taught to respect the right of others to state their views and should—if they disagree with certain views stated—be shown how disagreement can be expressed respectfully. They should be taught not to interrupt (parents' example is one of the best teaching methods, as always) and, in general, to follow rules of communication such as those described in this book. Two decades of such daily experiences are going to provide them with an excellent foundation for their later efforts to establish good communication in their "new" families.

## 10. "I DON'T WANT TO START ANYTHING."

*Rule 10: Be open and honest about your feelings. Bring up all significant problems, even if you are afraid that doing so will disturb your partner. Do not walk on eggs.*

Having learned how to prevent a discussion from turning into an argument, you can no longer use the fear of starting an argument as an excuse for avoiding a discussion. You must resolve—if you want a truly intimate and trusting relationship with your partner—to be open and honest about your feelings, to "level" with your partner, and to bring up all significant problems, concerns, and worries. This you must do even if you are afraid that discussing them will prove embarrassing or otherwise disturbing to you or your partner.

To leave a significant problem or concern undiscussed is similar to leaving a festering infection untreated. The problem will not go away; on the contrary, like a spreading infection, it will get worse. The problem must be brought up and discussed tactfully (Rule 14) with due regard for the feelings of the partner; it will only hurt more in the long run if you try to protect your partner—or yourself, perhaps—from becoming upset by avoiding a touchy topic.

Another way of stating this communication rule is: DO NOT WALK ON EGGS! Walking on eggs is often confused with tactfulness, although in a certain sense it is almost the opposite of tactfulness. Walking on eggs implies: "I distrust your ability to handle a sincere comment and I fear that you will react negatively and therefore I will not tell you." In other words, the anticipated negative reaction of the partner is used as an excuse for not being open and sincere. Thus, in walking on eggs there is an implied contempt for the partner.

Tactfulness, on the other hand, implies respect for and trust in the partner. The message involved in a tactful approach is essentially: "I trust you to be able to handle my sincerity as long as I show respect for your feelings," and the feared reaction on the part of the other person is not used as an excuse for not being open and sincere.

Thus, walking on eggs is a destructive approach, a way of avoiding a problem and not being intimate with one's partner, in addition to showing distrust and contempt for one's partner. Tactfulness is a constructive approach which meets the problem and leaves the door open to intimacy, in addition to showing respect for the partner.

The technique of walking on eggs is often used by "fight-evaders" who stay out of fights because they are unconsciously afraid of losing the battle or afraid of the unpleasant facts about themselves or about their partners which might emerge from such fighting. Rather than risk having such unpleasant facts, weak excuses, or unwarranted assumptions exposed, they avoid discussion with the pretext that they don't want to "spoil a nice day" or they "don't like to argue." In the case of frequently recurring problems, the excuse "I don't want to nag" is often used (nagging is discussed in Rule 17). Walking on eggs can also be combined with Unfair Technique 11-XIV (the destructive use of silence).

Walking on eggs usually leads to intensification of conflict, since the feelings that are "bottled up" will become stronger and stronger. They may then express themselves either suddenly and explosively or gradually and in an "underhanded" manner (by "forgetting," passive resistance, or coldness, for example). Bottling up of feelings can also lead to serious psychosomatic symptoms.

Accommodating to the other person's wishes may be courteous and nice and lead to smoothness in living and to "getting along." But to accommodate or acquiesce when important issues are at stake, or when you yourself feel strongly against the other person's position, can be costly and dangerous. It can be costly because the price of accommodation is often chronic inner resentment and a feeling of being a "second-class citizen." It can be dangerous because the bottled-up resentment may take pathological forms of expression, as described in the previous paragraph, or the partner may start taking advantage of the fact that you give him a green light, in which case your relationship is in danger of becoming that of leader-master and follower-slave rather than that of two intimate companions of equal worth.

Thus, the statement "OK, have it your way" or "OK" accompanied by a sigh and/or a resigned tone of voice is a danger signal. No discussion should be allowed to end with such resentful or resigned accommodation. To "OK, have it your way" the only safe reply is "I appreciate your wanting to please me, but are you sure that you won't feel resentful about it? I don't want for us to make a decision you might find hard to live with."

Not bringing up significant problems for serious discussion can, in extreme cases, be lethal. I am not referring merely to the development of bleeding ulcers, the exact psychosomatic etiology of which is still uncertain. I am referring to clear cases where avoiding an honest discussion actually invited death. Let me give you an example.

Some time ago I was contacted by a family who had experienced the death of one of their children in a tragic freeway accident in which no one else received significant injuries. This is what happened:

The father, Jim, was a quiet, passive man who kept postponing matters indefinitely. His wife, Betty, kept nagging and pushing him but she never had a serious discussion with Jim about the basic problem of postponing because she was afraid of embarrassing him and making him upset. She was also reluctant to take matters in her own hands, because this could be interpreted by him as being "shown up." And *eventually* he would usually "get around" to doing the things that needed to be done, such as paying bills, buying a suit, or having the car fixed.

One day when Betty was going to pick up her children from school, she found that the family car with which she had taken her husband to work that same morning had a flat tire on the left front wheel. A retired neighbor offered to help her change tires but found that the spare tire was unusable. A tow truck had to be called and the car was taken to a garage. Betty was in a hurry and the mechanic put a patch on the left front tire. At the same time he warned her that the patch was temporary and only good for driving home on; it would not be safe at high speeds.

Every day during the following week Betty begged Jim to buy a new tire, but Jim kept postponing it. An inner voice kept telling Betty that she should do it herself, but she did not want to show Jim up! Then came Sunday and the family was invited to one of Jim's friends for dinner. The friend lived rather far away and Jim wanted to use the freeway to get there in time. Betty thought for a moment of refusing to go, but again decided that it would hurt Jim's feelings if she put her foot down.

On the way to Jim's friend, while they were traveling at high speed, the bad tire exploded. The car crashed into the freeway divider and one of the three children, the oldest boy, flew through the windshield and received a fatal injury.

This tragedy was especially terrible because of the fact that it could so easily have been avoided. The reason it took place at all could be traced to the fact that Jim and Betty did not express their feelings to each other openly and sincerely. They bottled up their grievances; they were "fight-evaders." Not that daily fights are necessary or, in my opinion, even desirable. What is necessary for an intimate and satisfying relationship is openness and honesty expressed in a tactful manner, but with a willingness to put one's foot down if the partner persists in a definitely dangerous pattern. Betty in our example should have stopped nagging Jim about his procrastination. Indeed, she should have insisted on a serious discussion of the problem—and on a workable solution. In the case of the tire, she should never have risked the lives of the whole family just to avoid hurting Jim's feelings. In the end, this avoidance turned out to be the most cruel thing she could have "done," because Jim will never be able to forget that he was the indirect cause of his son's death. Betty should have served notice on Jim that she will not get into the family car until she considers it safe; until it is fixed she will use a cab. Jim may have been angry, he may have been hurt, he may have felt henpecked, he may have pouted, but his son would have lived!

Death is perhaps a rare consequence of avoiding discussions of significant problems. But there are other tragic consequences. Countless divorces can be traced to such avoidance, and many child-raising problems also. Vast numbers of people are prevented from having an open, honest, and intimate relationship with another person because of the fear of expressing feelings and discussing problems.

The statement, "It would hurt (upset) him, so I won't tell him how I feel," is only partially based on a genuine and sincere conscious desire to protect the partner. When analyzed in psychotherapy this statement is almost always found to be an excuse designed primarily to protect the person making the statement from having to face basic and anxiety-provoking issues rather than to protect the partner from being "hurt." The statement itself implies distrust of the partner, or at least a lack of confidence in the partner's ability to handle sincere communication. It also implies pessimism with regard to the relationship ever developing into one of intimacy and trust, since intimacy and trust are dependent upon openness and sincerity of communication.

The statement, "It would hurt (upset) him, so I won't tell him," can also be seen as an example of the neurotic tendency to think in extremes. The person making the statement is, in effect, choosing one of two extremes: "I can't express my feelings without my partner becoming upset, so it's best that I don't bring up those feelings at all!" Although this statement may sound logical on the surface, it does not make sense because of two reasons:

1. The partner and the relationship will, in the long run, be hurt more by the silence than by bringing out the

feelings, even if the feelings are expressed in a destructive manner.

2. The feelings do not have to be be expressed destructively; they can be brought out tactfully and sincerely in such a way that the partner is not realistically hurt.

Reason number one is undeniable. Reason number two is often rejected by neurotic individuals with the excuse: "He would get just as upset whether I was tactful or not." The excuse must then be met by a factual observation: "If your partner gets upset when you express your feelings openly, sincerely, and tactfully, that is due to *his* neurotic problems, for which he should seek help. But you are not to use his neurotic problems as an excuse for not being open and sincere about your feelings, because such avoidance is in itself neurotic and destructive."

The reason the neurotic avoids the tactfulness-alternative is that he unconsciously knows he will hurt the partner most effectively by choosing either extreme: by being destructively open with his feelings (like the bull in the china shop—see Unfair Technique 11-VIII) or by being silent. Avoiding the tactfulness-alternative and engaging in one of the extremes (which can be guaranteed to make the partner upset) can then serve as a means to prove that the partner is an unreasonable person: "You see, there is no way to please him, if I express my feelings and scream at him he gets just as mad as when I am quiet, so what can I do? Of course I would rather be quiet, because I am a peace-loving person" (unconsciously: "because my being quiet will hurt him more").

The approach: "It would hurt him, so I won't tell him"— especially when it is chronic—amounts to accepting or "taking" too much negative behavior from the partner and can thus be seen as the opposite of faultfinding. The neurotic purpose of such long-term "swallowing" of the partner's unacceptable behavior is to "heap coals of fire" upon the partner's head and to let him accumulate a long list of crimes, which the "swallower" can then use later as an excuse for his own destructive actions. Let us take an example.

Mr. E. has for more than twenty years "silently endured" his wife's nagging, whining, and incessant demands for more money. Then one day when the children have gone away to college and his wife is out for the day, Mr. E. gathers up all his belongings, leaves a brief note ("I can't take it any longer") and leaves the house and the marriage for good. To his friends he later brags about how he—for the children's sake —"took" his wife's destructive behavior for so many years without saying anything! When asked about the reason why he never voiced his feelings or why he made so few attempts to voice his feelings, he may use the standard excuses: "I have no right to change another person" or "it would only have led to arguments; this way at least I had a little peace once in a . while."

Mr. E.'s destructiveness is at least equal to that of his wife's. Letting a person get away with destructive behavior is in itself destructive. It was Mr. E.'s duty in the marriage (1) to attempt to bring out the best in his wife and in himself; (2) to point out her destructive behavior and help her overcome it, even at the expense of arguments; (3) to ask her for ways in which he, himself, could improve; and if the first three failed, (4) to insist on professional help for the relationship. His failure to do so resulted in tragedy for both his spouse and himself.

Using the anticipated negative reaction of another person as an excuse not to be open and sincere is thus destructive to both parties. The excuse involved is weak, since knowledge of how the other person will react should be all the more reason why you can prepare to deal with his reaction constructively! If you know, for example, that a sincere remark will most probably be met by sarcasm, then you can prepare yourself to handle that sarcasm constructively, either by ignoring it and continuing to be reasonable in your own statements or, better, by saying something like: "It hurts me when you make sarcastic comments like that, but I know that I do things that hurt you, too, so let's both try to avoid that kind of thing," and then you go on being reasonable in your statements and sticking to the subject at hand.

Egg-walkers are often hypocrites who attempt to cover up the existence of hostility and tension with sweetness and superficial use of words of endearment. They will say "honey" when they mean "bitch," "darling" when they mean "bastard," "sweetheart" when they mean "swine." The destructive meaning of the words of endearment shows up either verbally in emotional explosions from time to time or nonverbally in destructive behavior or lack of desirable behavior. In either case, the destructive message is later explained away by "I didn't really mean what I said (or did)." The hypocrisy is, of course, usually unconscious and is experienced—often by both parties—as "really trying" (to be good, that is).

Pretense in a relationship supposed to be intimate is seldom constructive, except when exercised in front of other people, and then only if it is not obvious and sarcastic. Pretense, even when unconscious, can be most infuriating, as when an otherwise inconsiderate person pretends to show compassion or concern.* It is best, however, to respond to the overtly positive behavior rather than to the suspected unconsciously destructive motivation. The reason for this is twofold: (1) It is unfair to blame a person for something of which he is not aware, and (2) if you do blame a person for probably unconscious destructive motivation, he is likely to use such blame as an excuse to "give up": "Why should I bend backwards to try to be nice to you? You just find fault with anything I say or do anyway!"

People who are afraid of being open and sincere about their feelings are often quite manipulative in their approach even to supposed intimates. They see the spouse or the child not as another person with important feelings which must be understood, but as a set of buttons which must be pressed in the right combination so as to produce the desired response. Their concern in psychotherapy is thus expressed in statements such as: "What should I tell him exactly?" or "How should I phrase it?" or "I want to be certain that I say the right thing," or "When should I bring it up?" etc. The answer to all these questions is that you bring it up however you please and whenever you please, as long as you follow the communication rules given in this book and as long as you do not choose a time that is particularly inauspicious (such as when the other party is leaving for work, or suffering from a terrible headache, or in the middle of an interesting television program, etc.).

Showing one's negative feelings only in one's voice, facial expressions, gestures, or in a sarcastic phrase is not being honest and open. Consequently, it is injurious to the development of closeness and intimacy in a relationship. Let us take the feeling of irritation as an example. For every irritation there is a source (sometimes several sources) which

---

*Cf. the case of Joe and Carol, p. 237.

leads to the feeling of being irritated. This irritation is likely to show up in tone of voice, choice of phrases, facial expressions, or sighing, etc., and may then lead to an angry, sullen, or likewise irritated reaction from the partner. The result is then often a destructive argument into which both partners are "drawn" without really knowing how it happened. Since both partners feel drawn into the argument, each partner is likely to feel that it was the other one's fault and may thus feel indignant and resentful. Indignation and resentment, on the other hand, are among the worst enemies of closeness and intimacy (indifference being the "very worst").

To avoid such destructive interchanges, it is important not to show the irritation in voice, manner, or in any other "underhanded" ways, but to state it openly: "I feel irritated because. . . ." In other words, both the feeling and the *source* must be stated openly. If the source is not conscious, that fact must be stated: "I feel irritated but I don't know why. Maybe we can both try to find out what it might be that makes me feel this way?" Sometimes a person may even show irritation without being aware of the feeling consciously. In such a case, the partner has a choice between ignoring the irritation ("living with it") and pointing it out. Ignoring it may be dangerous, if the irritation is chronic or recurrent, since that may lead to resentment building up in one or both parties. On the other hand, if the irritation is temporary it may indeed be best to ignore it in order to avoid nagging or "playing therapist." Every human being must learn to accept and overlook temporary irritations, "moods," and minor rejecting behavior in other people. Only when such behavior becomes—or is in danger of becoming—chronic, must it be brought up and dealt with. When the rejecting quality of the other person's behavior is pointed out, it must be done in a compassionate and understanding manner, not in the form of picky accusations, nagging, or playing therapist. The attention should always be on the *source* of the irritation; its manifestation in behavior should only provide the stimulus to find the source and to eliminate or modify it.

A good rule of thumb in connection with recurrent problems is to *discuss them in advance*. If a problem has occurred often in the past, it is likely to recur in the future. It is best to attempt to prevent its recurrence through discussion now (even at the risk of being "drawn" into an argument), rather than to wait until the next time it comes up. If both parties can agree in advance on procedures to follow when the problem shows signs of recurring, then the problem will most likely be prevented altogether. Again, however, the partners must beware of the excuse "I don't want to start anything." They must also beware of using the advance discussion as an opportunity to heap further accusations on the partner.

In connection with Rule 5 (be realistic and reasonable in your statements) we warned against employing exaggerations in accusing your partner. Let us now show how accusations can be made—and, consequently, how anger can be expressed—with constructive results.

Accusations can be most destructive if the primary (conscious or unconscious) purpose is to hurt the partner, pick on him, make him feel bad, tear down his self-concept, or avoid facing one's own part of the blame. However, if the primary purpose is to solve a problem, an accusation can be not only desirable, but necessary.

Accusations per se are not incompatible with good and positive discussion. However, to insure that accusations are not going to lead to destructive arguments, both parties have to agree on certain conditions:

1. The primary purpose of an accusation must be to help solve a problem.

2. Accusations must be made one at a time, so that each one can be discussed fully.

3. All accusations and "gripes" must be specific and must be accompanied by specific demands for reasonable change.

4. The accuser must look at his or her own part in contributing to the condition of which the partner is accused.

5. The accused is not to use the fact that he is accused as a pretext for venting his anger.

6. No counteraccusations are allowed until the issue has been discussed fully. If the accuser is "guilty of the same crime" with which he charges the accused, the latter must wait until the end of the discussion before he can make his charge and thus himself become the accuser.

Accusations are often met by angry responses. Therefore, just as you must be open to your own feelings, it is important that you be open to the feelings of your partner. If your partner gets angry with you when you state your feelings openly and sincerely or when you accuse him of something which has made you angry, you must respect his feelings *even though he may state them destructively*. You are not to use his destructiveness as an excuse for becoming destructive yourself or for not recognizing the value and importance of his feelings. On the contrary, if your partner—in accusing you or in responding to your accusation—communicates his anger in destructive ways, the probability is that you yourself (because of your present or past behavior) have contributed to making your partner feel angry as well as to his becoming desperate enough to use destructive ways of communicating. Thus, deal with the feeling expressed in an understanding, constructive, and problem-solving manner, rather than "hitting back." And do not fool yourself that such reasonable behavior on your part means that you are a "doormat" or that you "have to take it lying down." Such attempts at self-deception are designed to give you an excuse to be destructive yourself.

When accusations are dealt with in a reasonable and constructive manner with the attention focussed on solving a problem, they can lead to most fruitful and rewarding discussions. Once parents have learned how to accuse and how to deal with accusations constructively, they should not hesitate to accuse each other in front of the children (as long as the subject is not how the child should be handled). Children learn a lot through listening to adults solving problems and if they hear their parents discussing problems constructively, they will benefit even when anger and raised voices are involved.

Many parents are afraid of bringing up problems in front of their children. They either wait till their children are away or asleep, or they go to the bedroom, close the door, and whisper angry words to each other!

There is, of course, some merit to this protective attitude. If parents do not follow sound rules of communication and are unwilling to learn to do so, their discussions are, indeed, best conducted out of earshot. Otherwise, the parents will be teaching their children destructive techniques of communication. But it must be kept in mind that the children of parents who do not at all show anger and/or discuss problems in front of them are disadvantaged. They are not taught constructive and helpful ways of showing anger, nor are they given examples of how problems are discussed and worked out through mutual give and take.

To discourage children from becoming manipulative and "playing one parent against another," it is important to present a united front with regard to how the children should be handled. To side with the child against one's spouse is an example of "dirty fighting." The negative feelings or disagreements you may have concerning the way your spouse is handling the children must be communicated after the children are out of earshot. However, if the discussion is not about how to deal with the child (or about sex or other matters which could be of no benefit to the child), the discussion is carried on reasonably, and the verbal fighting—if present —is fair (does not employ destructive techniques), then the children should be allowed to listen. One of the main factors in developing maturity and good judgment in children is the observation of how the parents solve problems through discussion. This is an invaluable gift for the child and he should not be deprived of it. Of course, you need to see to it that "raised voice" discussions do not become chronic and are not allowed to interfere with the general cheerfulness of the home atmosphere.

Cheerfulness is one of the most important qualities in "running" a home. Cheerfulness will make other people feel good and will help them accept minor frustrations much more readily. However, cheerfulness must be coupled with openness about one's feelings, otherwise it will become false and will lead to the bottling up of resentments which will then express themselves insidiously and destructively.

Similarly, the ability to control one's feelings in terms of the old Victorian "stiff upper lip" can be a great asset, a sign of emotional security and strength of character. But the stiff upper lip was used by some Victorians to avoid intimacy, and in those cases it was a destructive quality. The stiff upper lip is meant to be reserved for adversities coming from *outside* the family; then it is indeed a wonderful quality and one which we should teach our children.

Thus, it should perhaps be stressed that Rule 10 applies only to relationships where intimacy is involved. In superficial relationships it is often imprudent and/or rude and/or cruel to be honest about one's feelings. It may be damaging to the other person and it may be damaging to oneself. Complete and indiscriminate honesty about one's feelings is not the goal. The goal we must strive for is the *ability and willingness* to be honest about our feelings when such honesty is called for.

Finally, we should point out that there is an important exception to Rule 10 which should be stated as a subrule: *Never Communicate Thoughts Which Clearly Stem Either From Your Own Psychopathology or From Insufficient Repression of Impulses Which Are Normally Checked By Strong Taboos.* Examples:

Henry was an obsessive-compulsive patient who suffered from incessant thoughts of killing his wife. He would even at times go to the kitchen and weigh a sharp knife in his hand while having these thoughts. Henry was extremely frightened by his obsession even though he knew he would never act it out. He was also particularly puzzled by his murderous fantasies because not only was he a mild-mannered and kind man, but his relationship with his wife was warm, close, and loving, and he felt no significant conscious resentment toward her.

Henry's problem was severe and he suffered terribly from it. Constantly plagued by the idea of murdering his wife, he was unable to sleep without taking sedatives, lost weight, and his performance on the job began to deteriorate. To his wife's questions as to what was the matter, he only gave the explanation that he had problems at work.

There is no doubt, however, that it would have created a much worse problem if Henry had told his wife about his thoughts, because she would then have lived in constant dread of his killing her. Instead, Henry sought psychotherapeutic help at my office. I encouraged him to speak openly to his wife about everything *she did* which made him resentful but to say nothing about his thoughts of killing her. We soon found that these thoughts were actually revivals of death-wishes he had had toward his mother when he was a boy. This insight (together with other insights he made in psychotherapy) had the initial effect of removing the compulsive and frightening aspects of the thoughts and later led to the disappearance of these thoughts altogether.

Mrs. A. had incestuous feelings toward her teen-age son, with whom she had lived alone since her husband deserted her when the boy was just a baby. As in the example above, it would have been disastrous if she had been open and frank about these feelings to her son. He would have been badly frightened and his psychological development could have been affected most adversely. Instead, Mrs. A. came to psychotherapy to work on her problems. She found out that the normal repression of the taboo against incest had failed in her case, primarily because of a strong fear she had of involvement with any man. This fear made her avoid relationships with eligible adult males and caused her to turn *all* her attention to the only male in her life: her son. The fear, in turn, was due to her past relationships with men (especially her father and stepfather, both of whom had been brutal and unfair but at the same time rather seductive) and to her mother having imbued her with a hatred against men during her childhood. The insights Mrs. A. achieved in her individual psychotherapy removed her conscious incestuous feelings entirely, at the same time she worked on her hatred against men in group psychotherapy.

The point is clear: thoughts and feelings which are due primarily to pathology within oneself are to be communicated only in a professional psychotherapeutic setting. If there is any doubt as to the degree of pathology involved, a psychologist must be consulted.

A last word: Rule 10 should never be used as an excuse to communicate feelings destructively. There is no honesty involved in choosing a destructive rather than a constructive way of communicating one's feelings.

# 11. "NO WONDER YOU HAVE A BROTHER IN A MENTAL HOSPITAL."

*Rule 11: Do not use unfair communication techniques; do not engage in "dirty fighting."*

There is a famous play by August Strindberg called *The Dance of Death*. Not only is it a great drama, it is also an extremely perceptive study of destructive communication in marriage. In Strindberg's play there is none of the crudeness and vulgarity of Edward Albee's *Who's Afraid of Virginia Woolf?;* instead, there is an insightful description of the subtle techniques which two spouses who know each other intimately are capable of using against each other to inflict agony. In the various subheadings of this chapter we are going to describe such subtle techniques, as well as the crude ones.

My hope is that some readers who may—knowingly or unknowingly—be using one or more of these techniques will be influenced through recognition to discontinue their use. Others will need professional psychological help to stop using destructive techniques; still others will remain unmoved and will continue hurting others through unfair means.

The list is by no means to be considered complete. Some techniques, such as nagging, preaching, and using excuses have been treated under separate "don't-rules" in this book. Others, such as outright lying, betrayal of another person's confidence, and physical fighting, I have deemed too obvious to be included here. The destructive techniques listed here should, however, serve to provide ample examples of what constitutes taking unfair advantage and being a "dirty fighter."

In the discussion of Rule 10 (be honest about your feelings) we warned against using excuses for hiding feelings of anger. I hope that the very existence of the destructive techniques described in this chapter will not be used as such an excuse. Anger is a normal, necessary, and healthy emotion that should be expressed. But it can be expressed fairly, without the use of unfair methods and without destructive effect. To put it in other words: you can learn to stay reasonable when you are angry. The illusion that reasonableness and anger are incompatible is responsible for many tragedies.

When you feel angry toward a family member, it is best to tell him or her about it honestly and sincerely, at the same time mentioning the reasons for your anger. It is unreasonable to demand that you inhibit all nonverbal expressions of anger. Healthy anger is often accompanied by such expressions as flushed face, angry (but not threatening) gestures, and raised voice* (but not screaming). But it is also unreasonable to behave like a bull in a china shop (Unfair Technique 11-VIII) and use the excuse of just being honest about one's feelings (Rule 16).

Anger is not to be hidden, it is to be expressed honestly without hurting the other person unfairly. However, if the anger is chronic or if it is precipitated by minor matters which all people must learn to take in their stride, then the person feeling the anger will need to seek professional help.

Some people, especially those involved in destructive game playing (Rule 20), are characterized by a seemingly irresistible need to engage in destructive fighting. Consider the following example.

> David and Bessie have "fought dirty" all through their marriage and have used several of the destructive and unfair techniques which will be listed in this chapter. Both have made especially heavy use of sarcasm. However, Bessie has begun psychotherapy and has recognized the destructive techniques she has been using. She now wishes to stop her underhanded tactics and to state her feelings openly and sincerely; in other

---

*A raised voice *can* be used as a destructive technique if the partner for some reason is allergic to yelling or if the tone is perceived as menacing or threatening. There are some people who had an unhappy childhood, where the parents were constantly yelling at each other, and who are now very upset by being yelled at. If you raise your voice on communicating with a person that you know is allergic to a loud voice, you are being cruel and using a destructive communication technique (see Rule 12: It is the effect of your communication that counts, not your intention).

words, to "level" with her husband. In these efforts she understandably "slips" from time to time.

David, who has not entered psychotherapy, is unconsciously afraid of this new development and of the revelations about himself which openness and frankness in the relationship may entail. Accordingly, his response to Bessie's attempts to express her feelings sincerely is to use more of the "old" destructive techniques. This happens especially on the occasions when Bessie slips:

*David:* "What was that you said?"

*Bessie:* "Gee, Dave, I slipped again and I am sorry. It was a sarcastic remark and . . ."

*David* (interrupting with a sigh): "Never mind, I'm quite used to it by now."

David's conscious excuse for this sarcastic response is: "Well, it is *true*. I am in fact used to it by now." The truth, however, is not to be used as an excuse for being destructive (p. 174). What David is actually communicating—without knowing it—is: "I think sarcasm is a much better idea, so I will use a sarcasm myself." More indirectly, David is communicating: "Don't stop using sarcasms, Bessie, because those have protected us from honestly facing ourselves for a long time and I am simply scared of your becoming more open and sincere."

How would David have responded if he had not had an unconscious need to keep the relationship on a destructive level? He would either have ignored Bessie's sarcastic remark or, when she apologized, he would—in a sincere tone—have said something like: "Gee, I think it is great that you recognized that you slipped. I will try to work on my use of sarcasm, too."

If Bessie keeps improving and David does not respond constructively, they will come to a point where David will have to enter psychotherapy himself (which he should have done together with Bessie in the first place). If he does not, the marriage will be in danger, because Bessie may decide that she no longer wants to live with such destructiveness now that she herself has worked out her own problem of being destructive.

David's sarcastic remark to Bessie's conciliatory apology shows that an unconscious part of David's personality *needs* destructive interaction. In our discussion of Rule 20 (beware of playing destructive games) we will examine in detail what some of the needs are which account for such implied refusal to cooperate in efforts to improve a relationship.

# "Am I Supposed to Jump Up and Down and Lick His Boots?"

*Unfair Technique I: Pretending that the other person has made an unreasonable statement or demand.*

This technique could be given various names, such as "The Ridiculous Alternative" or "Building a Straw Man." Essentially it involves drawing a caricature of the other person and then acting as if the caricature were, in fact, a realistic picture. Let us illustrate the technique by examples.

> Bill was a skilled mechanic who lived in a nice suburban home with his wife, Marilyn. Their two children, a boy and a girl, were in their teens and doing poorly in school. Bill and Marilyn had several problems in their marriage, only one of which we will go into here.
>
> Bill, like Jim in a previous example (Rule 10, p. 84), was a postponer when it came to fixing things around the house. His great love was a 1928 Pontiac which he was rebuilding in the garage, and that hobby occupied all of his spare moments. He resented taking time out from his hobby to do things that his wife asked of him. He felt her demands were unending anyway, so it did not make much difference if he met them or not.
>
> Marilyn, in contrast to Jim's wife in the previous example, did not care whether she hurt Bill's feelings or not. She slammed into him almost daily with violent reproaches for the things he had left undone around the house.
>
> For over a month Marilyn had asked Bill to put in a new garbage disposal they had bought and to remove the old one. Bill constantly promised that he would "get around to it," but the new disposal remained in its box. Marilyn nagged, begged, and threatened, but Bill simply answered "tomorrow," or "as soon as I get a chance," or "when I get around to it."

One Saturday afternoon, however, when his wife was out shopping with the children, Bill felt in a good mood and decided to put in the garbage disposal, so that Marilyn would have a nice surprise when she came home. He worked rapidly and efficiently and had it installed and working long before he expected Marilyn to return. He left the box and some tools on the floor in front of the sink, so that Marilyn would know that the new disposal was installed, and then went to the garage to continue on his labor of love, the 1928 Pontiac.

Bill's appointment with me was on the following Monday and he looked rather sad as he came into my office. He had had a depressing weekend. This is what he said: "Here Marilyn has been bugging me about that stupid garbage disposal for such a long time, nagging me and pestering me about it constantly, day in and day out, and when I finally did it, do you think she said even one word to thank me for putting it in? No sir! She just went right ahead and used it and didn't say anything about it. Instead, she bawled me out for leaving my tools on the kitchen floor and gave me a bad time for not fixing the screen door while I had my tools out! How do you like that for friendly treatment?"

After Bill's session was over, I had an appointment to see his wife and during the course of the session I asked her: Marilyn, why did you not thank your husband for putting in the garbage disposal?"

The question made Marilyn angry. She looked defiantly at me and half shouted, half sighed: "Well! After all that waiting and postponing and all those excuses, after I have had to practically beg him on my knees for over a month, how can he expect me to suddenly start jumping up and down for joy and licking his boots?"

The last sentence of the example above constitutes the technique which uses The Ridiculous Alternative and is based on Building a Straw Man. Marilyn reacts as if Bill had said: "I think you should jump up and down and lick my boots." He had, of course, said nothing of the sort. He had indicated that he would have liked some recognition from his wife, some word of appreciation or even acknowledgment, but he had received none.

In this kind of neurotic interaction there are no innocent victims. The more Bill postpones, the less appreciation Marilyn will give him when he does do the things he should. And the less appreciation Marilyn gives him, the more Bill postpones doing things, using the excuse: "She doesn't appreciate it anyway, so why bother."

To break the vicious circle Bill could stop procrastinating. Marilyn could show him appreciation without jumping up and down or licking his boots. Both of them can make an agreement to cover such situations in the future. An example of such an agreement would be this: Marilyn agrees to tell Bill about what needs to be done and then to write it on the bulletin board in the kitchen with the date affixed. She also agrees to refrain from nagging Bill about it. Bill agrees to take care of the matter within fifteen days from the date; otherwise Marilyn is free to call in someone to do the job. Agreements like this do wonders in cutting down on nagging and make daily life a great deal more pleasant.

The basic purpose behind the use of The Ridiculous Alternative is to hide one's own crime (in Marilyn's case: not showing appreciation) behind the pretense that the other person is making an unreasonable demand (you must jump up and down and lick my boots). Pretense is an obstacle on the road to intimacy and must be abandoned. Sincerity and tactfulness must be its replacement. What Marilyn could have said in the case above is that she realizes she should thank Bill for doing the job, but that it is difficult for her to show even a little gratitude, because she is still mad about his putting it off for so long. No matter what Bill would have replied to such a statement, Marilyn would at least have known that she had tried to be open and sincere in her communication without attempting to hurt Bill.

> Some husbands seem to find it difficult to show their wives affection and, conversely, wives sometimes behave in a manner which discourages their husbands from showing affection. This was one of the problems that confronted Barry and his wife Lorraine. Barry apparently could not or would not show Lorraine any affection in daily living; the only time he showed her affection was when they were having sex. On one occasion Lorraine confronted him with this problem point-blank and said: "Barry, why is it that you can't show me any affection other than when we are having sex?" Barry's reply was: "You should know by now that I am not the over-emotional gushy type!"

The use of The Ridiculous Alternative is eminently unfair. Barry in the example above is building a straw man (or perhaps we should say "straw woman") who is unreasonably demanding and then he attacks and ridicules his own creation. Lorraine has obviously never said to her husband: "Please be over-emotional and gushy with me!" But Barry pretends that she has in order to cover up his own short-coming. He paints her as making a ridiculous and unreasonable demand, so that he will have justification for not meeting it.

What Barry in our example could have said instead, if he had followed sound rules of communication, would have been something like: "Gee, Lorraine, I know you have a good point there and I am going to work on it, and just to show you I mean business I am going to give you a hug right now." (When this was suggested to Barry in his psychotherapy, he used the excuse that it would go against his "nature," it would not be "he"! This type of excuse, unfortunately very common, is dealt with in Rule 16.)

> Dr. T., whom we have met in a previous example (Rule 6, p. 50), felt that his wife was doing too many things independently without consulting him. When he told her so, she said: "I know, you want me to become your slave and fall on my knees and beg you for permission for everything I do!"

The appropriate response would, of course, have been something like: "I think it is good that you told me what you feel about it. Let's discuss it and come to an agreement about what things we should consult each other on and what things we can do without asking or informing each other."

As we have seen in all three examples above, the destructive and dishonest use of The Ridiculous Alternative can easily be replaced with something honest and constructive.

The Ridiculous Alternative is sometimes used by a patient to ward off the remarks made by his psychotherapist, as in the following examples:

> A mother is talking to me about her son, who has just started in psychotherapy.
> *Mrs. X.:* "Ronny never does anything normal, he never does anything we ask him to do."
> *Dr. Wahlroos:* "Mrs. X., Ronny has complained about your exaggerating. Don't you think that you may be exaggerating when you say that he never does anything normal?"*

---

*There would be many other possible reactions on the part of a psychotherapist to Mrs. X.'s statement. In this case I chose to go into the matter of the mother's exaggerations, since that constituted the main conscious irritant for Ronny.

*Mrs. X.:* "I don't see why we have to wait till he is in a mental hospital before we start to worry."

In other words, in order to avoid facing the fact that she has a tendency to exaggerate, this mother pretended that I had suggested: "Mrs. X., I think you should wait until Ronny is in a mental hospital before you start worrying!"

Further examples of pretending that the therapist has made an unreasonable demand:

> *Dr. W.:* "Have you ever asked your wife what she felt about this before you married?"
> *Husband:* "No, I'm not going to start *prying* into her past!"

> *Dr. W.:* "Couldn't you suggest that he try another method?"
> *Company President:* "No, I'm not going to *dictate* anything to him."

This technique is often used with the unconscious purpose of discouraging the partner from being open and honest about his feelings, as can be seen in these examples:

> *Wife:* "I don't like it when you read the paper at the breakfast table."
> *Husband:* "I know, I know, you don't like anything about me."

> *Husband:* "Would you mind if I had an evening out with the boys next week?"
> *Wife:* "What are you asking me for? You always do as you please anyway!"

The use of this technique can be seen as a violation of Rule 5 (be realistic and reasonable in your statements) as well as Rule 6 (test all your assumptions). It also involves a definite element of sarcasm (Unfair Technique 11-XIII). However, it is a very specific technique in itself and I have therefore given it separate discussion. It is much used by people who try to be witty but who confuse wit and clever repartee with brutal assault or sarcasm:

> "Could you mail this letter on your way to the office?"
> "What do you think I am? Your errand boy?"

"There should be a little more salt in the mashed potatoes."
"Lousy dinner again, eh?"

One final word which, I trust, requires no elaboration:
*do not ever use this technique with children!*

# "You Did It Only Because
# You Feel Guilty!"

*Unfair Technique II: Mind reading, psychologizing, jumping to conclusions. Pretending that one single motive constitutes complete motivation. Divination.*

Rule 8 states that your family members are experts on you and your behavior. This is especially true of their observations concerning what impression you give them and how you "come off," but they may also have some interesting and valuable ideas regarding what your unconscious motivations might be. This fact, however, should not be used destructively. Theories regarding conscious or unconscious motivation, if mentioned at all, must be presented tactfully and with a genuine and compassionate desire to help the other person gain more insight into himself. The use of such theories as weapons of attack is grossly unfair, since it is impossible for anyone to read another person's mind.

We could call this technique Mind Reading, or Psychologizing, or Jumping to Conclusions, but no matter what we call it, it remains unfair and sometimes even dangerous. Yet it is widely employed, often well-meaningly and with the conscious purpose of indicating understanding of the other person's feelings. As a matter of fact, with all respect to my colleague, the late Haim Ginott, it seems to me that he—unwittingly—comes close to recommending daily use of this technique in his book, *Between Parent and Child.** Let us take some examples of the types of comment Ginott recommends that parents make.

*Child:* "I am not good in arithmetic."

| *Some comments recommended by Ginott:* | *Possible dangers:* |
| --- | --- |
| "Arithmetic is not an easy subject." | The child might use the alleged difficulty as an excuse for poor performance. |
| "The teacher does not make it easier with his criticism." | Children blame teachers enough nowadays. For parents to encourage such blaming can only be destructive. |
| "He makes you feel stupid." | Here the parent is playing an all-knowing God. The child may well feel stupid after such statements if he did not before. |
| "I bet you can't wait for the hour to pass." | The child may, on the contrary, have wished for *more* explanation from the teacher. A very dangerous statement, since it implies that a math lesson is *in fact* unavoidably boring or frustrating. |
| "You must be worrying about what we will think." Or: "You must be afraid we'll be disappointed in you." | If the child has a good relationship with his parents, he will feel no such worry. But he might begin to worry after such statements.† If the relationship is not satisfactory, statements like these will only serve to further "rub in" this unpleasant fact. |

*New York: Macmillan, 1965.
†In our discussion of Rule 9, we pointed out that if a person says: "I don't see an elephant in this inkblot," he must have seen an elephant and then consciously rejected the idea. Similarly, if a person says to you: "You know, I do not hate you," you know that the idea of hating

The well-meant recommendations are designed to help the child feel that his parents understand him. But understanding can be shown much more effectively and constructively, with no attendant dangers, by an attempt to help solve the problem. Following the principles of positive and constructive communication outlined here, I would suggest that when your child says: "I am not good in arithmetic," you say to him: "Let's see what the problem is and discuss what we can do to help." This statement shows a more genuine understanding of the child than mind reading or "rubbing-in" statements which still leave the child without any constructive solutions.

In fairness to the author of that particular best seller I should point out that his aim is positive: he wants parents to try to understand the feelings of their children. Such attempts cannot be made safely through mind reading, however. It is much better to show one's desire to understand through confronting the child—in a friendly and compassionate manner —with the feeling he actually communicates through his behavior (including facial expressions and tone of voice): "You look worried; please tell me about it; maybe I can help you," or "I can see you are angry; how about telling me why and then maybe we can do something about what it was that made you get mad," or "The way you said 'all right' makes me think that you don't want to do it; tell me what your feelings are about it." These are all responses to *observed* communicated behavior and thus cannot be considered mind reading.

At least the statements recommended by the best seller are well-meant. Many mind reading statements cannot be defended on the basis of good intentions, however. Let us consider an example of the type of mind reading which accuses the other person of negative motivation even when the precipitating action is positive.

Robert is driving home from work after a good day at the office. He has been having problems in his marriage lately,

---

you has occurred to him. If a parent says: "We don't think badly of you" or "We are not disappointed in you," the child gets the message, unconsciously if not consciously: the parent *has* thought badly of him and *has* been disappointed in him, although he (she) has rejected those thoughts.

but he is now in psychotherapy and feels things are going to be all right.

He feels happy and lighthearted and looks forward to spending a nice evening at home with his wife, Carolyn, and the children. Robert thinks about how fortunate he is to have such a nice family. He would like to show his appreciation to his wife for all the things she does for him and for the children. He also feels a little guilty for having been in a grumpy mood lately and for so seldom showing his wife any appreciation. He remembers that his wife some time ago said that she would like it very much if he sometimes brought something home for her. So he stops at a florist's and buys her some flowers.

When he comes home he hands the flowers to Carolyn with an embarrassed smile. Carolyn looks suspiciously at him and says: "What do you feel guilty about?" An argument ensues which ruins the evening and Robert decides that this is going to be the last time he ever brings something home to his wife again!

Carolyn's response may be understandable, but it is nevertheless destructive. She assumes that she can read her husband's mind and that guilt is the only reason for his gesture of goodwill. The fact is, as we have seen, that guilt was only a partial reason for Robert's action and it was healthy guilt at that: Robert *should* have felt guilty for his grumpiness and *should* have tried to make amends.

Is Robert an innocent victim? To many husbands reading this book it might appear that way, but such is nevertheless not the case. Carolyn's semirhetorical question, "What do you feel guilty about?" can be seen as an unconscious invitation to argue (Rule 9). Robert can decline the invitation by openly and honestly stating his motivation: "Yes, Carolyn, I feel guilty about having been so grumpy lately. But today when driving home I thought of how much I do appreciate you and I wanted to do something to show my appreciation." If Carolyn continues being suspicious (which is unlikely), Robert still does not need to use that as an excuse for entering into an argument. If he is truly appreciative, he will *show* it by staying reasonable and concerned and letting his wife get in a little revenge for his recent grumpiness.

Chuck has been nagging his wife, Connie, about keeping the house in better order. One day Connie decides that she wants to give her husband a nice surprise when he comes home that evening. She works very hard and efficiently all day to get everything the way he (and basically she, too, although she is less particular) would like to have it. When the time for his arrival comes, the house is spick and span.

Chuck, who is a faultfinder of the first order, comes in and (unconsciously) starts looking around for potato chips on the floor or sweaters thrown over chairs. Finding nothing to criticize he says: "Not bad. The only reason for this must be that your mother is coming over tonight!" Connie throws a temper tantrum and decides that her efforts have all been in vain!

Chuck is unfair in four ways:

1. He pretends he can read Connie's mind, and with certainty! ("The only reason for this must be. . . .")

2. He accuses his wife of a motive that does not exist. (Connie's mother is not coming over.)

3. He implies vaguely that such a motive for cleaning the house would be undesirable in any case.

4. He claims that there could be no other motivation to account for Connie's action.

Even if, on the basis of past experience, Chuck must suspect that his mother-in-law is coming over, his reaction is still destructive, hostile, and self-defeating. It certainly has the effect of discouraging Connie from trying so hard again. Following the principles of positive communication (Rule 3), Chuck should only show appreciation. If he feels he must bring up the mother-in-law he can do so later, but only in terms of a confession: "You know, I must confess something which really shows what a problem I have with faultfinding. My first thought when I came home tonight was that your mother was going to come over. That just shows I must work harder on this negative attitude I have so often." This "confession," if made sincerely, is likely to have a positive effect. If it does not, if Connie gets upset by it, Chuck must remain reasonable, concerned, and willing to mend his ways.

But Connie is no helpless victim of Chuck's faultfinding. She seldom keeps the house in reasonable condition and usually only when her mother is expected for a visit. In other words, she herself adds fuel to Chuck's critical attitude. When he makes his sarcastic remark about Connie's mother coming over, Connie can say something like: "No, she is not coming over tonight, but I can see why you might think so. It is true that I have usually made an extra effort only when we expect her. But today I decided to change and keep the house nice for us and no one else." If Chuck does not respond positively to that statement, he needs professional help. But even if Chuck responds negatively, Connie does not need to become unreasonable. She can honestly tell him that she is angry about his faultfinding, but does not need to use any destructive techniques to accomplish this purpose.

Andy, a 17-year-old high school student, has for a long time been careless about his chores and his homework. His parents have kept nagging him about it. One day Andy decides that his parents are really pretty good anyway and that he should do something to make them happy. He knows his mother's birthday is coming up soon and each time he has asked her what she wants for a present, she has said that all she wants for a present from him is that he become more responsible. Andy also feels guilty about setting a bad example for his younger brother who used to keep his room neat but is starting to imitate Andy's irresponsible behavior. Furthermore, Andy knows that his chances of borrowing the car on weekends are greater if his parents are in a good mood.

In other words, Andy has at least four reasons for deciding to "behave." He does his chores—and a few extra ones—cheerfully all week and spends a lot of time on his homework and on writing reports. His mother is happy about it but does not tell her husband, because Andy's good behavior might not last and her husband could stop it in its inception because of his "sarcastic tongue." But when Friday afternoon comes around and Andy has behaved in an exemplary manner all week, his mother can no longer hold back her enthusiasm. When her husband comes home from work, she tells him about everything Andy has done all week and how proud she is of him.

Andy's father looks at him (with a facial expression that says "You are not fooling me") and says: "Well, it certainly is high time that you straightened out. I don't suppose you did this to butter me up so you could borrow the car?" (The last statement is said in a tone indicating that that is exactly what the father does suppose.)

The destructiveness of the father's reaction should be crystal clear. Through his unreasonableness and sarcasm he has probably had a large part in creating the problem with Andy's irresponsibility in the first place. The father's reaction can only have negative consequences:

1. Andy will feel resentful (and maybe even revengeful).

2. He will be confirmed in his opinion that his father is unreasonable and unfair.

3. He may feel "What's the use of trying anyway" and, as a consequence, may give up trying to improve altogether.

There is, however, one more thing to be said about the father's reaction. Suppose it has been a pattern of long standing that Andy *only* behaves well when he needs a favor such as borrowing the car. In that case it may be desirable to indicate to him that you do know and understand what is going on, otherwise you run the risk of encouraging him to think that he can manipulate people at will. However, you have to show him your understanding of his behavior in a way that is constructive, fair, and has a chance of finding his acceptance. For example, you can wait until he has neglected his chores a few days in a row. At that time you praise him again for his recent accomplishment and simply let him understand that you would like him to be consistent about it and let it go at that.

In this last example, was Andy then an innocent victim of his father's cruelty? To some people it may appear that way, but my answer would be: Not really! Andy is seventeen years old and knows his father thoroughly. He may have been disappointed and discouraged by his father's cutting remark, but it could hardly have been any surprise to him. Andy has for a long time added fuel to his father's fire and cannot reasonably expect his father to change overnight. And he certainly has the choice between whether to continue doing well despite the discouragement or whether to use it as an excuse for giving up. (On the other hand, the father is not to use these last considerations as an excuse for not changing *his* ways. See Rule 16 for a thorough discussion of excuses.)

Dr. T., whom we have met in two previous examples (Rule 6, p. 50, and Unfair Technique 11-I, p. 101), had a wife who would do things and buy things without consulting him. Whenever he became aware of her having done something "behind his back," he would tell her: "You did that only because you knew it would make me mad!"

Actually, Mrs. T.'s conscious reason was the opposite: she fooled herself over and over again into thinking that she knew what her husband would like and she just wanted to give him "nice surprises." Unconsciously, however, she was expressing her anger against her father, who had been a tyrant. In other words, Dr. T.'s accusation was correct but it was nevertheless unfair, because Mrs. T. could not be blamed for a motivation of which she was not aware. Thus, instead of unfairly blaming his wife, Dr. T. could have suggested that the two of them discuss the issue and come to an agreement as to what matters the two of them needed to consult each other about and what matters they each could take care of without consulting the other.

Divination is a variant of mind reading. This technique consists of pretending to be able to read the future and is often employed in order to punish the partner before he has committed a crime. It is illustrated by such statements as:

"Why should I tell you, you wouldn't understand anyway."

"We can't take you to Disneyland, you wouldn't behave yourself there."

"I just know you are going to spoil the fun for all of us."

It is a good idea to discuss problems in advance, especially if they are repetitive or forseeable on the basis of previous experience. But to suggest that the outcome is inevitable and that you *know* it is inevitable is destructive both because it precludes problem solving and because it indicates distrust and contempt for the partner. It is much better to say: "I am afraid that you will do such and such. Let's discuss how we can both prevent it from happening."

# "Anyway, Look at How Filthy Your Room Is!"

## *Unfair Technique III: Switching the subject. Using counteraccusations.*

Switching the subject without finishing the topic at hand or without the partner's agreement is obviously a devious way of avoiding a solution to the problem being discussed. Its crudest and most common form is the technique called *counteraccusation*. A counteraccusation is simply a primitive way of avoiding personal responsibility in solving a problem and of hurting another person "back." The most immediate objective in the employment of counteraccusations in direct interchange (as in "Well, what about yourself? You are no angel, you know!"), is to "bounce off" the attack and direct the attention to the other person's faults, at the same time making him or her seem like the pot who is calling the kettle black, as in this example:

> *Wife:* "How long are you going to postpone fixing that fence?"
> *Husband:* "Look who's talking! What about you and your ironing? I don't even get to wear a clean shirt to the office!"

The underlying principle behind counteraccusations is often that to do something bad is a privilege or "goodie" that you should be entitled to if others are. Your misbehavior, in other words, is somehow justified by theirs. Consider the essential similarity in the following seemingly very different examples:

*Friend:* "Why do you embarrass your wife like that in public?"
*Husband:* "Oh, Bob, if you only knew what *she* has done to humiliate *me* in front of others!"

*Mother:* "Why did you take cookies from the jar without permission?"
*Johnny:* "Gee, Mother, Mary took many more than I did!"

The first two examples use counteraccusations to avoid personal responsibility. The questions—admittedly ineffective and difficult to answer—are deflected by calling attention to someone else's misdeeds. In all three examples there is the additional implication that behaving badly is a "goodie" (literally, in the third example) which the speaker would like to have since someone else has already helped himself to the same kind of "goodie."

One way to stop the use of this technique is to propose an agreement with your partner that you will both discuss fully the initial accusation before moving on to another problem. An open and sincere accusation is not hurtful in itself (unless it employs exaggeration or belittling of the other person or other destructive elements); on the contrary, it may sometimes be necessary and desirable to bring up an accusation about something that bothers you and "have it out" in order to "clean the emotional air." But additional accusations are not to be brought up by either party until the first one has been dealt with. If necessary, the partners can take notes for future discussions if other problems come up during the discussion of the original accusation.

Some accusations are, however, in themselves so unfair and destructive that their unfairness must first be exposed. This, however, must be done through sincere questions or statements of fact and not through counteraccusations or rhetorical questions that are really disguised counteraccusations.

*Husband* (to wife on Sunday morning): "Let's go for a drive."
*Wife:* "No dear, thank you, but I would rather sew today."
*Husband:* "You are trying to ruin my day!"

The husband's accusation is unfair by definition since it involves the use of an unfair technique (mind reading). Ineffective and/or destructive answers to the husband's accusation would be:

*Wife:* "How can you say such a thing!"
"No, I am not. I just want to sew today, *if I may?*"
"Don't be a baby about it."
"I suppose it isn't my day at all, is it?"
"No, it's you who are trying to destroy mine."

Potentially effective and/or constructive responses would be sincerely asked questions, such as:

*Wife:* "Do you really mean that it is just your day? Please explain."
"But if so, would I not be ruining mine at the same time?"
"I am married to you and I would like to see it as *our day.* Maybe we could do both?"
"But what would be the advantage for me to do that?"
"Maybe you feel I say 'No' to you too often. Would you like to discuss it?"

A particularly insidious and anger-provoking way of using counteraccusations is the technique of switching the subject the very moment you are losing a point. The purpose here—at least as far as accusations are concerned—is to keep the partner on the defensive without getting a chance to recuperate. Consider the following conversation:

*Father:* "I am going to ground you, because you came home past midnight last night."
*Son:* "But Dad, a week ago you said it would be all right for this one time and mother, too, remembers that you said it."
*Father:* "Anyway, look at how filthy your room is."

Techniques such as this one are discouraging and destructive to children and adults alike, but especially to children. The very use of an unfair technique implies that the object is not to solve problems and gain understanding but to win points in a game. To teach such techniques to children is to ensure that they will grow up to be similarly destructive and similarly concerned with one-up-manship in their communication with others, especially with intimates.

Parents often wonder why their children do not confide in them more and communicate more of their feelings. The parents find consolation in vague explanations such as "generation gap," instead of looking at the destructive communication techniques they themselves may be using and which their children may have adopted both to use with others and to stay away from trying to communicate constructively with their parents.

Switching a subject because it is getting touchy or embarrassing is unfair as well as being destructive to communication. A touchy subject is not to be avoided; it is to be discussed with observance of the rules in this book. If you are too angry or upset to discuss a subject reasonably at the moment, you can suggest a postponement, but not for long. If the other person does not come back to the subject, *you* must bring it up for discussion until the issue is settled.

A more subtle way of employing this technique, used by experienced cloak-and-dagger fighters, is to get the partner to do the switching. This can be accomplished by the use of an exaggeration which is actually incidental to the main issue being discussed. Here is an example:

> *Husband:* "I get mad at you when you don't have a clean shirt for me in the morning."
> *Wife:* "I don't understand what you are talking about. I try my best to have everything ready in the morning while you go around screaming and yelling at the kids and——"
> *Husband* (falling for the ploy, interrupts): "I don't scream at the kids."
> *Wife:* "Oh, yes you do! The other morning, for example. . . ." etc.

The wife, by employing an exaggeration ("while you go around screaming and yelling") has succeeded in getting her husband to interrupt her as well as in making it appear that it was he who changed the topic (to one where it is he who is on the defensive). Thus, the husband has unwittingly accepted his wife's invitation not to discuss the shirts. She is the "real" subject-changer but he cooperates with her.

There are three ways of dealing with subject-changers:

1. Insist on keeping to the subject while indicating willingness to discuss the other topic later. In the example above, the husband could have said: "I want to discuss that, too, but what about the shirts?"

2. Ignore the switch, exaggeration, or incidental unfair accusation and ask for a constructive solution. *Husband:* "Is there anything I could do to remind you about the shirts?"

3. Respond to the main feeling in the partner's response while proposing that the original subject be discussed later. This is probably the best approach. In the example above, for instance, the husband could listen to the essential feeling in his wife's message and respond to it by saying, for example: "I know you must feel frustrated with so many things to do in the morning. And you must be angry with me when I lose my temper on top of everything else you have to deal with. Maybe we should discuss that first and then we can talk about the shirts?" This approach shows respect for the wife's feelings and turns her destructive method into constructive use.

All three of these approaches help the husband in our example to avoid falling into the trap which his wife—unconsciously—has dug for him; he remains tactful and respectful of her feelings and—in approach 3—openly asks for her permission to change the topic. All three approaches can be used in communicating with subject-switchers, but the third approach has the greatest chance of success.

An excellent auxiliary technique designed to prevent destructive switching of topics is for the partners to have a sheet of paper headed AGENDA FOR FUTURE DISCUSSIONS. Whenever one partner brings in an extraneous or tangential topic, that topic is written on the agenda as something to be discussed at a future time. In this way a topic cannot be used by one of the partners to avoid discussing another topic and, thus, diversionary tactics are stopped efficiently and constructively. Both parties must keep in mind, however, that sometimes a topic is merely a specific case of another, more important, issue, in which case the more important issue should be discussed first. If the partners disagree on which topic is more important, a coin is very useful in making the decision.

## "You Never Let Me Finish!"

### Unfair Technique IV: Bringing up more than one accusation at a time, or the kitchen sink attack.

As we pointed out in discussing Rule 4 (be clear and specific), it is important to discuss subjects one at a time and not digress all over the place. Problems are much less likely to be solved if they are all talked about at the same time. Yet, digression in itself cannot be said to be unfair—it is merely ineffective. There is, however, a type of digression which involves accusations and is eminently unfair. It is often referred to as the "kitchen sink attack."

The kitchen sink attack is a favorite tactical maneuver with many dirty fighters. It consists of bringing up so many accusations at the same time ("everything but the kitchen sink") that the other person does not get a chance to defend himself. The experts in the use of this technique employ an additional stratagem: they start off with the most unfair or exaggerated accusation, so that the other person will feel indignant and will interrupt the accuser. Then, when the other person falls into the trap and interrupts, the accuser can slap him with the other side of the hand and say: "There you go again, you never let me finish!"

Accusations, as we have said, are not only acceptable but necessary at times. However, they must be realistic and unexaggerated and they must be brought up *one at a time,* so that the other person has a chance to defend himself, challenge the fairness of each accusation, and offer explanations for different ways of looking at each issue presented.

If the accuser will not follow this rule but persists in hurling long lists of accusations at you, there are two ways you can deal constructively with the problem:

1. You take notes on the accusations and then defend yourself with respect to each one, asking for the same privilege of not being interrupted. (This technique, if used good-naturedly, has the advantage of injecting some humor into the interchange.)

2. You make sure that you remember the *first* accusation in the list and then you discuss that issue as soon as the accuser is through with his list.

When *both* partners use the kitchen sink approach, we get into a variant of Unfair Technique 11-III (switching the subject, using counteraccusations) and, thus, into wildly flailing fights such as this one:

*Husband:* "Why has this bill not been paid? How irresponsible can a person be?"

*Wife:* "Look who's talking! You never do what you are supposed to do. Just the other day you left your heart medicine out where the baby could get to it."

*Husband:* "All right, all right, so I made a mistake. At least I don't hate the kid like you do. You sure learned to hate, didn't you, from that mother of yours?"

*Wife:* "Don't you bring mother into this. Your own mother lives like a pig; that's probably why you are so messy all the time."

*Husband:* "Messy? I can't even bring home my business associates because I am ashamed of the filth here."

*Wife:* "You goddamn dictator. If one little thing is out of place you torture me for days about it. But you just wait, you'll be sorry."

*Husband:* "You wait yourself. I'm not going to watch quietly while you drive me crazy like you did your first husband."

*Wife:* "You are a fine one to talk about earlier marriages. Don't think I haven't noticed how lovey-dovey you have been with your first wife lately."

*Husband:* "That settles it. You are paranoid. I can't take any more of this; I'm getting out of here. I know you are doing this so I will have a heart attack, but your scheme isn't going to work."

To counteract the kitchen sink approach is easy: keep discussing the first issue until it is solved and change topic only after having asked permission of your partner. If your partner keeps bringing up other issues, suggest that he (she) select *one* and indicate your willingness to discuss it. If your partner is unwilling to do so, *you* suggest an issue, preferably one in which you yourself have been negligent (because your partner is likely to be more eager to discuss that issue than one in which he [she] has shortcomings). If your partner is too upset to discuss anything reasonably now, you suggest a continuation of the discussion at a specific time later the same day or the next day. But do not use the suggestion to get in another dirty blow ("I think we should postpone the discussion since *you* are so upset"). The suggestion is to be made tactfully: "Don't you think both of us are too upset to continue the discussion now? How would you feel if we continued it tomorrow evening?" Never suggest a postponement after having been asked a question; that amounts to begging the partner to accuse you of wanting to avoid an answer.

# "I Try Much Harder Than You."

*Unfair Technique V: Bragging or playing the numbers game.*

Another way of accusing the partner destructively is by bragging or playing the numbers game. You are undoubtedly familiar with the person who says: "Just look at how many times I have put myself out for you; when have you ever done anything for me?" The question is rhetorical and impossible to answer, since no impartial objective person has been present to count and keep records of such incidents.

The bragging involved is usually not obvious to the person employing this technique, but is often reluctantly acknowledged if an impartial person, such as a psychotherapist, points it out. The unfairness and destructiveness involved is inherent in the derogatory comparisons and in the stress on making the other person "look small" instead of discussing possible solutions to the problem.

Thus, instead of saying: "Look at how many times I have put myself out for you; when have you ever done anything for me?," a more constructive statement would be: "I would very much like you to help me with the dishes (or whatever the specific demands are)." If the other person then has objections, they can be discussed one at a time.

Some people simply refuse to use this straightforward, honest, and constructive approach. They usually justify their refusal by such excuses as "It just does not mean the same to me if I have to ask for it" or "It would just lead to an argument if I asked him to do anything to help me." What they are really saying—without knowing it—is: "I am unwilling to work daily on improving our relationship; I would much rather just play the role of a martyr."

The numbers game is used as a favorite auxiliary technique in nagging (Rule 17): "Haven't I told you a thousand times?" inevitably involving exaggeration and an attempt at rubbing in the partner's negligence or misbehavior.

The way to deal with a person who plays the numbers game is not to comment on the actual number, but to agree with the main message: "I know you feel I don't do things for you often enough and I would like to do what I can to solve that problem. Let's see if we can come to some specific agreements as to what I can do. I suggest, for example, that I . . . (here you mention something you know you should do more often for your partner)." Or, in the case of nagging: "I know you have had to say it too many times. It's almost as if I begged you to say it over and over when I don't do it. Here's what I plan to do from now on to remind myself: . . ." (Here you put in some mnemonic device such as a list, or you offer some other solution.)

When bragging or playing the numbers game is used defensively against an actual or expected accusation, it is often called "whitewashing." Whitewashing is designed to cover up or to minimize the importance of a destructive action by stressing its infrequency. At the same time, whitewashing relies on a pretense of inevitability or of having reached the limits of human endurance and thus constitutes quite a heavy and somewhat underhanded attack on the partner. Examples:

"I seldom use that kind of language, but . . ."; "I am a polite person, but this time I . . ."; "I hardly ever lose my temper but . . ."; "It really takes a lot of provocation for me to do something like that." Whether the statements in these examples are informative or merely defensive must be determined by a person who knows the speaker well, such as a spouse.

# "Why Make a Big Deal Out of Nothing?"

## Unfair Technique VI: Using logic to hide from emotional reality.

There are two ways of looking at reality: Analytically-logically-objectively and intuitively-emotionally-subjectively. People differ in their ability and willingness to perceive logical aspects of reality and they also differ in their ability and willingness to look at and understand emotional aspects of reality.

Sometimes the reality itself seems different at different times and in different contexts. For example, one hour in a person's life is objectively defined by the movements of the hands of a clock and is normally not too difficult to estimate even without a clock. However, subjectively an hour can be an eternity: for example, if you are waiting for the outcome of your child's surgery. An hour may also seem like five minutes if you are engaged in an interesting conversation with a friend.

In intimate communication it is the emotional, subjective perception that counts, not the logical or objective aspects of the situation. To use the logical aspects in order to hide from or cover up the emotional aspects is a destructive technique which interferes with good communication and prevents a truly intimate relationship from being formed.

An example of the use of this technique is the husband who every morning leaves the shaving suds in the washbowl for his wife to clean up, despite the fact that she has asked him repeatedly to clean it up himself when he is finished shaving. When his wife brings it up again, the husband accuses her of "making a federal case out of it," and shows her how illogical it is for her to worry about the little time it takes for her to clean it up and how logical it is for him to forget to do so, since he has to make himself ready to go to the office.

Another example is provided by the wife who lets food waste in the refrigerator, despite her husband's repeated pleadings with her to stop this practice. When the husband brings it up again, the wife accuses him of penny-pinching and shows him how illogical it is to worry about such trifles when he spends large sums taking his business friends out to lunch every week.

Some people are so deeply afraid of emotional reality that they are unconsciously unwilling, and therefore for practical purposes unable, to perceive it. This inability to perceive emotional reality may be due to reasons which are buried deep in the person's developmental history. It is even possible that such seeming inability is hereditarily influenced, although it is demonstrably possible to overcome it (often completely, sometimes only partially) in psychotherapy. An example of a man who was for all practical purposes such an "emotional imbecile" will be given later (the case of Dr. N., p. 297). In the case of such people it is perhaps not fair to speak of their using "unfair" techniques, since they do not consciously know of the existence of other ways to deal with reality.

Other people are perfectly able to perceive emotional reality, but block it out (with various degrees of consciousness) for some immediate advantage or because they do not want to give more of themselves. Take, as an example, the woman who will not get up to fix breakfast for her husband and who uses the excuse: "All he wants is cereal anyway and I don't see why a grown man cannot pour some cereal from a box into a bowl himself!" Logically there is nothing the matter with such a statement. Logic, however, is not the same as realism, and the statement completely ignores reality. The emotional reality is that this woman, through her rejecting attitude, has contributed to a condition in which her husband desperately needs symbolic signs of affection, loyalty, and support. To him, her not getting up to fix breakfast communicates: "I am not with you, I will not support you, I will not let you start the day feeling loved and appreciated."

How, then, do we differentiate between a person who is for practical purposes unable to perceive emotional reality and therefore is limited to a logical-intellectual approach, and a person who is able but unwilling to perceive emotional reality? The differentiation is usually easy to make. The "emotional imbecile," "emotionally retarded," or "emotionally blunted" person is not aware of any deep emotional needs in himself, either, because most emotions, whether in others or in himself, frighten him (usually there are partial exceptions, such as love for children, or anger as a result of frustration). We cannot, therefore, accuse him of using an unfair technique when he stresses logic, although we most certainly can point out to him the destructive effects of his doing so. However, there are people who are seemingly unaware of emotional reality as far as other people's needs are concerned but who are very keenly aware of their own needs. Diane's parents, whom we met in discussing the dangers of making assumptions (Rule 6), appeared singularly oblivious to their daughter's needs and did not even bother to inquire into what they were, yet they were very much aware of their own feelings of being rejected by her. This seeming unawareness of other people's feelings and emotional needs must be due to an *unwillingness* (to what degree it is conscious or unconscious can be debated in each individual case), since the awareness these people have of their own emotional needs demonstrates that it could not be due to a lack of ability. Such people can therefore legitimately be said to employ an unfair technique, even if they—to the extent that they are unaware of it—cannot be blamed.

And then we have the true dirty fighter who does indeed perceive the other person's needs, at least on a preconscious level. He will use logic to suit his own purposes, whether these are to "cover up" the emotional reality of the situation, to "win," or to get his own way. A typical example of attempting to cover up the emotional reality of the situation will be given below in the case of Joe and Carol (Rule 20). Joe has—through underhanded means—provoked Carol into a seething anger and then, just before he leaves, he attempts to cover up this fact by saying, "Well, aren't you going to wish me good luck" and "Good-bye, honey, remember I love you." Later, Joe will use these statements to prove—*logically*—that he was the one who tried to be reasonable and to make up!*

Logic is also used by the dirty fighter who demands satisfaction of his own irrational wishes (which he will present as being logical, "natural," or modest) while denying such satisfaction to his partner (whose wishes he will present as being illogical, unreasonable, or selfish). His approach, in other words, is purely manipulative, even though his awareness of his own manipulations may only be preconscious.

> Burt almost always got his way by demonstrating that his way was the logical one and that his wife's (or son's or daughter's or employee's) way was illogical and unreasonable. There were several examples of this. If Burt wanted to go flying (which was one of his hobbies) and his wife did not, he would ask her for the reason. If she replied: "The weather is bad," he would say: "That's exactly why I want us to go: it is much more challenging and, besides, it will be much easier to rent a plane." If she replied: "I would much rather stay home and read today," Burt would say: "Darling, you stay at home too much, it isn't good for you. The flight will do you a lot of good." If his wife said: "I would much rather we go and visit the Joneses," Burt's reply was: "We have seen the Joneses too often, they are going to get tired of us, besides we could see them tonight when we return" (how about that for a sample of logical thinking!).
>
> On the other hand, if Burt did not want to go flying when his wife did, he would use "reasons" which were the same ones he had rejected when he wanted to go: "The weather is bad, it would be too dangerous," or "Darling, you need some rest, I have noticed that you have been tired lately and I don't think you should go out this weekend," or "I think it is much more important for us to go and see the Joneses, otherwise they will think that we don't want to associate with them."
>
> Whether it had to do with the use of weekends or how to deal with the children or how often to see the in-laws or what was needed for the house, Burt could be counted on to present his wishes as logical and reasonable while painting his wife's wishes as illogical or unreasonable. On the occasions when

---

*"Making up" is not achieved by a sudden switch to sweetness. It involves an admission of one's own destructive part in the interaction and a sincere apology for it, as well as a resolution to do one's best not to be destructive again.

this did not suffice for him to get his way, he pouted and moped for days, giving his wife the silent treatment in punishment for her "unreasonableness." This caused his wife to give in rather than put up with several days of unpleasant tension in the home.

Burt showed the same type of behavior toward his children and their resulting frustration was already beginning to show up in symptoms of emotional disturbance. The pattern was also clearly discernible outside the home: Burt had been fired from three jobs and had lost out on several opportunities for promotion because he was unwilling to acknowledge the validity of other people's needs.

When Burt's wife finally suggested that he go and see a psychologist, Burt—true to form—initially tried to show her how illogical her suggestion was. However, he had a great deal of faith in his "power of logical thinking" and therefore finally agreed, expecting to be able to convince the psychologist to join him in persuading his wife that she was being illogical, irrational, and unreasonable in her demands.

In the very first session, it became clear that Burt felt incensed, humiliated, embarrassed, and terribly upset whenever one of his "ploys" or "maneuvers" was pointed out. He accused me of taking his wife's side and it was not until we had several joint sessions (with both Burt and his wife in the office) that he became convinced that I pointed out her destructive operations as well. In the joint sessions, Burt would do everything to attempt to keep the status quo. Whenever his wife wanted to bring up an example of his destructive behavior or what she termed his "tricks," he would counter with such statements as: "There we go again, you see she just can't forgive and forget," or "What's the use? If you are going to bring up that thing again, I don't have one more word to say," or "My wife always makes mountains out of molehills," or "I feel like giving up on this marriage if I have to watch every little word I say," etc.

Burt's progress in individual and joint psychotherapy was slow. However, when he—most reluctantly—had entered group psychotherapy things started moving. The group would buy none of his excuses and there was no way Burt could stay "logical" and still assume that they were *all* on the side of his wife. The group members insistently pointed out the destructiveness of his pouting, and—although they showed compassion about the embarrassment he felt when his "tricks" were exposed—they also showed him in definite terms how there would be no need for embarrassment if he would stop using the tricks in the first place. In the group, Burt for the first time learned that there were deeper satisfactions in interpersonal relationships than the momentary triumph of having gotten one's way. He began to see the destructiveness of his manipulative attitude and to appreciate the validity and value of other people's feelings and wishes as well as the rewards inherent in sincerity and openness. Since his wife also participated in therapy (she *was* actually terribly unforgiving and had an unfortunate tendency to embarrass Burt in public), the relationship improved steadily until both of them could say that, on the whole, they were now experiencing a satisfying and rewarding marriage.

Before psychotherapy Burt had sometimes been conscious of being manipulative; at other times the purpose of his tricks, operations, and excuses had been preconscious ("in the back of my mind" or "like a secret voice whispering to me what I was really doing"). At still other times he had been totally unconscious of using any excuses or trickery: on those occasions he definitely believed that he was "right" in demanding that he get his way. There are, however, people who, consciously and deliberately, consistently seek to manipulate others through "logically designed" behavior or statements. It is as if they saw another person as a machine with a set of buttons and the task is to press the right buttons in the right combination in order to get the other person to behave as they want him to. Many parents who try to "use psychology" on their children follow this pattern. There are even some parents who use what in the vernacular is referred to as "reverse psychology." This means that they communicate one wish or command in order to manipulate the child into executing the opposite (aimed for) wish or command. Even if this method leads to desired results in terms of outward behavior (which it seldom does), the parent who uses this method is at the same time hiding from the emotional reality that the long-term effects of such manipulation are destructive, since the manipulativeness in itself precludes the development of openness, intimacy, and trust and, in effect, teaches the child to become a con-artist. A manipulative attitude toward other people is a sign of emotional disturbance (see Part II, Characteristic III), and a person who is characterized by such an attitude can never experience the deep satisfaction involved in a close and trusting emotional relationship with another human being.

# "But That's Not True, I Didn't . . ."

## Unfair Technique VII: Interrupting.

The destructiveness of interrupting another person, except in an emergency, is apparent. Yet this is one of the commonly used unfair techniques. Certainly, few experienced "dirty fighters" miss the opportunity to engage in the interrupting game, the reason being that it usually affords both parties great neurotic benefits. If the interrupting is one-sided with one partner, John, interrupting the other, Martha, then John gets at least four benefits:

1. He may protect himself against realizing or facing up to some specific unpleasant truth which Martha is leading up to or which is inherent in her communicative message.

2. He may have an unconscious general fear of establishing effective and open communication, with all the unpleasant or anxiety-provoking facts about himself which such openness might bring out. Interrupting Martha makes effective communication impossible and thus allays John's fear.

3. He may—consciously or unconsciously—enjoy the power of cutting Martha off and thus fulfill any need he may have to be a bully.

4. Since interrupting is often made under the conscious pretext of "correcting," "adding," or "explaining" something, John can feel indignant over having been the victim of Martha's unreasonableness if she objects to his interrupting.

In a neurotic sense, Martha (whose speech is being interrupted) is in an even more favorable position, being able to gather at least five benefits from being interrupted:

1. She may be able to fulfill any needs she may have to play the martyr.

2. She can make John seem unreasonable and at the same time get support for her own unreasonable statements ("You never let me finish").

3. She can feel justified in falling silent altogether (Unfair Technique 11-XIV), perhaps the dirtiest maneuver of all, and later blame John for it since he "did not let her talk."

4. She can, if she feels her own point is weak, actually provoke (usually unconsciously) John into interrupting her by interspersing a particularly unfair, incorrect, or exaggerated statement in her communication. When John falls into the trap, Martha says: "There you go again; what's the use talking to you since you never let me finish!"

5. She can, in any case, feel indignant and justify any consequent destructive reaction of her own with: "Well, who wouldn't get mad being interrupted like that constantly? I am never allowed to say what I want to say."

Because of these considerable neurotic "benefits," interruptions are often unconsciously invited or provoked. The speaker may, for example, use Unfair Technique IV (bring up more than one accusation at a time) and thus provoke the partner into interrupting in order to "defend himself," or the speaker may break Rule 15 (do not preach), thus provoking the partner to interrupt merely to break the monologue. Breaking Rule 5 (be realistic and reasonable in your statements) will very often lead to being interrupted by an indignant exclamation.

Interruptions do not, however, always have to be verbal. One can interrupt effectively by drumming one's fingers against the table or looking away with a glassy stare or making a disgusted grimace. Such interruptions are even more insidious and destructive than verbal interruptions because they require interpretation before they can be met appropriately and because of their very underhanded nature.

Interrupting is often mutual, which means that both parties get all the benefits in turn. A trained observer can well see how the partners, while consciously being angry and attacking each other, unconsciously are engaged in a mutually protective pact which prevents them from ever facing the real underlying issues. This is especially apparent when one considers how reluctant the partners are to give up this kind of behavior when it is pointed out to them by the therapist.

There are at least two good ways of guarding against interruptions and the provocation of interruptions. One is to agree to use an egg timer while talking (no one can then speak longer than three minutes at a time without asking for his partner's permission); the other is for one partner to take notes while the other one is talking. Both methods are highly effective when used singly and virtually foolproof when used in combination. They have the added advantage of introducing an element of humor into the interchange and constituting overt evidence of a mutual desire to cooperate in solving a communication problem.

## "All Right, We'll See What You Say When I Divorce You!"

*Unfair Technique VIII: Using the atom bomb. The bull in the china shop. Intimidating. Yelling, screaming, and "exploding."*

The technique of intimidation which I have called "Using the Atom Bomb" is, unfortunately, as widespread as it is destructive. It effectively stops, at least for the moment, all constructive communication and leaves the other person with a feeling both of anxiety and resentment (and perhaps an unconscious neurotic feeling of relief over not having established sincere communication). The purpose of using this technique is often to "batter down" the other person to a point where he will no longer oppose you or behave in ways you consider undesirable. Or the purpose may be to "drown out" any unpleasant or anxiety-provoking messages from the partner.

Unfortunately, one of the most widely used "bombs" is the threat of separation: divorce in the case of spouse vs. spouse, "sending away" (to boarding school, foster home, or corrective institution) in the case of parent vs. child, and "running away" in the case of child vs. parent. Such threats are unfair and "below the belt," because they hit at the very core of human security: the comfort and solace a human being derives from being in the presence of someone he loves (even if the love is mixed up with feelings of hatred).

As with all other destructive techniques, the threat of separation or "sending away" must never be used against children. The anxiety engendered by the thought of being separated from a loved one is strong enough in adults; just consider how terrible such a thought is to a child and, consequently, how much damage the anxiety engendered by the threat of separation can do a child. However, not only is this technique destructive and hurtful: like most destructive techniques it backfires and achieves the opposite result from the one consciously intended. The threatened person unconsciously feels that he wants to prove that the "threatener" does not really mean what he (she) says and, thus, he may intensify his provocations to show that no matter what he does, the threatener still loves him and would not use the ultimate weapon on him.

The most terrible way of threatening to abandon another person is through the threat of suicide. All other forms of abandonment, even divorce and marriage to another person, are reversible, at least theoretically, but suicide is the ultimate irreversible abandonment and, moreover, means that the survivor will have to spend the rest of his life in the torture of his own guilt feelings. Thus, to threaten suicide to an intimate partner is the ultimate weapon, worse than threatening homicide.

Unfortunately, many people counter the atom bomb technique in destructive ways, either by matching or surpassing the threats or by daring the other person to carry through with his threats ("Good riddance, see if I care" or "Go ahead, I have had you up to here"). Such daring may, if the threatener is emotionally disturbed, actually provide the trigger for him to act out his threat.

The atom bomb technique is best handled by suggesting a postponement of the "discussion" to a later specified time: "We are both upset now; let's discuss this tomorrow instead, say at nine-thirty." Or, if postponement is not desirable or if the partner strongly opposes postponement: "It hurts me when you say that, because I feel it would be a terrible tragedy if you. . . . It also shows me how deeply unhappy you must be and I want to do everything I can to help. Let's discuss what I could do to make you feel less desperate about the situation."

There are other ways of dropping the atom bomb, some of which are covered in Unfair Technique X (humiliating the partner). A wife screaming at her husband: "No wonder you are impotent, you goddamn homosexual" is stabbing him "in his vitals" and thus (unconsciously) inviting him to do the same to her, which he indeed may, sometimes literally! The same is true of a husband accusing his wife of having had intercourse with her father, etc.

The use of the psychological atom bomb must be banned if communication is to have any chance of developing along positive channels. Certainly, its use against children is indefensible and inexcusable under any circumstances. Even employment of "milder" forms of the bomb, such as "exploding," yelling, and screaming must be condemned for several reasons:

1. When used against a child, it transmits the message that it is a good idea to lose one's temper and be unreasonable, thus inviting the child to behave in the same manner.

2. It invites the partner, adult or child, to "tune you out" ("There she goes, screaming her head off again") and not really listening to what it is that bothers you.

3. It encourages the development of excuses for clamming up or walking on eggs: "I'd better keep it to myself so I don't start anything."

A person who has frequent temper outbursts must ask himself: "Why do I not get mildly annoyed instead of violently angry?" Excuses employing some mystical biological necessity ("That's my nature," "I have a short fuse," "I have always been a yeller," etc.) or focussing on the frequency of the irritant (or provocation or trigger) are to be discarded as explanations. The likeliest explanation is that such a person, due perhaps to some early childhood frustrations, harbors a deep-seated anger, the origins of which he does not want to recognize. Thus, he needs to find "outside" excuses to be angry so that he can say: "I am not angry; it was you who *made* me lose my temper." For a person who gets very angry when mild annoyance is called for, psychotherapy is often the only solution, since each incident leading to the strong feeling or display of anger is at the moment seen by him as completely justifying an angry reaction.

Among the bulls in the china shop we should also include those who just talk incessantly without letting the other one get a word in edgewise. Such "steamrolling" behavior is definitely unfair since it monopolizes the time available for commuincative interchange and shows contempt or disregard for the partner and his feelings. Therefore, people who engage in "steamrolling" have to agree to use an egg timer whenever they engage in discussions about problems. In ordinary conversation they have to agree to respond to some kind of signal, such as the partner's giving a "halt" sign with his hand.

## "You Are Just Like Your Father, That No-Good Bum."

*Unfair Technique IX: Blaming the partner for something which he cannot help or cannot do anything about now or for something you do yourself. Refusing to forgive.*

One would think that blaming another person for something he or she cannot help is so blatantly unfair that the technique would be used rarely. On the contrary, this is a technique relished by many "dirty fighters." There are untold numbers of husbands who say to their wives: "Anyway, look at that creep you have for a mother, she . . ." and then present a list of the crimes committed by the mother-in-law. The purpose is to hit the wife "below the belt" and (unconsciously) to invite her to do the same. The wife, in turn, might then hit her husband in the belly by countering with: "Well, you are a fine one to talk! Just look at your father, that drunken slob, he . . ." and then follows a list of the crimes of the father-in-law.

Again, such a destructive technique is especially disastrous when used against children. A child identifies with his parents, especially with the parent of the same sex, and this technique therefore interferes with the normal identification process. When identification with the same-sex parent is interfered with, the results can be most severe. Yet this technique is used appallingly often against children, especially by parents who are divorced or in the process of divorce.

An important class of matters that cannot be helped are *past crimes*. There are married couples who—twenty years after the wedding—are still fighting about what happened during the honeymoon or during the time the wife was pregnant. Wives, especially, often have a tendency to keep dwelling on their husbands' past crimes and seem determined not to let their husbands forget those crimes. Husbands tend to have an equally destructive tendency not to want to discuss their past crimes at all, not even in a constructive attempt at learning something from them. Husbands often do not—or do not want to—grasp the fact that a full realization of the impact of their past destructive behavior may be necessary in order to understand their wives' present feelings. Such a realization is also important in that it enables the husbands to examine more realistically whether they still may be behaving in ways which remind their wives of those crimes.

Similarly, there are parents who, whenever their child misbehaves, go through a long list of his past misdeeds and thus —unwittingly—teach him that one should never forgive and forget! Such "rubbing in" also has the unfortunate consequences that the child is unlikely to come to his parents with his problems. Children who keep their problems to themselves have often told me that they would be willing to discuss them with their parents if it were not for the fact that they know in advance that the parent would then launch into a long list of all the bad things the child has done in the past.

The best way to deal with this problem is to agree on setting a *statute of limitations on past crimes.* In the case of adults, the rule can be that *no crimes, faults, or misdeeds can be brought up which are more than three months old* (even one month should be ample time to discuss any destructive act or omission thoroughly). Recurrent misbehavior can be discussed on the basis of its present manifestations without going into the past. In the case of children, it is even more important to have a statute of limitations, since their learning and their self-concepts are involved. Because time is longer for children, the statute of limitations should be shorter for them than for adults, say one or two weeks at the most.

It is striking to observe how much such a simple rule alone can cut down on arguments and "dirty fighting" in families. Observing a statute of limitations gives the participants in communication a chance to "start fresh" instead of being burdened with past sins that are never forgiven and always held against them. Children, especially, are much more likely to go to their parents with problems if they have a guarantee that they will not have to listen to a long list of past offenses.

There are, of course, times when a feeling (of being deeply hurt, for example) cannot be explained or properly understood without going into past history. In those cases, the rule can be broken, *provided both partners agree.* In such a case, one partner must ask the other's permission to break the rule and tell him (her) why it is necessary. For example: "I know it is hard to understand why I feel this way, but I think I can explain if we can break the statute of limitations rule for a moment. Would you agree to that?" The past can also sometimes be instructive to learn from, in terms of causes and consequences, and in those cases the rule can also be broken, but again only with the agreement of both parties. The exceptions to the rule, in other words, are to be made only when it is necessary to achieve further understanding and learning from past events which can then be applied to the understanding of the partner's feelings and to the correction of present and future behavior. No exceptions are to be made for the purpose of attack, blame, or "rubbing in."

The feelings of anger or dissatisfaction which give rise to blaming the partner for something he cannot help now must, of course, be expressed. However, they must be related to something the partner is doing *now* and must be expressed constructively ("It makes me mad when you . . .") as well as being accompanied by specific demands for change (". . . and I wish that you would . . .").

In an intimate relationship each partner must be willing to forgive and forget past sins after they have been adequately discussed and a way has been found to prevent the likelihood of recurrence. Sometimes, however, a partner in a relationship finds himself unable (i.e., unconsciously unwilling) to forgive and forget. When such is the case, he is not to use this inability to keep rubbing the partner's face in the past crime. Rather, he is to present his inability as a problem which should be discussed and corrected. If the unconscious resistance against forgiving and forgetting is strong, psychotherapeutic intervention may be necessary.

A statute of limitations will cut down on a lot of useless fighting, but it will not take care of the problem which arises when one or both of the partners is unforgiving *in general*. Such a person will stay sour, pouting, or grumpy long after the incident which set him off. In this case, we are dealing with a neurotic game in which the sourpuss is constantly—through his behavior—inviting the partner to a destructive fight. Such a situation can be dealt with only by an analysis of the game itself or by psychotherapy with the sourpuss (and with his game-partner if the latter "falls for" the invitation to fight destructively).

Some vicious "dirty fighters" combine a violation of Rule 10 (be honest about your feelings) with Unfair Technique 11-IX which we are discussing. They are the ones who "go along" for the moment without mentioning their negative feelings about the incident or situation and who then save up these incidents for later use as weapons. Their technique actually amounts to cleverly setting a trap and then springing it, although the design itself is not conscious. Consciously, these dirty fighters feel very self-righteous (as do most dirty fighters). The self-righteousness comes out in connection with the springing of the trap and expresses itself in indignant statements, such as (husband after shopping with his wife): "Here I let myself be dragged by you from one stupid store to another, waiting around while you drone on in ridiculous conversations with idiotic salesladies, without my saying one word about it, and instead of your appreciating my going along with you, you have the stomach to . . . insult me, . . . object to my having just one more drink so I could relax a little, . . . tell me that I am too silent, etc." Or: "Here I have slaved for you for years, hating every minute of it, picking up your dirty underwear from the floor, keeping the food warm for you when you don't tell me you'll be late, putting up with all your disgusting demands, and did I ever say a word about it? No, but you have the stomach to come and tell me that you don't like the tone of my voice!"

Note in these examples that the dirty fighter makes a virtue out of the crime of not having been open and sincere about his feelings at the time he experienced them. His attacks can be met only on this basis: "Please tell me about your feelings at the time you have them."

Although most people would agree that it is clearly unfair to blame somebody else for something you do yourself, the fact is that such blaming is a frequent occurrence. Parents who cannot control their own temper outbursts lash out at children who cannot control theirs. Husbands who think nothing of buying a two-hundred-dollar golf set blame their wives for extravagance when they buy a new dress. Teenagers who are prejudiced against the "Establishment" blame their parents for prejudice against long-haired hippies.

Such unfairness must be stopped if the emotional health of the family is to be preserved. The parent who has difficulties in controlling his own emotions must, of course, continue to correct the child for misbehavior but should, for the sake of fairness, indicate that he himself is also willing to work on controlling himself. If he finds himself unable to do so, he must seek professional psychological help. The extravagant husband who blames his wife for extravagance must present the problem as one which should be solved jointly by discussion and agreements. The teen-ager should be helped to see prejudice as a phenomenon which is not restricted to any particular age group or establishment.

The victim of such blaming is not to use the fact that the blamer himself is guilty as an excuse to continue with the behavior in question. On the contrary, he should propose that both the blamer and he work on the problem simultaneously. If the blamer cannot see that he himself is engaging in the same behavior (thus breaking Rule 8: other family members are experts on you and your behavior), he must be encouraged to seek psychotherapeutic help.

# "How Can You Be So Stupid?"

*Unfair Technique X: Humilating the partner. Using insults and epithets. Rubbing in. Exposing dirty linen in public. Comparing unfavorably—and favorably.*

Epithets, destructive labels, and other insults have some destructive effect on anyone regardless of age. In the case of an adult, however, the destructive effect of an epithet will depend primarily on the emotional health of the "recipient." If you hurl an epithet or an insult at an emotionally healthy person (who, by virtue of this health is likely to have a reasonably positive self-concept), he may feel sorry for you or he may feel a little angry or annoyed, or he may be disappointed in you, but he will *not* feel deeply hurt, because he knows you are mistaken in your judgment. Or else, if he himself did something he should not do or said something he should not say, he will feel that he has contributed to provoking your anger and, thus, that he—for the moment at least—has "deserved" the destructive comment (or "asked for it") himself.

On the other hand, if you hurl an insult at an emotionally disturbed or insecure person (whose self-concept is likely to be poor), his reaction will be quite different. He will either feel deeply hurt and perhaps depressed, or else he will react with strong anger and indignation, perhaps with demands for apology or retraction; in other words, he will "make a big deal" out of it. A person with a poor self-concept will find it difficult or impossible to take insults without becoming unreasonable himself. However, in an adult the permanent damage from such an attack is relatively slight, compared with the damage done to a child subjected to a similar insult. The self-concept of the adult is already formed and can be changed only slightly, unless he undergoes psychotherapy, experiences a religious conversion, or finds a life companion who supports him significantly (or, conversely, constantly undermines his self-concept). A child, on the other hand, is in the process of forming his self-concept and is therefore extremely susceptible to influence in a positive or negative direction.

Whatever you call a child will become part of his self-concept. If you call a boy "Johnny" every day, he will think "I am Johnny." If you call him "stupid" with significant frequency, he will think: "I am Johnny the stupid." Even if he consciously resists the idea and says to you, "I am not stupid," there will still be a part of him that thinks: "If my parents consider me stupid, that is what I must be." These statements have much less power, of course, when they come from brothers or sisters whom the child does not consider as authoritative as his parents.

Epithets such as "stupid," "lazy," or "bad" have a most destructive influence on the child's self-concept and thereby on his whole future life. For one thing, when Johnny goes to school, he will expect to fail since he sees himself as stupid. His expectation of inevitable failure is going to make him try less hard and his trying less will lead to poor performance which he will take as further proof that he is stupid, so he will try even less hard and the vicious circle is started and keeps getting more vicious. Or, if Johnny consciously reacts against the idea of being stupid, he may project this characteristic onto the teachers or the whole school instead and use the stupidity of the teachers and the system as an excuse for not doing well himself.

The long-range effects of epithets and destructive labels applied to children are most severe, because the resulting damage to the self-concept tends to influence all choices in life: friends, spouse, career. A person is likely to choose what he feels he is worthy of and, if his self-concept is poor, his choices are likely to be equally poor and therefore self-confirmatory.

Thus, *do not ever use this technique with children!*

Any insult ("Shut your big mouth," "Go to hell," "Fuck you") is destructive even if it is not used repeatedly to destroy another person's self-concept. It is destructive for the following reasons:

1. It communicates: "I do not recognize your value as a human being."

2. It communicates: "I am a rude person and I do not want to discuss things reasonably."

3. If said by a parent, it communicates: "I am, in fact, teaching you to become a rude person, too."

There are only three possible ways of reacting reasonably to an insult from another adult with whom you have or wish to have an intimate relationship:

1. By ignoring the specific insult for the moment and saying: "We are both upset; let's discuss this later. What about tomorrow at _____ o'clock?"

2. By recognizing the insult and saying: "It hurts me when you say something like that."

3. By accepting the kernel of truth behind the insult or your own provocation of the insult, and saying something like: "Maybe I deserve being told that; I am sorry I made you upset."

In the case of insults hurled by a child against his parent, the parent must decide whether he deserved or asked for the insult by his own unreasonable behavior. If so, the parent should not punish the child but point out to him that he should express his feelings without resort to dirty tactics. If the parent decides, however, that the insult was undeserved, he can deal with it in one of the following ways:

1. By reprimanding the child.

2. By warning the child about what will happen the next time he is insulting (and then following through on the warning).

3. By giving the child an immediate slap or swat.

Slapping or swatting a child in response to an insult is, by the way, not as destructive as some psychologists would have you believe. Sometimes it is the only effective method, as with a badly spoiled child who does not respond positively to attempts at verbal communication. It should only be used when all other techniques fail, however, because its communication value is not only positive (I will help you control your impulses if you won't; I want to teach you how insults are often handled in our society; I care strongly about you and want to stop you from being destructive; I understand the value of swift punishment; etc.) but also negative (hitting is good; acting out your negative feelings is good). If slapping or swatting does not work *soon,* say within two or three weeks, then professional help must be sought without delay.

Some people engage in destructive labeling under the excuse that the label is "true," that it "fits." Truth, however, is not to be used as an excuse to be destructive (see p. 174). If your partner is neurotic, it will not help him or you to call him neurotic. It *may* help, however, to call his attention to the specific behavior (or behaviors, one at a time) that you object to. If that is not sufficient, perhaps he needs professional help (or, more usually, both of you do), but that, too, is to be suggested compassionately and helpfully, not humiliatingly ("You are crazy, you ought to have your head examined").

A person's tone of voice can, of course, be just as insulting as any words he might use—and worse. Even words which ordinarily carry a message of respect or affection, such as "sir" and "dear," can be most insulting when uttered in a contemptuous or impudent tone of voice. A phrase such as "Well, *I* didn't do it" can be said in a tone which carries the message "How stupid can you be!"

Since it is sometimes difficult to judge one's own tone, it follows that a person may be insulting without consciously meaning to be. When this is the case, there is no use denying the fact that the tone *sounded* insulting to the other individual (see Rule 7: each event can be seen from different points of view; and 8: your family members are experts on you and your behavior) even though it was not consciously meant to carry such a message. The person who sounds insulting to others without meaning to must work on his problem, preferably with the help of a tape recorder. However, since such a person probably rejects other people on an unconscious level, psychotherapy (especially group psychotherapy) may well be necessary for a successful solution of the problem.

Parents are often guilty of humiliating their children by "talking down" to them. The parents who do this are—usually unwittingly—communicating that they consider their children to be inferior beings, not merely in their physical size but in their value as persons. Teen-agers are especially sensitive to being talked down to and will develop fierce resentments against their parents as a result of such treatment.

There are multitudes of ways of insulting a person without using epithets. Some are covered in connection with other unfair and destructive techniques; others will be mentioned here. Comparing a person unfavorably with someone else, for example, is an obvious insult which does not need elaboration. However, what some people do not realize is that it is also destructive, and in a deeper sense unfair, to compare a person *favorably* with one of his relatives or close friends. Consider these statements: "Boy, am I gald that you don't talk in that vulgar way your mother does"; "Gee, I am so glad you are not like that creep who calls himself your father"; "I really appreciate your honesty. You are not at all like that pathological liar, Harold (close friend of the one who is being addressed)."

These statements are not compliments. They are, in fact, thinly veiled insults, even when the person being addressed does not consciously feel insulted. The reason is that any close associate (parent, sibling, child, spouse, friend) becomes a part of you whether you want to recognize it or not. Even when you consciously hate a parent, for example, that parent is still part of your psychological makeup and, when another person attacks that parent, part of you will feel hurt and insulted whether you are consciously aware of the hurt or not.

Another insulting technique consists of "rubbing in." Overtly expressed, it takes the form of statements such as: "You mean you didn't do it yet?," "Oh no, not again," "I knew it." But it can also be expressed through a sigh, facial grimace, or "helpless" gesture with the hands.

"Exposing dirty linen in public" is another insulting technique. It is usually used by a partner who is not embarrassed over such exposure against a partner who *is* embarrassed. The person using the technique gets an unconscious (sometimes even conscious) pleasure out of seeing the partner squirm and may also enjoy the attention and/or possible shock value the exposure of the dirty linen affords. It is particularly often used in marital fighting and is a favorite technique used by dramatists, probably because of the shock value. As a matter of fact, a whole play has been written in which this technique is used almost exclusively by the hero and heroine: *Who's Afraid of Virginia Woolf?* by Edward Albee. George and Martha in the play, however, use this technique very crudely, like bulls in a china shop. Only rarely do "real" people expose dirty linen with such gross vulgarity. It is more often done in such "jabs" as the following, uttered in front of other people:

> *Husband* (in a group discussing a stage play): "I think it expresses a kind of cynical view of marriage" (= "I want all of you to know that my wife and I have a good marriage").
>
> *Wife:* "From my experience I think it is a realistic view" (= "Don't you believe a word of what he is saying: we actually have a bad marriage").
>
> Or, less subtly:
>
> *Wife:* "I like my mother-in-law very much."
>
> *Husband:* "Yes, especially when she stays away."

Underhanded fighting in public is just as injurious to a marriage relationship as overt dirty fighting in private, perhaps even more injurious. If a marriage relationship in which such fighting takes place is going to have a chance of improving, the partners must agree that they will do all their fighting in private or in a psychologist's office.

# "That's All in Your Mind!"

## Unfair Technique XI: Crazy-making. "Bugging." Unpredictability.

Crazy-making* refers to a variety of techniques which all have one thing in common: they are designed to make the partner doubt his sanity and/ or make him feel like climbing the walls. An extreme form of crazy-making was illustrated in the movie *Gaslight* (Metro-Goldwyn-Mayer, 1944) starring Ingrid Bergman and Charles Boyer and directed by George Cukor. In the movie, Charles Boyer attempts to drive Ingrid Bergman crazy by dimming the lights in the house, at the same time claiming that they shine with their usual brightness and thus implying that she can no longer trust her senses, that she must be hallucinating. *Gaslight* can thus serve as a prototype for a most common form of crazy-making which employs the strategy: set up an expectation, then see to it that it is not validated.

A crucial difference between the crazy-making shown in the movie *Gaslight* and ordinary or everyday forms of crazy-making is that whereas the former was consciously deliberate, the latter are unconsciously deliberate. All crazy-making operations, however, are repetitive and involve elements of neurotic games (see Rule 20). A crazy-maker often becomes addicted to his operations because of the power it gives him over his squirming victim who, it should be kept in mind, unconsciously gives him full cooperation, as is required in any game-type operation. There are many forms of crazy-making

*In writing some parts of this chapter I have used terms and concepts originally introduced in George R. Bach and Peter Wyden, *The Intimate Enemy* (New York: William Morrow & Co., Inc., 1968).

apart from the *Gaslight* variety; for example: "bugging," unpredictability, plain inconsideration, and playing therapist. We will here mention only the most common varieties of crazy-making. The ones listed below are all universally used techniques which "work" on anyone who does not spot them right away and openly demand that they be discontinued. There are also multitudes of "tailor-made" techniques which simply take advantage of the other person's "weak spots" (we all have such weak spots simply because we are human beings). The tailor-made techniques can be fought successfully only if the "victim" admits to the weak spot and demands that the partner stop pressing it.

1. *Denying a feeling which the partner can clearly observe.* This is a real *Gaslight* crazy-maker and it is easily recognized through the paradigm: "What's the matter?" (= "The lights seem dim"), leading to an irritated and curt or a nonchalant and shoulder-shrugging "Nothing" ("No, they are burning clearly"). The implication is, of course, that the partner is hallucinating, it is "all in his mind."

To be angry without verbally admitting it and telling the partner why is eminently unfair. It leaves him wringing his hands, filled with all kinds of fantasies, and not knowing what to do to remedy the situation. Showing anger surreptitiously (through silence, irritated or bored voice, refusal of sex, etc.) and simultaneously denying its existence is perhaps the most cruel crazy-making technique of all. It can be dealt with only in the way that Ingrid Bergman *should* have dealt with it in the movie: "I *know* the lights are dim and I insist on knowing why"="I *know* you are angry and I want to discuss it with you and see how we could solve the problem together." (This, by the way, does not constitute mind reading since the feeling—anger, depression, irritation—has been communicated through behavior, albeit surreptitiously.)

However, expert dirty fighters do not easily give up their weapons. When the pretense "Nothing is the matter" becomes untenable, they can admit to being angry but still refuse to tell the partner the cause for the anger. This is usually done by employing some phrase which rubs in the partner's insensitivity or stupidity ("If you don't know, what's the use of telling you?"), or uses divination ("You wouldn't understand anyway"), or expresses outright defiant refusal ("If you don't know how you hurt me, I'm certainly not going to tell you"). Pleading with such expert dirty fighters is usually hopeless and professional help must be sought.

This technique can also be employed "in reverse" through the use of mind reading. The partner is accused of having a feeling or attitude of which he is consciously unaware ("You really hate me, don't you"). Then, when the partner honestly and sincerely denies having such a feeling, the crazy-maker can refer to the principle stated in Rule 8, namely that he, as a family member, is an expert on the partner's behavior. The only way this type of crazy-making can be fought is by demands for evidence: "How do I show this hatred which you think I have?"

2. *Contradicting an issued demand*. This is a *Gaslight*-type of crazy-making even though the crazy-maker is unconscious of what he is doing. It involves setting up an expectation in the partner that everything will be all right if he fulfills a certain demand; however, when he does, it actually turns out that everything is wrong!* Examples: The wife who gets angry when her husband does not show her affection and then when he does, tells him that he is bothering her. Or the boss who one day tells his secretary to open and screen his mail, so that he does not have to go through a lot of trivia, and the next day gets angry with her for having invaded his privacy by opening his mail. Or the wife who tells her husband to "act like a father" to the children and then, when he does, tells him that he is interfering.

An all too common application of this crazy-making technique is illustrated by the following interchange:

*Wife:* "I would never have anything against your ·coming home late if you would only call first to let me know."

(Late that same afternoon the husband calls his wife to tell her he will be home late.)

*Wife:* "You goddamn sonuvabitch, are you going to do that to me again?!"

3. *Finding fault with the execution of an issued demand*. In this approach the crazy-maker tries to create the illusion that there is, indeed, a way to please him, whereas the

---

*Actually, *any* contradictory messages have a crazy-making quality about them and lead to confusion in the partner (see Rule 1), if not to his climbing the walls. In this chapter, however, we are concerned with specific techniques rather than with general tendencies.

reality is that there is absolutely no way to please him
Examples:

*Husband:* "Why do we never have fish for dinner?"
*Wife:* "But we had fish last Friday, dear."
*Husband:* "Yes, but it wasn't fresh fish."
Or:
*Son:* "I cleaned up my room, mother."
*Mother:* "Why did it take you so long?"

4. *Denying something which has been fully discussed and agreed upon.* Example: "I never said any such thing; that is all in your mind." Or: "You must be crazy to think that I would have agreed to something like that."

The frequent use of this technique can only be fought by making a record of all agreements in an "agreement book." However, sometimes an agreement is implicit rather than stated in so many words. Suppose, for example, that a wife demands that her husband clean up the garage, where he keeps the tools and workbench for his wood-working hobby. The spouses argue angrily for hours about this issue, the implication being that at least the spouses agree on its importance: the demand that the garage be cleaned is extremely important to the wife and the refusal is extremely important to the husband. When the husband then finally says: "All right, I'll do it from now on," thinking that he is being very generous, the wife says (usually with a sigh): "Never mind, it's not important, I'll do it myself!" If she is an expert dirty fighter she may add: "If I have to go through arguments like this to get you to do something any husband would do for his wife, it just isn't worth it to me."

Such breach of an implied agreement is best fought by confrontation ("The fact that we have argued so long about it shows that it *is* important to both of us") followed by a constructive comment ("But maybe my not cleaning the garage shows inconsideration to you and your feelings and I don't want to be inconsiderate toward you, so I want to do something about it").

Some people habitually deny what they have just said, thus causing the partner to doubt whether he can trust his senses. As an example, let us take the following interchange between a mother and her teen-age son.

*Mother:* I want you to clean up your room before you do anything else. I can't stand this terrible filth any longer; I am ashamed to have company over, the way it looks. And see. to it that you put away those half-finished models; I don't care where you put them as long as they are not in sight.

*Son:* (cleans up the room)

(One hour later.)

*Mother:* Why haven't you started on your homework yet? You know you have that exam tomorrow that you must study for.

*Son:* But Mother, you said for me to clean up my room before I do anything else.

*Mother:* I said no such thing. I said that your room needed cleaning and that it should be done soon. But I didn't say that it should be done before your homework. (Inspecting the closet.) Anyway, why did you put your models in here with your clothes, you idiot? Don't you realize that your clothes will start to smell from that terrible glue. How stupid can you be?

*Son:* But Mother, you said you didn't care where I put them as long as they'd be out of sight.

*Mother:* There you go putting words in my mouth again. I said you have to put them out of sight and in a place where the smell and wet paint won't do any damage. I know exactly what I said, so you. stop giving me static about it. Now get to your homework. You are a very intelligent boy and there is no excuse for your not getting A's in your subjects.

*Son:* Mother, you just said I was a stupid idiot.

*Mother:* What? You know I never use that kind of language. What I said was that you didn't use good judgment when you put away your models. Anyway, your room is not important but your education is. Just think how much money we spend every year so that you can go to a good private school!

*Son:* But I never asked to go to an expensive school. I would rather go to a public school.

*Mother:* Why don't you ever listen to me? I just got through saying that it is your education that is important, not money or other things. You kids nowadays, you just don't appreciate anything. You are going to the finest school in all . . . (launches into a sermon). (etc., etc.)

Is this mother deliberately lying when she "doctors up" her previous statements? No, not at all. She sincerely thinks that what she remembers she said is what she actually said. But nevertheless the fact is that she is driving her son to climb the walls. As a result of the mother's—unwitting—crazy-making, the son may come to doubt himself and his ability to understand or even perceive correctly, learn that his mother cannot be trusted to tell the truth, withdraw into smoking marijuana, or rebel openly by outright refusal to obey any commands or requests. Whatever the consequences, they are likely to be negative. And yet, the mother *is* well-meaning— she loves her son and wants the best for him.

In the case of a habitual denier of previous statements, often the only recourse is a tape recorder.

5. *Refusing to take half the responsibility for joint agreements; or "Have your way now; pay later."* Examples: The husband who lets himself be "talked into" buying a certain house and then spends a great deal of time blaming his wife for its disadvantages. The parent who agrees to let his child choose the color of his room and then keeps criticizing him for having chosen black. The wife who insists that her husband choose a restaurant and then spends the evening making sarcastic remarks about his choice.

6. *Building up the partner's hopes and then shattering them by changing one's mind without an acceptable reason having been offered.* Example: For over a month, Arnold has not only agreed to have his wife's daughter from her first marriage live with them, he has actually insisted on calling her and inviting her himself. Then, five days before his wife's daughter is to move in, he announces in the middle of a conversation: "By the way, I have changed my mind about Judy, I can't let her move in." Any attempts by his wife to find out the reasons for his change of mind are met by clichés such as "A person has a right to change his mind, doesn't he?", or "I'm just telling you my honest feelings, I don't want to have her here and that's all," or "Why do you always have to have a reason for everything, isn't it enough that I don't like the idea?"

Another example: A father has promised his son that he will take him to Disneyland on Sunday. When Sunday comes around and the son asks him when they are leaving, the father is surprised and says: "Where? To Disneyland? I don't feel like it today, son." If the son insists on being given a reason, the father says: "Enough of that nagging now. I don't have to give you any reasons. You must learn to show some respect for your elders!"

An unfortunately common example of this type of crazy-making occurs when one partner in a marriage has finally persuaded the spouse to come in for professional help in working out the marriage problems. After the first few sessions the reluctant partner, having built up the spouse's hopes by finally agreeing to come in, shatters them by saying: "I am tired of trying, I give up, we are in the wrong office; we should see a lawyer instead." To prevent the use of this dirty technique I ask most patients who come in with marriage problems to consider the subject of divorce taboo for at least six months.

7. *Insisting on exact wording and refusal to allow re-phrasing; or "Sticking to the letter and denying the spirit."* Examples: "I told you you could call him but I did not say you could call him today." "I said we should be nice to her but I didn't say we should buy her flowers." "I didn't say you were lying, I just said that you were not telling the truth. You never listen to what I actually say." A typical example of a crazy-maker using this technique is provided by Mr. N., whom we met in discussing Rule 6 (p. 55).

8. *Putting words in the other person's mouth.* This is usually done by using Unfair Technique 11-I and 11-II excessively. Examples: *Partner A:* "Could you please bring me a cup of coffee?" *Partner B:* "You want me to jump whenever you whistle, I know, but I have told you I am not going to become your slave." *Partner X:* "I feel we should discuss how to spend Thanksgiving." *Partner Y:* "There you go trying to worm out of seeing my parents again."

9. *Accusing the other person of consciously vicious or sinister motivation.* Examples: "Where did you hide my socks?" "You knew where we should have turned left and didn't tell me." "You conveniently forgot to reserve tickets, so you wouldn't have to go to the concert with me." This technique is a particularly diabolic variant of mind reading, since it implies that the other person is a sadist. If used in the absence of anger it borders on paranoia.

10. *Blaming the other person for one's own destructive behavior.* Examples: "You made me lose my temper." "It was your chatter that made me forget to make that important phone call." "If you hadn't argued so much last

night, I could have had a good night's sleep for a change!"

11. *Ignoring the other person's wishes.* Examples: The wife who just will not make herself ready to leave on time. The husband who just won't help his wife so she could get ready to leave on time. The father who constantly breaks his promises to play a game with his son, fix his bike, or take him to a ball game. The mother who through her rude behavior keeps embarrassing her children in front of their friends. The school-age child who will not put away his toys (this happens mostly in homes where there are no reasonable rules or where the rules are not enforced firmly and kindly).

12. *Repeating the same point or question over and over again.* This technique is usually employed in connection with a violation of Rule 15 (do not preach or lecture) and can be very effective in producing irritation in the partner or making him interrupt ("If you'd only let me answer"). When used chronically it constitutes definite crazy-making of the "bugging" variety.

   Repetition of the same point or question is permissible only when an opportunity has been given for the partner to respond and the response has not adequately dealt with the point or fully answered the question. Even then, however, the repetition must be preceded by a specific demonstration of how the response was inadequate.

13. *Insisting on seeing a hidden psychological significance behind everything that is said or done.* Examples: "You made a Freudian slip again," "Your crossing your legs that way means you are an introvert," "People who prefer maroon as a color are emotionally disturbed." Such "psychologizing" can make life unbearable for the partner, even if there is no destructive mind reading involved in the sense of specifically attributing negative unconscious motivation to the partner.

14. *Frequent use of the nondirective ("client-centered") therapeutic technique variously referred to as "active listening," "mirroring," or "reflecting."* Although some people like to have their statements rephrased because it gives them the feeling of "being understood," many people get frustrated over being paraphrased, especially if it happens often and leads to no resolution or decision. In our discussion of the importance of listening, we will have an example of the potentially destructive effects of transposing such a therapeutic technique into the home situation.

Crazy-making of any type is a symptom which can be most difficult to deal with by any do-it-yourself methods. Absolute insistence on reality, abstaining from retaliation by unfair methods, and nonsarcastic humor are the ingredients of a constructive defense against crazy-making, but are often not effective. Good-natured, nonhostile sarcasm, employing truly absurd alternatives will sometimes work if the crazy-maker is not allergic to sarcasm. Examples:

*Crazy-Maker:* "Why do we never have fish for dinner?"
*Wife:* "But we had fish last Friday, dear."
*Crazy-Maker:* "Yes, but it wasn't fresh fish."
*Wife:* "You are right and, come to think of it, I didn't serve it with a peacock feather, either."
Or:
*Crazy-Maker:* "Where did you hide my socks?"
*Wife:* "This time I hid them in a place where you will never find them."

Usually, however, crazy-making is resistant to being treated at home. As a matter of fact, it is difficult to handle even in intensive individual psychotherapy. Crazy-making is best dealt with in group psychotherapy where it is most likely that at least some members of the group will have intensely negative emotional reactions to the operations of the crazy-maker. In a psychotherapy group, the crazy-making operations (and their preconscious and unconscious purposes) as well as the "allergic" reactions to them can be analyzed with simultaneous benefits for both the crazy-maker and his "victims." After such repeated exposures and analyses, only the conscious sadist will persist in his use of crazy-making to destroy the human identity of his partner.

## "Boohoo-Boohoo."

*Unfair Technique XII: Having one's feelings hurt at the drop of a hat. Guilt induction. The destructive use of crying.*

Attempts to control others through the induction of guilt are most destructive to communication. The employment of guilt-manufacturing techniques (playing martyr, sighing, crying, the "suffering look," etc.) encourages the partner to walk on eggs and provides the partner with an excuse for not being open about his feelings (see Rules 10 and 16).

The term "martyr-complex" is applied to a condition in which the individual constantly communicates verbal or nonverbal messages designed to induce guilt, such as: "I do everything for you without getting anything in return," or "I am fragile and you are a brute," or "You always take advantage of poor defenseless me," or "I try so hard and yet you never appreciate it." The martyr, either through "putting up" with everything and "suffering in silence" or through oversensitivity and touchiness, attempts to control the other person by making him feel guilty. A skillful martyr can make the most reasonable person appear to be an insensitive brute.

There are many ways to rule through guilt induction, but the most obvious way is through crying. Crying—at all ages —can be a healthy and normal way of showing grief, sorrow, or compassion. In infants and very young children it is also a normal way of showing frustration, disappointment, and anger. However, as soon as a person is capable of an intellectual understanding of what is realistic, reasonable, and feasible (usually at the age of five or six), crying in frustration, disappointment, and anger can become a destructive technique, the employment of which may be a sign of retarded personality growth.

When used as a destructive communication technique, crying can be employed for the following purposes:

1. To induce guilt: "Look what you have done to me."

2. To achieve power if the guilt induction has been successful: "I will stop only if you do what I want."

3. To show frustration: "Perhaps my frustration will be alleviated this way, the way it is for babies."

4. To show anger: "Maybe this will hurt him if nothing else does."

5. To show fear: "I am afraid of getting hurt."

6. To avoid constructive discussion: "I don't want to talk about this; discussion could lead to a solution that may deprive me of some pleasure that I have now."

7. To express a feeling of inadequacy, usually with the implication that the other person's demands cannot be met: "You should have married someone better than me" or "How did you get stuck with a stupid child like me?"

Crying can also serve as a danger signal: "Stop, you have gone too far." If this is the case, efforts should be made to encourage the person to give a *verbal* danger signal instead. If the danger signal is not verbalized, there will always be a suspicion that the crying serves merely to avoid constructive discussion. As we pointed out above, crying in one partner is often used by the other partner as an excuse for "walking on eggs."

For cultural reasons which we will not attempt to analyze here, crying as a destructive communication technique is mostly used by women ("boys don't cry"). There are, however, exceptions to this rule. As a matter of fact, in my practice I have seen a fair number of families in which the father, not the mother, "rules by tears."

Certainly the role of martyr can be played by a person of either sex and any age. Martyrs are difficult to deal with by "do-it-yourself" methods. Certainly, being cold and indifferent to the martyr's complaints is destructive since it plays right into the martyr's game and serves to confirm to him (her) that he (she) is indeed being treated cruelly. The best thing to do is to try to deal with problems in advance: "Don't you think that you might feel put upon if . . . ," or "Are you sure you won't feel resentment over my . . . ," or "I want to be sure that you yourself want to. . . ."

Martyrdom as a way of life is, however, seldom cured by such home remedies. Both the martyr and the partner in whom he (she) tries to induce guilt should therefore seek help from a psychologist.

# "Sure, Sure, I'll Bet."

## *Unfair Technique XIII: The use of sarcasm and ridicule.*

The destructiveness of using sarcasm is—or ought to be—so obvious that we should not need to allot much space to the topic in this book. The sad truth, however, is that many people use sarcasm daily without being aware (or being insufficiently aware) of the destructiveness of its effects.

If it is destructive to use sarcasm in communicating with adults, it is unforgivable to use it with children. Let us take an example. If a child says "I'll try to do better next time" and his parent replies "Sure, sure, I'll bet" with the concomitant sarcastic tone, there are at least five likely destructive consequences:

1. The child will feel beaten down and will lose confidence in himself, since he will feel that the parent has no faith in him at all.

2. The child may give up trying altogether, since his attempts to improve merely lead to destructive attacks from the parent.

3. The child will see the parent as an unreasonable person, one with whom one cannot reach any positive results through discussion.

4. The child may also come to see the parent as hypocritical, because he knows that if he himself were to use sarcasm against his parent, the latter would probably get angry and accuse him of being sassy.

5. The child has been taught poor communication and will therefore most probably learn from this type of lesson to communicate poorly and negatively. If the lessons are frequent, the learning will be thorough and the child will himself grow up to be a parent who communicates negatively and teaches *his* children to do the same, etc. The consequences for future generations of what we do or do not do today are staggering to the imagination!

If a *child* uses sarcasm with the parent, it is best for the parent not to react with repressive anger, but to point out to the child how sarcasm will usually backfire and to help him discuss the issue openly and frankly instead of through underhanded means. For example, if the child says, "Yeah, yeah, you are always right and I am always wrong," do not deny that that is how you "come off." If you deny it, you will actually be *confirming* what your child is saying, namely that he is always wrong in your eyes! Instead, tell him that sarcasm is not a fair way of discussing, but that maybe he has a good point: perhaps you do not admit your own mistakes enough. Ask him to *specify* where he feels you are mistaken and then try to see the situation from *his* viewpoint. If you follow this course, your child is more likely to see you as a reasonable person and he is less likely to use sarcasm in talking with you in the future.

Sarcasm can sometimes assume sadistic proportions. One of my patients, the attractive wife of a professional baseball player, used sarcasm to ridicule almost everything her husband did, especially his profession. When he finally threw a temper tantrum in which he emptied the contents of his chest of drawers onto the floor of the living room, his wife sat and leafed through a magazine and said, calmly: "You are a real big boy, aren't you!" And when—probably as a direct result of his resentment—he became impotent, she would say such things as "Perhaps you would like me to buy you a miniature baseball bat instead" or "What's the matter, little boy, afraid to grow up?"

Of course, we must make a distinction between destructive sarcasm and sarcasm as a form of humor. A witty repartee often contains sarcasm, yet a person who masters the art of repartee is usually admired and sought out rather than detested and shunned. When, then, is a sarcasm destructive and when is it not?

The answer is simple: *A sarcasm is destructive whenever your partner in communication reacts unfavorably to it*. The relative destructiveness of a sarcasm, in other words, is measured by its effect on another person. It follows, of course, that you can use a sarcasm with a person who may react by laughing and enjoying it and giving you one right back. But someone else may feel quite hurt and offended by the same remark.

In this connection we should mention the subject of good-natured kidding. There are people who love being kidded and there are others who resent it vehemently and there are all shades in between. But this is a book on communication in the family and in the family there is no excuse for not knowing how much kidding another family member can "take." The kidding must stop immediately when the partner signals, verbally or nonverbally, that he has had enough and no longer enjoys the kidding. More on this subject in Rule 18 (learn when to use humor and when to be serious).

People who habitually use sarcasm will often hide behind the excuse that what they have said is true. For example, if a sarcastic person has just said "Well, since you are such an expert on . . . ," he may later justify this by saying that you are indeed an expert. You must then point out to him that the truth can be told in both constructive and destructive ways. "Well, since you are such an expert on . . ." can also be expressed positively, for example by saying *in a sincere tone:* "I feel that you know more about . . ." or "I feel kind of inadequate about . . . so I would appreciate if you. . . ." If the sarcastic partner insists that this is "splitting hairs," you can say that it would indeed be splitting hairs for you to make an issue of it if he used sarcasm very seldom, but since he uses it often (for heaven's sake don't say "always"), you must point it out because you resent it.

When a person denies having been sarcastic, it is often best to take the denial at face value and proceed as if there had been no sarcasm. If, however, the use of sarcasm is chronic, it has to be pointed out or the person using it will not have a chance to change his approach. It is then often useful to ask him to repeat what he said. If he says it non-sarcastically the second time, you show him that you appreciate his change by responding positively to what he has said. If it is still said sarcastically, the sarcasm involved should by now be more obvious even if the "user" is reluctant to admit that such is the case. In order to give him something to work on, however, you tell him *how* you would have liked him to say whatever it was and then you respond as if he had actually said it the way you would have liked him to.

At all times, you must be careful that you don't make the situation worse by "picking" on your partner. Perhaps you are unduly sensitive to sarcasm. Perhaps you are a fault-finder. In your response to a sarcastic comment, try to be helpful and forgiving rather than picking and "rubbing it in." Under no circumstances should you respond to a destructive technique by using one yourself.

"_____"

## Unfair Technique XIV: *Silence, ignoring, sulking, pouting, "cold shoulder treatment."*

One of the strongest needs of a human being is the need for recognition and acknowledgment. We have already dealt with the need for recognition and acknowledgment of accomplishment and improvement. But there is an even more basic need: to have one's very presence, existence, and significance as a human being recognized and acknowledged by another person. The withholding of such recognition denies one's value as a human being. As a matter of fact, not to have one's presence acknowledged is one of the severest insults to which a human being can be exposed. This is the reason why the cold shoulder treatment can be the most vicious of all destructive techniques used in communication.

Maybe it sounds strange to say that silence can be a communication technique, but the fact is that silence is a behavior and all behavior is communicative if it carries a message, intended or unintended, to another person. All behavior can also be *used* for specific purposes of communication.

Silence can communicate many things. It can communicate satisfaction, well-being, and mutual understanding and love. But silence can also communicate contempt, pouting, sulking, indifference, "coldness" or, what is perhaps worst: a cruel refusal to cooperate in solving problems. Silence precludes any possibility of solving problems cooperatively and effectively prevents the development of any true intimacy, since the latter can only be achieved through sincere and tactful openness and frankness in communicating feelings and thoughts.

People who use silence as a weapon often hide behind such excuses as "I don't like to argue," or "Frankly, I have never been the chatterbox type," or "I am just not much of a talker," or "What I say never makes any difference anyway," or "I talk all day at the office; why can't I be allowed some relaxation when I come home?" No matter what the excuse, silence can be a most destructive weapon. It can be seen as the ultimate in contempt for another person, worse than spitting in his or her face (which at least shows strong involvement, despite the destructiveness of the act itself).

Even when it does not offend the other person, in fact even when the other person consciously welcomes it, silence may give the impression of a compliance and agreement which is not there and which hides a resentment. Since the resentment is unexpressed, it may grow to the point of explosion in terms of violent acting out, divorce, or even suicide!

To be angry and not let the partner know why is a variant of the first technique we listed under crazy-making, since it leaves the other person wringing his hands and not knowing what to do. Especially when the anger is denied under questioning (implying: "You must be hallucinating") the crazy-making intent is obvious.

It should be pointed out that there are cases where the employment of silence is entirely unconscious and not the slightest trace of conscious ill will is present. Some people who clam up when they are upset do not consciously want to do so, but feel compelled to: they are "tongue-tied." No matter how much they consciously want to answer a challenge by the other person, they are seemingly unable (actually: unconsciously unwilling) to get a word out. This is a neurotic reaction and is characterized by the absence of excuses and—usually—a willingness on the part of the person who is tongue-tied to seek help for his difficulty.

Children of all ages sometimes use sulking and pouting as a means of showing displeasure. It is an ineffective technique (at least it *should* be ineffective) and it is destructive, but it should not be countered by another destructive technique, such as ridiculing ("Boy, that's the biggest baby I have ever seen") or sarcasm ("You are really taking it like a man, aren't you"). Sulking and pouting are best dealt with openly and sincerely, with compassion and firmness, and with a constant readiness to discuss the other person's and one's own feelings.

The "silent treatment" is particularly destructive when directed against children (whose need for recognition is extremely strong), but unfortunately I know of many examples of families where the parents, especially often fathers, have used this technique in order to punish the child or to show their displeasure. In such cases it should go without saying that professional help is urgently needed.

Silence usually cannot be stopped by one partner demanding "Talk to me." The usual response to such a general demand is more silence or an anger outburst. Silence is best stopped through a recognition that silence in itself communicates and confronting the partner with this fact. For example, instead of the ineffective "Talk to me," you can use such openings as:

"What do you think about . . .?" or "Why do you think it is that . . .?" (asking for an opinion). The former question is preferable since the latter is too easily avoided by answering "I don't know."

"I wonder what you are trying to tell me by being silent?" (but beware of "playing therapist" if you use this approach).

"I'd like to discuss silence and what effect it has on me and on other people. What do you think about silence?"

"I wonder if there is something I do that discourages you from talking to me."

"I am mad at you for being silent so often and I want to fight about it if we can't discuss it."

Finally, a few words on the subject of "walking out" on an argument. To avoid an argument by walking out is usually destructive and may show contempt for the partner, unwillingness to come to a conclusion, or fear of facing an issue. Consciously it is often defended by such excuses as: "You can't talk with her anyway when she is in that kind of a state!," or "I had had it up to here; I just couldn't take any more," or "I am not going to just stand there and let him talk to me that way." Walking out is a most insidious and underhanded technique since it leaves the partner seething with emotion without an opportunity to communicate his feelings. It can engender a terrible feeling of hopelessness in the partner; as a matter of fact, many a suicide has been triggered by the partner walking out.

There are occasions, however, when walking out is permissible and even constructive. For example, if the partner has previously said: "I wish you would just let me alone for a while when I get upset and give me a chance to simmer down," then fulfilling the partner's wish is the reasonable thing to do, provided the issue over which the argument arose is discussed fully later. Even when the partner objects, walking out may be permissible if the partner is given a reasonable explanation (without blaming him) and a promise to continue the discussion at a specific time, for example: "I am too upset to be reasonable now [not "you are too upset . . ."], so I suggest that we continue the discussion tomorrow after dinner."

# 12. "I DIDN'T MEAN ANYTHING. YOU ARE TAKING IT WRONG."

*Rule 12: Let the effect, not the intention, of your communication, be your guide.*

We have earlier discussed the fact that family members and other close associates become experts on your behavior. There is a corollary to that fact which deserves to serve as the basis of another rule. The corollary is that if a family member gets upset by something you often do or say, then the conscious intention behind what you did or said is of little consequence. Notice the word "often" in the preceding sentence. From time to time there can be semantic misunderstandings which are, indeed, corrected when the conscious intention is stated. However, if there is a chronic problem, such as one partner being inconsiderate, selfish, or covertly hostile, then his statement of positive conscious intent ("I didn't mean anything bad") will not solve the problem, because the other family member knows or senses the destructive tendency which led to the partner's upsetting words or actions (or lack of action) in the first place. Let us take an example.

Suppose a husband ignores his wife in the course of a dinner out with another couple. Suppose further that the wife bawls him out because of it when they come home. Now, if this is a rare event and the husband is otherwise considerate, a sincere apology and a statement of conscious intention such as: "Gee, honey, you are right; I really did not mean to do that; I'll see to it that it doesn't happen again," will satisfy the wife* and that will be the end of it.

_____
*If it is a rare event and not symbolic of other inconsiderations, and the wife still does not accept the apology and statement of conscious

However, if it is not a rare event, if it is just another example of frequent inconsiderate behavior on the husband's part, the statement of conscious intention will not be enough, nor should it be enough. The husband then has seriously to accept the fact that he—unconsciously, to be sure—has hurt his wife on many occasions and he must come to terms with his inconsideration. The wife, similarly, must seriously examine whether she has not in some way—again unconsciously —invited such inconsiderate behavior from her husband (by being sarcastic, for example).

In no case should the husband belittle his wife's concern, such as by saying: "Why do you have to make a federal case out of it?" That is a counteraccusation and is not to be brought up until the accusation itself has first been thoroughly discussed. After that, it would certainly not be destructive for the husband to say: "Honey, I wish you would tell me about these things without bawling me out," if that is what he feels. The manner of bringing up accusations can then be discussed and decisions made for future handling of such situations.

You often hear such remarks as: "I was just kidding; can't you take a little humor?" or "God, you are thin-skinned, why do I always have to walk on eggs around you?" These are again counteraccusations and therefore destructive both in timing (they should be brought up *after* the original accusation has been discussed) and in form (they ridicule and belittle the other person).

The remark, "Can't you take a little humor?," for example, cannot be justified under any circumstances (see Rule 18). If it is said to a stranger, it is rude and should be replaced by "I was just kidding; please forgive me," or something similar. On the other hand, if it is said to a person you have known for a long time, it is not only rude but it also indicates insensitivity or inconsideration on your part. It shows that you are either insensitive to the other person's feelings (which, if you were sensitive, you would know by now) or you are unwilling to tailor your communication in such a way as to take the other person's feelings into account.

Let us take another example. Suppose a member of your family perceives a remark you have made as being insulting.

---

intention, then the wife probably has a personality problem which should be treated professionally through psychotherapy.

If you then reply: "It wasn't insulting at all; I just meant such and such; why do you *always* read things into what I say?," you are breaking at least three of our rules: Rule 8 (family members are experts), Rule 12 (it is the effect that is important), and Rule 5 (be realistic and do not exaggerate).

Instead, when someone finds what you say insulting, say something like: "I am sorry it came out that way, let me try to say it in a different way." If it *still* comes out as an insult, you have to ask your partner to tell you wherein the insult lies if you cannot see it yourself. If he then says that it is your tone of voice, for example, you *must* accept that as a fact, even though you suspect that the partner is exaggerating. However, there is a faint chance that the partner feels that *any* mention of the topic at hand is insulting. Then again, instead of accusing him of being unreasonable, you must ask him to discuss with you how the topic should be dealt with if it is important to you to have it discussed. It should go without saying that if you find yourselves unable (i.e., unconsciously unwilling) to communicate without upsetting each other, then it is high time to go to a psychologist or psychiatrist for professional help.

In this connection I would like to repeat my warning against seeing these matters as trivia. They may be "small matters" on the surface but that does not make them less upsetting or less dangerous. A virus is a "small matter," but it can be deadly. The same is true of the "inconsideration-virus" or "hostility-virus": it may be small, but it may be so destructive in its effects that it can lead to ruined relationships and ruined lives. How matters are communicated can make the difference between whether a marriage breaks up or lasts or whether it is happy or unhappy; it can determine whether problems are solved or allowed to accumulate and eventually lead to an explosion; it can have a major influence on whether a child ends up as a prison inmate or as a responsible member of society.

An important fact which should be brought up at this point is that the listener's picture of you as a person is going to "color" what you communicate to him. If the listener sees you as a critical and faultfinding person, for example, he might read criticism into what you say even if you neither consciously nor unconsciously intend to be critical. If this is the case, there are three measures you must take in working on your communication:

1. You must "bend over backwards" to see to it that your speech is noncritical.

2. You must realize that there is no realistic cause for your being upset about being "misunderstood." The other person probably has good cause to see you as a critical person and, thus, you are just making installment payments on past sins.

3. You must develop a long-term program to change the other person's view of you, not just by stating your conscious intentions, but by behaving toward him in an accepting, noncritical manner.

The same principles apply to *any* picture the listener has of you which may color or otherwise influence his perception of what you are trying to communicate. If he sees you as prone to exaggerate, for example, he may not believe your story is realistic no matter how accurate it is. It is then important that you realize that his disbelief was largely created by you. Again, you are paying for past sins and must be prepared to do so for a long time, until your nonexaggerating behavior has had a chance to change the other person's picture of you.

Similarly, if a child is used to being hit by his father, he will cringe when his father approaches even if the father has no intention of hitting him. If a parent has had several experiences in which his child has lied to him, the child may tell the truth and still not be believed by his parent. If a wife is used to her husband's being unrealistic and overly optimistic, she may think he is just fooling himself when he tells her about the excellent chances he has of being promoted.

When your conscious intention is not accepted by a family member or by anyone who knows you well, it is useless to "feel misunderstood." It is much more fruitful to examine what there is about your own behavior which causes the other person to gain a different impression from the one you consciously intended to convey.

# 13. "SHAME ON YOU FOR SAYING SUCH BAD THINGS ABOUT YOUR SISTER."

*Rule 13: Accept all feelings and try to understand them; do not accept all actions, but try to understand them.*

At the end of our discussion of Rule 1 (actions speak louder than words) we gave an admonition: express your positive feelings in both actions and words but your negative feelings only in words! A reciprocal rule would be that you should accept all the feelings expressed by another person but not necessarily all his actions. This rule is especially important to follow in the process of raising children, although it applies just as consistently to adults.

Children often complain that their parents don't understand them. When you question these children a little more closely, it often turns out that they simply demand that their parents let them do whatever they want. A prohibition is interpreted by these children as a lack of "understanding." And then both parents and children, instead of differentiating between understanding feelings and accepting actions, begin to hide behind the current universal excuse for poor or destructive communication called "generation gap."

Problems do exist in communication between age groups as well as between any groups or individuals. These problems arise mainly from not following rules of constructive communication. In understanding problems between age groups, as well as between any groups in a hierarchical position, the matter of differentiating between understanding feelings and accepting action is important. Children, employees, racial minorities, etc., often claim that they are not "understood" if their demands are not met. Adults, bosses, and racial majorities, on the other hand, often tend to reject demands without attempting to understand the feelings leading to the demands, sometimes just to "show who is boss." This is a major cause of communication problems between hierarchically arranged groups.

Perhaps we as individuals cannot do very much to prevent conflicts between groups in society. But we can certainly contribute to such prevention by teaching our children to respect and try to understand other people's feelings even while disapproving of their actions. Likewise, our children can be helped to understand that disapproval of an action does not necessarily mean lack of understanding of the feelings which led to the action. Such teaching must start early, however, and is best accomplished through the parents' example in handling everyday situations. As a paradigm, let us take the following situation and analyze it in detail.

> Tom, eight years old, has hit his sister Mary, five years old. Mary is howling and mother asks Tom why he did it. He says: "Because she broke one of my models again. I hate Mary, she is a creep and I just wish she'd drop dead." Now it is up to the mother to respond and thereby make the situation better or worse or leave it in status quo.

Many mothers would say: "Tom, how *can* you say such horrible things about your little sister? You know it is wrong to hate and Mary is such a nice little girl. She loves you and she did not mean to do any harm to your model. You must remember that Mary is so much younger than you and she does not understand things well yet. But *you* are older and you should know better than to hit your sister. Go straight to your room and stay there until you are sorry for what you said and did and then you apologize to your sister and to me."

Such a response is well-meaning, but nevertheless destructive. The mother is committing at least five serious mistakes, which are going to lead to a lot of similar—and worse—trouble in the future:

1. She is scolding Tom for his feelings as much as for his action and therefore is saying, in effect, that Tom *should not tell her about how he feels* in the future. Without

realizing it, she is asking her son not to communicate meaningfully with her!

2. She is making no attempt to understand his feelings. On the contrary, she implies that they are totally incomprehensible since Mary "obviously" is such a nice girl. By implying that Tom's feelings are completely incomprehensible the mother is saying, in effect, that *feelings cannot be understood*. And since understanding feelings is an important aid to controlling them, she is thereby making it even more difficult for Tom to control his feelings in the future.

3. She takes sides in the conflict on the basis of the underdog fallacy: Mary is the underdog because she is a girl and because she is younger. The mother does not realize that Mary—through her behavior—may have been *asking* her brother to hit her, perhaps (consciously or unconsciously) to get him into trouble! Thus, she unwittingly tries to "con" her son into accepting the ridiculous idea that Mary—at the age of five!—did not know what she was doing! Under serious questioning the mother herself would not admit to believing such utter nonsense as that her daughter would not have known she was doing something she was not supposed to when she handled her brother's model. After all, she had broken some of them before.

The underdog fallacy assumes that a younger or weaker child is less skillful in getting someone else into trouble than an older child. The fact is that the ability to get someone else into trouble is fully developed by the age of about three or four. In other words, a three-year-old can be just as skillful getting someone else into trouble as a thirteen-year-old—or as an adult, for that matter. The statement, "Mary is so much younger than you and she does not understand things well yet," is not applicable to this situation because Mary understands quite well at the age of five how to get her eight-year-old brother into trouble. She is no underdog at all; on the contrary, she is more powerful than her brother, because she knows that her parents believe in the underdog fallacy and therefore support her because of her age. Her brother is comparatively helpless, because if he uses any effective way of stopping her, she can start screaming for her parents and be sure that she can count on their support.

Thus, if there is any underdog here at all, it is the older brother. Tom knows he is powerless and that he cannot get any help from his parents, and that knowledge increases his hatred toward his sister. An additional likely consequence is that he will behave in more and more immature ways, his unconscious purpose being to tell his parents—through his actions—that he is little and needs support, too.

4. The mother humiliates Tom and prolongs the humiliation by requiring him to apologize to his sister. The humiliation is particularly galling because it is not accompanied by the demand that Mary apologize for breaking the model. This will intensify Tom's feelings of hatred toward his sister. Consequently, what may have started as normal and ordinary sibling rivalry may end up in a neurotic love-hate relationship, the destructive effects of which can be lifelong.

5. She takes no action to help Tom protect his property in the future and is, thereby, in effect, seeing to it that this type of situation will continue forever, thus making Tom feel totally hopeless. It will also have a destructive effect on Mary, because she knows she should not have touched the model and she needs a parent to help her control herself by setting definite limits. As matters stand, she is likely to grow up to be a person who secretly enjoys the power of provoking others into behaving in an unreasonable manner.

How *should* this situation have been handled? Here we come to the encouraging part of the lesson to be learned and that is that although there are many ways of being destructive, there are also many ways in which to be constructive. Let us give two examples of how the situation can be handled constructively, one involving no punishment, the other involving punishment.

*Mother:* "Why did you hit Mary?"

*Tom:* "Because she broke one of my models again. I hate Mary; she is a creep and I just wish she'd drop dead."

*Mother:* "I understand you must be mad at Mary for breaking your model. And I am going to do everything I can to see to it that she won't do it again. If it is necessary, I will tell her that the next time it happens she is going to be punished. I know she can be difficult to handle, but let me help you to handle her. You must promise not to hit her again, and I will promise to do my best to help you protect your stuff. What do you think about that? Do you have any suggestions that we might discuss?"

Or:

*Mother:* "You know I told you that next time you hit Mary I will punish you and so I will. You are grounded for the rest of the day (or any other reasonable punishment). But *she* knows that she is not to touch your models, so she is going to get the same punishment. I think I understand how you feel about it and tonight we will all discuss what we can do to stop things like this from happening again. Let's all think about it and we'll discuss it tonight."

Despite the differences in the two replies by the mother, they are both constructive. The main difference is that the first mother decides not to punish, but the second mother is committed to punishment from what she has said before, so she must punish. However, she does it fairly and realistically by punishing both, rather than picking on the older one. Both approaches are reasonable. Another difference is that the first mother wants to discuss future measures right away, while the second mother prefers to wait and discuss them in the evening. There are advantages and disadvantages to both alternatives, but, again, both are basically reasonable and constructive.

The common elements in how these "constructive" mothers handle the situation are:

1. They respect Tom's feelings and do not scold him for them. If they had wished, they could have added that he should not use words like "creep" and "drop dead"; he can say that he is "boiling mad" at his sister without using bad language.

2. These mothers not only try to understand how Tom feels; they also know that trying to persuade him that Mary is really nice would backfire badly. They know that the only way he will ever really understand that Mary is nice is if Mary starts behaving nicely toward him and stops getting into his stuff and invading his privacy.

3. Both mothers avoid falling victim to the underdog fallacy. Consciously or unconsciously they realize how powerful Mary is, especially through the fact that she is younger, and they are determined not to add to Mary's power.

4. In both examples of a constructive approach, the mothers are aware of the need to help *both* children control their impulses and the very fact that they are aware of this need and determined to help them with this control is going to contribute to cutting down on future problems. I say "cutting down," because total prevention is unlikely. Total prevention may not even be desirable, because children

need you to teach them how to solve problems. If you do it well, with fairness, realism, and understanding, they are themselves likely to be good parents to their own children one day. It is exciting to think that you can influence future, unborn human beings in a positive way through what you do today in your own home. And it is at the same time frightening to consider the damage that can be done not only to our own children but to children not yet born through the destructive things we might do in everyday life.

5. Both "constructive" mothers are careful not to humiliate either child.

Through compassionate and understanding, yet firm, handling of such everyday situations, children are taught that feelings can be understood and respected even when actions are disapproved of. Likewise, children can be taught that the rejection of a demand does not mean a lack of understanding of the need which led to the demand. When a child demands a toy, for example, the parent who says no can sympathize with the child's desire and discuss ways in which the child can earn and save up the money for the toy. When a teen-ager demands to be allowed to go to an unsupervised party, the parent who says no can discuss various ways in which the teen-ager could meet the same friends and have just as much fun, including the possibility of his throwing a party himself.

The same rule applies, of course, to adult interaction. A wife cannot be required to accept her husband's neglecting her or abusing her, but she must try her best to understand the feelings which account for her husband's actions and the role she herself has played in engendering these feelings. A husband cannot be expected to put up with sloppy housekeeping or extravagant spending, but he must make a sincere attempt to understand his wife's feelings of dissatisfaction (or whatever) which account for her actions and he must examine his own behavior honestly in order to assess to what degree he may have contributed to his wife's dissatisfaction.

# 14. "YOU ARE STILL WET BEHIND THE EARS."

*Rule 14: Be tactful, considerate, and courteous and show respect for your partner and his feelings.*

This rule is, in a sense, a way of restating Unfair Technique 11-X (do not humiliate your partner) but it goes further by providing a "do" instead of a "don't." Tactfulness is so important a characteristic in interpersonal communication that it deserves a rule of its own rather than being implied in a section on the use of unfair techniques. One could even say that tactfulness, if it has become a way of life, embodies almost all of the qualities called for in listing these rules of communication.

Tactfulness, as used in this book, is defined as follows: tactfulness is an approach to another human being which involves being sincere and open in communication while at the same time showing respect for the other person's feelings and taking care not to hurt him unnecessarily. Tactfulness involves an implicit trust or faith in the other person and communicates the message: "I trust that you will be able to handle what I am going to tell you, as long as I respect your feelings and do my best to guard against my own destructive tendencies so that I don't hurt you unnecessarily."

As an excuse for not being open and sincere, many people confuse tactfulness with "walking on eggs." However, as we have mentioned earlier, walking on eggs is almost the opposite of being tactful. Walking on eggs means using the other person's sensitivities as an excuse for *not* being open and sincere. Walking on eggs shows contempt for the other person's feelings, while tactfulness shows respect.

Thus, tactfulness means *more* than just being courteous (listening without interrupting, avoiding offense to the other person, being diplomatic, etc.): it involves sincerity and implied trust. A person who "walks on eggs" can certainly be superficially courteous, but he cannot be said to be tactful because of the implied contempt of the other person and, in the case of a family member, the implied refusal to attempt to create an intimate relationship with him.

Tactfulness, of course, presupposes a conscious or unconscious *awareness* or sensing of the feelings of others. Furthermore, it implies attributing *importance* to the feelings of other people. However, a confidence man or a crooked salesman can often display both of these characteristics to a high degree. It is at the third requirement that the confidence man and the truly tactful person part company. The third requirement for tactfulness is a basic—preferably unconscious and automatic—decision *not to take advantage of another person's feelings* but to be compassionate and considerate instead. The confidence man and the crooked salesman manipulate the other person's feelings destructively for their own personal material gain, while the truly tactful person does not manipulate and does not take advantage of the other person's feelings.

Tactfulness implies a willingness to "save face" for the other person. Saving face is actually just another term for protecting the self-image. Protecting another person's self-image is just as much an act of kindness as protecting him from bodily injury would be.

There has been very little written on the subject of tactfulness in the psychological literature. Some psychoanalysts, especially in the United States, have shown a tendency to confuse it with inhibition in a destructive sense. Similarly, the recent encounter-type approaches have tended to view tactfulness as an obstacle to or a shield against intimacy. The fact is, however, that true intimacy can never develop where tactfulness is absent. Most psychotherapists who are not involved in any extreme type of psychological sectarianism know that it is futile to attempt to achieve intimacy in a relationship without working on each party's becoming tactful, considerate, and compassionate of the other person's feelings.

Tactfulness is often confused with pretense and with suppression of feeling. In actuality, neither pretense nor suppression of feeling is involved in being tactful. What has been interpreted as pretense in being tactful is actually nothing else than being generous and giving the other person the benefit of the doubt. Let us once more consider the example we discussed in connection with Rule 5 (p. 47) of the wife who reacted constructively to her husband's exaggeration.

> *Husband:* "How come you can never keep clean socks for me in the drawer?"
>
> *Wife:* "I know you feel it happens too often and it makes you angry. I will do my best to see that it doesn't happen again. You will help me, won't you, by remembering to put your clothes in the hamper?"

There is nothing "dish-raggy" or submissive in such a reply, nor is there any suggestion of pretense or suppression of feeling. What is present is dignity and tact. The wife reacts positively to her husband's gross exaggeration because she is willing to give him the benefit of the doubt; she generously recognizes that a significant part of him intended to be reasonable in his accusation. Her reply "translates" his accusation into a more reasonable one without hiding anything and thus cannot be seen as a pretense, certainly not in a destructive sense.

What has been interpreted as suppression of feeling in being tactful is actually healthy *control of the manner of expression* of one's feelings, not a hiding of the feelings themselves. Tactfulness in an intimate relationship certainly does not mean long-term accommodation to the partner's wishes if the latter are basically unacceptable. Such accommodation constitutes "fight evading," to borrow a currently popular term, and is in itself destructive, because it leads to a buildup of resentment and hostility (Rule 10). Suppressed or repressed feelings will eventually lead to symptoms which may be physical (ulcers, skin-disease) or behavioral (irritability, forgetting to wash the husband's shirts, avoiding the wife by watching television, etc.), or it may lead to explosive outbursts of anger in which nothing is accomplished except heaping abuse on the partner.

Tactfulness is an art that children should be taught early if it is going to become an ingrained, automatic characteristic in their personality. Tactfulness can also be learned later on in life, but then it takes a long time for it to become spontaneous and automatic. In our earlier discussion of destructive and unfair techniques of communication we had several examples of tactless, inconsiderate, and discourteous behavior. Here we will only point out that parents—who, of course, would like their children to become tactful and courteous—often unwittingly teach their children to be rude and discourteous. The parents do it by being rude and discourteous themselves, often by humiliating their child.

In many cases the humiliation is obvious, such as in the examples given in Unfair Technique 11-X (humiliating the partner). Parents who say to a teen-ager: "You are still wet behind the ears" or "You are getting too big for your britches" are obviously humiliating their child, whether they are aware of it or not. We must repeat that only destructive consequences can follow from humiliation:

1. The most serious consequence is the destructive influence humiliation has on another person's—especially a child's—self-concept. A child who is subjected to frequent humiliations from his parents will come to feel that he is worthless and thus does not deserve any better treatment.

2. Another destructive consequence is that the humiliated person, adult or child, will feel anger and resentment toward the humiliator and, instead of trying to correct his behavior, may concentrate his energies on how to "get back" at the humiliator.

3. A third destructive consequence is that when you use rude and disrespectful language, you are at the same time—unknowingly, but nevertheless—telling the other person that you are a rude and discourteous person. If the other person is a child, you are then by example (which is the most effective teaching method) teaching him to be rude and discourteous. Rudeness, disrespect, and sassiness in children's behavior does not come only from the influence of their friends, although that, too, can play a role. Very often you find that rudeness and disrespect are being taught the child in the home, without the parents realizing it! What happens in these cases is that the parent does not realize that his own behavior is disrespectful and that he is thereby teaching his child to be disrespectful.

For example, take a mother who has just noticed that her seven-year-old daughter went out to play without tidying up her room. She sees her playing with several other children in the backyard and she runs out and yells: "Joan, you come in

this instant. Your room is filthy and you have to clean it up."
Does this mother realize that she has just given her daughter
a lesson in how to be rude and discourteous? Does she realize
that her daughter feels humiliated? Probably not. But the
fact is that even though the daughter comes in to clean up
her room, the results will be destructive: she has been taught
to be discourteous* and her feelings of resentment over being humiliated will lead to more trouble in the future.

Take another mother in the same situation. She goes out in
the backyard, takes Joan aside, and says to her in a low and
friendly (but firm) voice, so the other children can't hear:
"Joan, you forgot to clean up your room. You know the rule
is that you have to do it before you can play. Please come
in and do it now." This mother has given the child a lesson
in how to be tactful and the child will probably be grateful
to her for not humiliating her in front of her friends. But
even if the daughter's response in this case is negative, forc-
ing the mother to issue a command and/or a warning, the
mother still knows that her daughter has had a lesson in how
to be tactful. Eventually, after a certain number of lessons,
the daughter will learn.

Sometimes the humiliation involved is hidden behind a
statement of truth, but it is there nevertheless. When, for
example, a parent says to a teen-ager: "You are too young
to know what is best for you," the statement may be true,
but the truth of a statement should never be used as an excuse for making it.

Some people humiliate others with the excuse that what
they say is true. However, the fact that something is true
does not give you permission to say it. Suppose that you meet
someone on the street who has had his face burned in a fire
and who, as a result, looks terribly ugly. This fact does not
give you permission to run up to him and say: "Hey you
there, you look very ugly."

The statement "You are too young to know what is best
for you" may be true, but it is humiliating and—moreover—
it is totally unnecessary. The same purpose can be accomplished without humiliation by showing the teen-ager in this
case *why* you feel a certain course of action is best for him.
He still may not see it or accept your recommendation or

---

*As with all teaching, it has to be repeated. One or two incidents of
this type will not teach a child to be rude. But if it is the rule rather
than the exception, the child will definitely learn to be rude.

ruling, but in that case it is up to him to show cause why your statement should not be accepted. In any case, even if he does not share your point of view, you have still avoided making matters worse by humiliating him.

The best rule of thumb, as always, is the golden one; in this case: talk to others as you would like to be talked to.

Truth is to be spoken judiciously and with careful and compassionate concern for the long-term effects on the other person. Sometimes it is best to let another person harbor an illusion rather than shatter it, as Ibsen shows us so dramatically in his moving play, *The Wild Duck*. Such is especially the case with older people. Why tell an older person some unpleasant secret from the past, the knowledge of which cannot possibly profit him in any way? Why rob an older person of the illusion that he was an innocent victim of adverse circumstances, if he can live out his life with more peace and happiness in ignorance of how his problems were self-created? Such knowledge can greately benefit a younger person but not an older one who, besides, is not likely to seek psychotherapeutic assistance in accepting and integrating such confrontations.

Finally, tactfulness implies an absence of "false pride," a readiness to sincerely and specifically admit one's own mistakes, a nondefensive attitude toward one's own contributions to creating a problem, as in: "I am sorry I was rude," "It was my mistake, will you please forgive me," and "I am sorry for my part in the argument." Sincerity is paramount in importance, however. An insincere admission of full or partial guilt is of no value and is, indeed, destructive to the development of an intimate relationship. The same is true of exaggerated admissions, such as: "It was all my fault." Insincerity can sometimes be seen as politeness or as diplomatically desirable in superficial relationships, but it cannot be seen as tactfulness and it is antithetical to intimacy.

# 15. "OH NO! DO I HAVE TO LISTEN TO THAT SERMON AGAIN?"

### Rule 15: Do not preach or lecture; ask questions instead.

Our fifteenth rule: "Do not preach or lecture," could have been listed under the heading of destructive and unfair techniques, except that it is not always destructive to preach or lecture. There are three cases where it is constructive:

1. Young children sometimes benefit from a lecture if it is *short and to the point.* Many "modern" self-styled "experts" will tell you otherwise, but don't you believe them! The young child still sees you as all-knowing and wise. To him you are still the ultimate decider of what is right and what is wrong and he may therefore take heed of what you say, if you are brief, relevant, and deliver your short lecture in a friendly manner. A young child still does not know everything about your value system; he *needs* to be taught values and often *wants* to be taught values if you just see to it that you don't make the teaching process too unpleasant or tedious for him.

2. A person of any age may occasionally need to be informed of something that he does not know, *whether he likes to be informed or not!* A teen-ager, for example, may need to be informed about the reasons why certain acts are harmful or dangerous, even though he may not like to listen to those reasons. In that case, you must inform him, you are forced to lecture. However, you must be sure that he *needs* it and does not already know it. And you must keep your lecture brief, to the point, and beware of humiliating the person you are lecturing to.

3. It is, of course, always permissible to lecture when you have been asked to do so. When a child asks for informa-

tion you must provide it. Just as in the conditions above, you need to see to it that your lecture is short and to the point and—if you can manage it—interesting to the child.

The temptation to preach is perhaps greatest when it comes to teaching values. As we indicated above, this is fine as long as the child is young. However, a teen-ager is not likely to accept your authority that easily, as those readers who have teen-age children may know. Secondly, it is usually a fact that by the time a child is fourteen, fifteen, or sixteen, there is very little that you can tell him that he has not heard many times before. He probably knows your value system—perhaps better than you are willing to admit—and much of what you have to say your teen-ager may be able to recite before you even start saying it. In other words, he knows your sermons by heart.

Therefore, if you preach to a teen-ager, he is likely to turn you off completely. Moreover, he might avoid coming to you with any of his problems because he is afraid that he will have to sit through another lecture again. This is likely to lead to a vicious circle. The less he comes to you with his problems, the more you may feel you must preach in order to "get through" to him. And the more you preach, the less likely he is to come to you with problems. So: what the teen-ager needs especially is not a lecture but a *listening ear* and *questions* designed to help him think through a problem himself.

With the exceptions given earlier, lectures and sermons in the family are generally destructive and self-defeating. Many parents would agree to this, yet they often preach to their children without knowing they are doing it! When their children accuse them of preaching, the parents are frequently quite surprised. Let us take an example.

A father had promised to take his fourteen-year-old daughter, Debbie, to a carnival one Saturday. By profession he was a salesman for a big corporation and he often had to meet with representatives from other companies and government agencies. Sometimes this happened on weekends with very little notice. And now it happened on the Saturday he had promised to take his daughter to the carnival and, to make matters worse, his wife did not drive. When the father called home in the morning and said that he would be unable to take Debbie to the carnival, she went to her mother and said that she was upset, because "Daddy broke his promise."

In handling this, Debbie's mother—well-meaningly—made a common mistake. She said to Debbie: "But Debbie, just think of all the things that Dad does for you and for the whole family." And then she went on to deliver a long sermon describing the good qualities of Debbie's father. All through the sermon Debbie had a blank look in her upward-directed eyes and an "Oh no, not again" expression on her face (this should have been a signal to her mother to stop preaching). When the mother finally was through with the long sermon, Debbie was angrier, more upset, and more indignant than at the outset and the mother was no further along than when she had started, because Debbie simply repeated, whiningly: "But he broke his promise!"

Older children especially do not like to hear sermons. That in itself constitutes no objection against preaching; necessary medicines must be taken whether they are liked or not. However, the trouble is that sermons—with the exceptions previously noted—are worse than useless: they usually backfire and make the child more resentful and oppositional or sullen and shoulder-shrugging than before. Preaching to adults usually backfires also. Preaching has a chance of working only if someone has volunteered to be preached to.

What should Debbie's mother do instead when her daughter comes and says: "Daddy broke his promise"? The answer is that the mother should use the opportunity to help her daughter think through problems and issues for herself. One way to accomplish that goal in this case would be to ask interesting questions, such as: "Do you think it is always reasonable to keep a promise?" (Beware of sarcasm here.)

If the daughter says "Yes, you should always keep a promise," then you can ask a new question, such as: "Suppose that you have promised to finish your homework before you do something else and, while doing it, you notice that the house is on fire. Now, wouldn't you agree that it would be unreasonable for you to keep your promise?" The girl would agree with you. (If she does not, she is either pulling your leg or else suffering from serious emotional disturbance.)

The girl has agreed that it is *not always* reasonable to keep a promise. Now you can ask her what she thinks about her father's situation. Would it be reasonable for him to risk his job in order to keep his promise? Would it perhaps be more reasonable for Debbie to release him from his promise? These are interesting questions to have Debbie think about. If you preach the answers to these questions to her, she will not think about them. But if you *ask* her what *she* thinks, there is a much bigger chance that she will come to a reasonable conclusion on her own.

I would like to further stress this last point. When I asked Debbie's mother if she had thought of asking Debbie such questions, she said: "But I had already *told* her all of that; it did not work." That is true: giving the answer to a problem does not help a person solve it. Suppose the mother says to Debbie: "It is not always reasonable to keep a promise. If you have promised to do your homework and you notice that the house is on fire, you would not keep your promise. And it is not reasonable for Dad to keep his promise and risk losing his job. It is much more reasonable for you to release him from his promise." This sermon covers all the issues elicited by the questions recommended. But it will most probably fall on deaf ears, because Debbie tunes out her mother. She does not really hear what the mother is saying; she is just waiting for the mother to be through, so she can repeat: "But he broke his promise." But if the mother asks Debbie questions, it is much more difficult for her to tune her mother out, plus the fact that the mother in that case is showing a definite interest in her daughter's opinion.

This brings us to another important advantage in asking questions rather than preaching: it gives you more information about your partner in communication and the way he or she thinks. Only if you ask questions will you know, for example, if your child engages in jumps in logic, circular reasoning, or non sequiturs which throw him off the track. These mistakes can be pointed out only when they have been demonstrated to exist.

Also, important problems may come up which need to be solved and which might remain hidden if questions are not asked. In the case of Debbie, perhaps the father has often broken promises in the past without reasonable cause. Then *he* must work on this problem and see to it that it does not happen again. Or perhaps Debbie does not really understand what a promise is and the conditions that are usually taken for granted when you give a promise. Or perhaps—like so many children—she has a tendency to call it a "promise" when all you have said is "maybe." There are many possibilities here which may remain hidden if you preach.

> Ricky said to his father: "Cindy [sister] is stupid." Father: "How can you say things like that about your sister? She is very smart, she gets good grades in school, why she even helps you with your math problems! I think it is very mean of you to say things like that and I don't want to hear any more ridiculous statements from you."

Well-meaningly, unwittingly, shortsightedly, this father almost contributed to his daughter's death! What Ricky had wanted to tell his father before he was cut off was that Cindy (who was fourteen years old) had secretly gone for rides on a motorcycle belonging to the most reckless teen-ager in the neighborhood. Ricky was worried about his sister and wanted his parents to stop her. Two weeks after his unsuccessful attempt to tell his father, the boy with whom Cindy was riding ran a stoplight and crashed into a car. He was severely injured and had to have a leg amputated. By some miracle Cindy escaped with a few nasty lacerations. But if the father would have said: "Give me examples," "Tell me more about it," or "What makes you feel that way?" his daughter may have escaped the danger entirely.

It is, of course, not often that preaching has such obvious and immediately serious effects. But preaching does shut off communication and the principle should again be clear: Ask questions, ask for examples, show interest and not disdain for the statements made by other people, especially your family members.

Millions of parents today are concerned with "getting through" to their children. A partial answer to their problem is just this: ASK QUESTIONS! It is through questions and posing problems that we teach children to think for themselves. At the same time we show our interest in what *they* have to say, thus helping them develop a positive self-concept. And we show confidence in their ability to work out problems on their own, a confidence they will eventually adopt and which will help them throughout life.

Although preaching is a technique used especially against children, it is also used between husband and wife. It may take the form of long-winded expositions or of telling the partner how he or she should feel about something or of extolling one's own virtues. Long-winded expositions can best be handled in one of the two ways we recommended earlier: (1) An agreement is made that an egg timer is to be used, so that neither gets to talk more than three minutes at a stretch without permission. (2) One partner takes notes while the other talks. Telling the partner how he or she should feel cannot, however, be "handled" by gimmicks; it must simply be taboo. The same is true of extolling one's own virtues, which is rude (except when you talk to nonintimates, such as a job-interviewer, or when you are a politician trying to get votes).

# 16. "I GOT A BAD GRADE BECAUSE THE TEACHER IS UNFAIR."

## Rule 16: Do not use excuses and do not fall for excuses.

An excuse* is a statement that hides a reason or avoids stating a reason fully. Many excuses are harmless and do not appreciably interfere with communication. For example, if you get to your job late and say to your boss: "I am late because my car ran out of gas on the way," you are technically using an excuse (even though you are telling the truth), because the *full reason* is that you were thoughtless and irresponsible not to look at the gas-gauge the evening before! However, if you are not often late for your job, your excuse will be accepted as if it were a reason and everything will be all right.

There are people who never or almost never run out of gas. But there are also people who chronically run out of gas or do other things to make themselves late (forgetting where they put the car keys, forgetting to set the alarm

*The slang term *cop-out* is currently popular, even in psychological literature. It seems, however, to have more limited meaning than the term *excuse*. Cop-out seems to refer mainly to excuses for not engaging in potentially desirable action, while the term excuse also covers attempts to "explain away" destructive actions.

clock, budgeting time poorly, etc.). For such a person it would *not* be sufficient to say: "I am late because I ran out of gas." He would have to face up to his *reason* (thoughtlessness, irresponsibility, secret disdain for authority) and solve the basic problem inherent in the reason; otherwise he would be out of a job!

Children need to be taught the difference between excuses and reasons. For example, the statement, "I didn't clean up my room because I didn't have time," is almost always an excuse which is—consciously or unconsciously—designed to cover up the reason which is, "I did not plan my time well enough to clean up my room," or (more basic and unconscious) "I am not going to have you tell me what to do," or "I want to get back at you for something by making you upset." The child is not to be given the possible unconscious reasons (that would constitute an attempt at doing psychotherapy at home, which is a bad idea), but he should be given the hidden conscious or preconscious reasons (in this case, "I did not plan my time well enough") which are obvious to others and should be obvious to the child upon reflection (although to save face he may not admit it).

Similarly, "I hit him because he called me a liar," would be a reason only if the child has been taught to act out physically when faced with verbal attack. The statement is an excuse if the child has been taught that there are other ways of dealing with such a situation (verbal denial or verbal expression of anger, or simply saying, "I am sorry you think so"). In the last case, the child must be shown that the epithet "liar" could not possibly have made him hit the other child; he had a choice of many ways of reacting to the insult and, thus, there must be another reason. The child may not be able to find the reason because it is buried too far in his unconscious ("I am looking for excuses to show my anger," "I am touchy because I already feel very badly about myself"), but the very fact that the parent helps him recognize excuses will, in the long run, help him both to become more honest with himself and to develop more effective control over his impulses.

Excuses differ in the extent to which the user believes in their validity. At one end of the continuum we have excuses which constitute a form of rationalization. These excuses are unconsciously designed to fool the user himself and thus protect him from the anxiety of facing some unpleasant truth about himself ("I did not think she would mind," "I would have done it if I had thought of it," "I thought one drink would not hurt," "That's the way men [women] are," "He'll grow out of it," etc.). At the other extreme of the continuum we have the excuses which the user knows are invalid and which are consciously designed to protect him from an unpleasant (external) consequence, fool someone else, or gain an advantage ("I never received your letter," "I know I had a green light, officer," "The market is in the process of a sidewards adjustment," etc.). The former involve hiding the truth from oneself or playing confidence tricks on oneself, the latter involve hiding the truth from others; in other words, lying or playing confidence tricks on other people. The vast majority of excuses are designed primarily to fool oneself, but any excuse may also contain an—unconscious, preconscious, sometimes even conscious—element of deceiving the other party.

Parents, unfortunately, tend to use a great deal of excuses in communicating with their children, thereby—unwittingly—teaching their children (who often see through the excuses) to use excuses themselves. A parent is likely to use excuses especially often on occasions when the child makes a request and the parent is reluctant or afraid to give the real reason for saying "No." The following example illustrates the conscious and deliberate use of excuses to avoid an anxiety-producing situation.

I once treated a family where both the mother and father had a fear of giving their children any information on sex. This led to many problems which I won't go into at this point, but here is an example of the excuses these parents resorted to in order to hide their real concerns:

In this family there was a fourteen-year-old son whom we might call Randy. Randy liked swimming and had been going on his bicycle to a public pool in the community rather regularly. One day, however, the mother heard from a neighbor that an older boy who frequented the pool had made some homosexual overtures to a younger boy in the neighborhood. Neither the mother nor the father had ever discussed sexual matters with Randy, even though he was already fourteen years old! They dreaded the very thought of any discussion involving sexual topics and, consequently, the idea of discussing sexual deviation such as homosexuality was unthinkable to them. Here is an example of one of the consequences of this avoidance, a conversation which took place one morning (following the day the mother heard about the "incident") in the kitchen while the mother was ironing:

*Randy:* "Mother, can I go to the pool today?"

*Mother:* "No, I don't think you should."

*Randy:* "Gee, mother, why not?"

*Mother:* "Well, . . . uh . . . uh . . . your bathing trunks are dirty."

*Randy:* "No, they aren't! I put them in the washer yesterday."

*Mother* (gives no answer, keeps ironing).

*Randy:* "Can I go then, mother?"

*Mother:* "No. Can't you ever take no for an answer? Stop bothering me now, you can see that I am busy."

*Randy:* "But why can't I go?"

*Mother:* "You went there yesterday, didn't you? I don't see why you have to go there so often. Anyway, I am not sure they have a lifeguard there."

*Randy:* "Mother! You *know* they have lifeguards there, two of them, in fact. And if they didn't why could I go there before, then?"

*Mother:* "Stop sassing me, you hear. I won't have anyone your age give me any back-talk. If you talk back to me once more, I'll take your bike away from you for the whole weekend."

*Randy:* "Gee, mother, I'm sorry, I didn't mean to be sassy. I just want to know why I can't go."

*Mother* (silent, keeps ironing, looks as if she had not heard).

*Randy:* "Mother, *why* can't I go?"

*Mother:* "Listen, will you stop pestering me with your whining!"

*Randy:* "But tell me why I can't go."

*Mother:* "It's too chilly outside and you'll get a cold, that's why, so there!"

*Randy:* "But mother, it is warmer than yesterday and I could go then."

*Mother:* "I just don't want you to go and I don't want to argue about it with you any further."

*Randy:* "I don't want to argue either; I just want to know why I can't go swimming today."

*Mother:* "I don't want you to go and that's reason enough."

*Randy:* "Gee, mother, that's unfair!"

*Mother:* "What was that you said? Are you being sassy again? All right, I have had enough of this, you can't use your bike this weekend and that's it."

This interchange breaks many of the rules of communication we have discussed. But the most important aspect of the conversation for our present purpose is that Randy's mother is hiding an important reason behind transparent excuses. Randy is well aware that his mother is using excuses and if he were more considerate he might let her off the hook. But children are not likely to do that; nor would it solve anything if they did. The only solution to the problem in this case is for the parents to overcome their fear and for one of them, perhaps the father, to tell Randy the real reason why his parents are concerned about his going to the public pool. By this age, certainly, the boy should be informed not only about normal sexual functions, but also about those abnormalities which he may encounter in life and therefore should be prepared to deal with or avoid altogether. In the course of their psychotherapy, Randy's parents had to face this fact and overcome their fear of discussing sex. This was accomplished through a three-fold program consisting of (1) each parent exploring his (her) reasons for the fear of sex, (2) each making a conscious decision not to let those reasons stand in the way, and (3) each participating in group psychotherapy, where intimate subjects were discussed with openness and frankness by all members.

Let us take another example.

A few years ago I saw a woman in her early forties, Mrs. G., who constantly complained that her children were using excuses to get out of doing chores, justify poor grades on report cards, get out of brushing their teeth, etc. Yet Mrs. G. would herself use very obvious excuses in dealing with her children.

For instance, if Mrs. G.'s fifteen-year-old daughter Robin asked her if she could go out on a date Saturday night, Mrs. G. would almost automatically answer "No." After the automatic refusal, she would then search her mind for "reasons," which would be presented for her daughter to tear apart. This process would then lead either to Mrs. G. being "broken down" and "giving in" or—just as often—to the daughter being punished for her opposition.

Frequently, when Robin asked if she could go out on a date, Mrs. G. would say something like: "You know very well, dear, that Aunt Millie is coming over on Saturday and that she would be *very* disappointed if you were not here." This excuse (which was only one of several that Mrs. G. kept on tap to cover all possibilities) was an especially primitive and transparent one, because:

1. Aunt Millie saw her niece rather often.

2. Aunt Millie usually arrived for lunch and left between eight and nine o'clock in the evening. Since Robin's date was in the evening, she would have plenty of time to be with her aunt.

3. Aunt Millie herself felt that Robin spent too much time cooped up in the house!

However, if Robin would dare mention any of these facts, Mrs. G. would immediately accuse her of talking back or of being insolent and send her to her room. Then her "backtalk" could easily be used as an additional "reason" for grounding her. The *real* reasons for Mrs. G.'s frequent refusals, as they were unveiled in psychotherapy, included the following facts, on different levels of consciousness:

1. Superficial, fully conscious reason: Mrs. G. did not like Robin's current boyfriend but was reluctant to say so openly.

2. Preconscious reason (secretly, "in the back of her mind"): Mrs. G. feared that Robin and her boyfriend—any boyfriend—would engage in sex play.

3. Unconscious reason (uncovered in psychotherapy): Mrs. G. was jealous of her daughter's youth and attractiveness (à la Show White's stepmother).

It required months of psychotherapy for Mrs. G. to realize that she was hiding behind excuses and—by using such obvious and transparent subterfuges—was actually teaching her children to use excuses. It was quite a shock for her to recognize that she was blaming her children for using a method of avoiding reality that she herself had taught them to use! As to Mrs. G.'s third reason, the unconscious one, it did not become clear to her until she had had a dream in which she actually saw herself as the Queen-Witch forbidding Snow White to use eye-shadow!

Mrs. G.'s reason number three brings us back to the important point that people are often not conscious of the reasons behind their excuses. Many people believe that the excuses they give are actually reasons and they may become quite angry if someone suggests that what they think is a reason is actually an excuse. Most people cannot stand the thought of being driven by unconscious impulses or of having hidden destructive motivations for their actions. They must, therefore, conceal the "true" motivation behind an acceptable subterfuge or pretext. This process, when it takes place automatically and unconsciously, is referred to by psychologists as *rationalization*. It is a normal process, designed to protect the self-image, but when it is used excessively or for the purpose of avoiding solutions to important problems, it can assume pathological proportions.

To illustrate the use of excuses in marriage, let us take the case of Nick, whose wife complained that he did not talk with her enough. When I asked Nick what his reasons for being so silent were, he said: "Look, I am a salesman and I have to talk to people all day. My wife should understand that I get tired of all that talking and want some rest when I get home, that's all!" I told Nick that just a few hours earlier another husband had sat in the same chair and had answered the same question with: "Look, I am an accountant and I sit alone in a cubicle all day and I get used to not talking with anyone. My wife should understand that I just can't turn on a switch when I come home and start talking; I am not used to it, that's all!" I asked Nick what he thought of the other man's statement and he saw the point and said: "I guess we are both using excuses." (As it happened, both men were using silence as a hostile weapon against their wives, but they had to abandon their excuses and face the real reason before they were able to change. Also, in both cases, the wives did not make it easy for their husbands to talk.)

Typical excuses for breaking Rule 10 (bring up all significant problems and feelings) are provided by the married couple in the following example.

Ross and Miriam were having serious problems in their marriage. Ross was an alcoholic whose drinking was done in periods which seemed unpredictable until psychotherapy was initiated. It was then discovered that Ross' drinking periods actually were highly predictable, being preceded every time by dreams of hiding bottles and by conscious feelings of strong resentment against Miriam.

In Miriam's concurrent psychotherapy we also discovered that she could "sense" when Ross' drinking was going to start up again. There were definite prodromal signs in Ross' behavior: he became more withdrawn, evasive, and irritated and less interested in sex before starting to drink.

However, before these insights regarding the feasibility of prediction could be put to use in controlling the drinking, we had to get Ross and Miriam to discuss the prodromal signs at the time they were present. Here we ran up against excuses from both:

*Ross:* "I do feel the resentment against Miriam building up before I start to drink, but I don't tell her how I feel because I know it would hurt her feelings if I did. And I can't tell her about the dreams because then she would be afraid that I'll start drinking again."

The "excuse-nature" of this statement is clear on the basis of two facts:

1. Ross knows that his starting to drink will hurt Miriam much more than his being open about his feelings, which she has at least *said* she would welcome.

2. Ross has been advised by me to be open about his feelings to his wife and to discuss them thoroughly with her.

*Miriam:* "I am afraid to talk about my fears to Ross, because I feel he would take it as my distrusting him and that in itself might precipitate his drinking."

The "excuse-nature" of this statement is clear from the fact that Miriam *knows* from previous experience that Ross will start to drink after a period of increasing withdrawal and decreased interest in sex. Thus, she would have nothing to lose by following my suggestion to be open and frank about her fears and discussing them with Ross.

Behind these excuses lies an unconscious "secret pact" between Ross and Miriam to keep Ross drinking. The purposes and neurotic advantages are manifold. Some of them might be mentioned here:

1. Ross wants (unconsciously, of course) to be a baby and the drinking is a most effective way of accomplishing this objective.

2. Ross (unconsciously) wants to hurt Miriam and knows from the past that his drinking will cause her conscious suffering, torture, and self-reproach. Seen in this light, the unconscious reasoning behind his excuse is actually: "Why hurt her a little now by mentioning my anger, when I can hurt her so much more effectively later through my drinking?"

3. Ross has a need (unconscious) to punish himself which is also eminently well fulfilled by his drinking. His indulgence in alcohol has in the past cost him several jobs and

can always be counted on to elicit verbal and even physical abuse from Miriam.

4. Miriam is afraid of sex and feels it is dirty and would therefore (unconsciously) rather play a mother-role with Ross. When he has been drinking, she can "legitimately" express her disgust, avoid sex, and treat him like a baby instead.

5. Miriam has a deep-seated unconscious contempt for men, mixed with anger. This contempt and anger can be expressed openly when Ross drinks.

6. Miriam, too, has a need to punish herself and she gets this punishment without having to take responsibility for it whenever Ross drinks.

Note that all these "benefits" from Ross' drinking are felt unconsciously. When they were explored in therapy—after the excuses had been "exposed"—Ross' drinking stopped. He has been dry for six years now and is not likely to resume.

As we pointed out in discussing Rule 10, using the other person's anticipated answer or reaction or lack of answer and reaction as an excuse for not expressing one's feelings and opinions or for not asking questions is common among patients with interpersonal difficulties. A patient who uses this excuse must be helped to accept the principle that one should try one's best even if others do not cooperate.

A patient often says that he did not bring up a certain problem for discussion or did not ask a certain question because he feared that this would elicit a verbal attack from his partner (wife, friend, business associate, etc.). The fact is, however, that if you have done nothing to provoke an attack, the attack is primarily the other person's problem and you must feel compassion for a person who launches into such unprovoked attacks, because he (she) must be deeply troubled. Verbal attacks do not need any defense or counter-attack at all, only a sincere and concerned effort to try to understand the other person and help solve a problem.

No human being has complete power over another. Your task is to see to it that *you* behave reasonably, lovingly, and constructively, and try your best to solve problems. If the other person then does not respond, he (she) deserves your compassion, not your wrath. But never use the *anticipation* of a negative reaction from the other person as an excuse for not doing your best to solve the problems in the relationship.

Children's excuses have to be dealt with appropriately, otherwise reliance on excuses will become a way of life for the child. The important thing with children, as with intimate associates of all ages, is to see to it that the excuses do not benefit them, but to do it in such a way that their self-concept (which the excuses are designed to protect) is not damaged.

If a child gives excuses for not being able to sleep, the conscious purpose may be to stay awake longer, but there might be unconscious purposes such as a need for more closeness with the parent, a fear of being alone, or simply a need to show power and make the parent into a servant. When an excuse is suspected, there must therefore be a kind and gentle —but firm—refusal. The refusal must be understanding and respectful, not hurtful to the child's self-image.

An example of an understanding and respectful refusal would be something like: "I understand that you would like to stay awake a little longer and that you'd like Mommy to be here with you. Tomorrow we'll spend more time together, but now you must try to sleep. If something bothers you, remember that it's good to learn to sleep no matter what and then tell me about it tomorrow. Good night and sweet dreams." (If this does not work, the next-to-the-last sentence must be stressed with increased firmness and notice must be served—and followed—that the parent will not come in again that night.)*

An example of a destructive refusal would be: "You are just using excuses to make me run back and forth. What kind of whining crybaby are you anyway? You keep your trap shut from now on or you'll be sorry." Unfortunately, a lot of parents alternate between the extremes of destructive refusals and the equally destructive pattern of, indeed, becoming the child's servant.

Remember that children who use excuses excessively may

---

*In the case of night terrors the parent must remain with the child and comfort him, but professional help must be sought if it happens more than once in a long while. After a scary movie or story or witnessing an accident, etc., a child may feel afraid at night and will need comforting, but if the fears persist, the likelihood is that the scary movie (or whatever) served merely as a trigger to release an anxiety which was already present in latent form. The child must then be taken to a psychologist for psychodiagnostic evaluation.

have learned to do so from their parents. This brings us back
to Mrs. G.:

> Mrs. G. was not only an excessive user of excuses and di-
> versionary tactics; she also—without realizing it—fell prey to
> excuses and diversionary tactics when they were employed by
> her children. Yet she actually thought she was challenging the
> children's excuses! The root of the trouble was that she did
> not know how to demonstrate to her children that an excuse
> was an excuse, not a reason.
>
> Mrs. G.'s twelve-year-old son, Neal, had received a failing
> grade in math on his last report card. His excuse was: "The
> teacher is unfair, he picks on me all the time, and he just
> doesn't like me, that's all." To this Mrs. G. answered: "Don't
> give me all these excuses. Your teacher is not unfair. I have
> met him and I know he is a fine man and he treats all the kids
> alike. It's just that you never do any homework and you never
> pay any attention to him when he explains things in class."

Apart from breaking Rule 5 (be realistic and reasonable in
your statements) through the use of "never," Mrs. G. has fall-
en into a trap. She has, so to speak, let her son choose the
battlefield and the result will be that she loses the battle due
to the son's greater knowledge of the "terrain." The terrain
in this case is the teacher Neal sees every weekday and on
whom he can therefore claim to be something of an expert,
at least compared with his mother, who sees the teacher very
seldom. Moreover, Neal can probably give his mother a long
list of his teacher's "unfairnesses," none possible to verify. No
matter what happens, the mother must lose, because she does
not know the teacher as well as her son does. (Actually, as we
shall see in our discussion of Rule 20, *both* parties lose in
this type of neurotic game.) Even if Mrs. G. knew the teacher
better than her son did, had been present at all mathematics
classes, and could "prove" that the teacher was not unfair,
the boy could still stick to his view as a "matter of opinion."
The point is that the mother is fighting on the wrong battlefield. The battlefield on which the mother *should* fight is the
issue of how to deal with unfairness without hurting oneself!
Mrs. G. would have avoided falling into her son's trap if
she had said something like this: "Neal, I have met your
teacher only a few times and he certainly seemed fair and
reasonable to me. But you work with him everyday, so
maybe you can see something in him that I can't. So, let's

just *suppose* that he is unfair. What are you going to do about it?" If Neal says that there is nothing he can do about it, the mother can ask: "Would you like for me to tell you how to handle unfair teachers?" When Neal has said "yes" (if he says "no," he is either "pulling his mother's leg" or he is emotionally disturbed to the point of needing professional help) and thus has given permission for the mother to deliver a brief sermon, the mother can say: "Neal, if your teacher is unfair, it's going to be a very good opportunity for you to learn to handle unfair people without your getting hurt yourself. You may have more teachers in the future that you feel are unfair, and you can't fire them, so you just have to make it extremely difficult for them to be unfair! Whenever you have an unfair teacher, just make it a point to study five times as hard and to behave so well that he really will have to go out of his way to find things to pick on. By studying five times as hard you will get more out of the class than you would otherwise, so you will benefit from it no matter what happens. And by doing so well and behaving your very best, you will make it as difficult as possible for the teacher to continue being unfair!" Thus the mother has *demonstrated* that the teacher's unfairness is not sufficient reason for Neal's poor performance and, accordingly, that his statement to that effect was an excuse.

There is a large category of excuses which are based on conditions that cannot easily be checked. Such excuses are best handled by drawing another conclusion from the premise than that which the person using the excuse expects. Examples:

| *Excuse* | *Expected conclusion* | *"Healthy" conclusion* |
|---|---|---|
| "My teacher is unfair." | "There is no use trying." | "Work extra hard, so as to make it really difficult for the teacher to be unfair." |
| "I have a headache" (or stomachache, etc., anything you suspect is being used as an excuse for staying home from school, but which is impossible to verify). | "I can play at home or watch television." | "You can choose between school and staying in bed all day. If someone is sick enough not to go to school, he belongs in bed." |

The same method can also sometimes be used with conditions which can be checked.

| | | |
|---|---|---|
| "I have very little time in which to do it." | "I should just skip it." | "If so, you'd better start doing it right now." |

There exists a somewhat facetious yet good way to deal with chronic and predictable excuses (the method was originally suggested by Parke Cummings\*). Suppose that your son is expected to mow the lawn every (or every other) Saturday morning, but that he usually tries to put it off or get out of it altogether through some excuse. For example, in the morning he can say that it is too wet, during the day it is too hot, and in the evening it is too dark. That covers the day nicely. What you do is to sit down with him (on any day other than Saturday) and discuss the difference between an excuse and a reason. Ask him what he thinks are good reasons for not mowing the lawn and what he would consider an excuse. Good reasons might be that he is sick in bed (although in that case no one would expect him to mow the lawn anyway), he has a severe allergy diagnosed by a physician, or that the lawn mower is broken. Wetness of the grass, heat, and a feeling of tiredness would really be excuses, since they have to do with comfort rather than with safety or possibility. Feeling that it is too dark or that the lawn does not really need cutting would be excuses by definition, since another person (the parent) has made a different judgment (the probability of an alleged "reason" actually being an excuse increases if it involves a judgment contrary to that of another, reasonable, person).

As a conclusion to this discussion, you list (in writing) all reasons you and your son can think of and classify them: 1 A, B, C, etc., and 2 A, B, C, etc. It will probably be a fairly short list. Then you list all the excuses the two of you can think of, number them, and classify them in a similar manner. This list should be very long and comprehensive. (Let your son do the writing; it will help him with his spelling.) As a matter of fact, you should encourage your son to make up as many excuses in advance as possible and you should ac-

\*Parke Cummings, *I'm Telling You Kids for the Last Time* (New York: Henry Schuman, Inc., 1951).

tually help him find more excuses! Draw on your previous experience and use your imagination freely. Then tell your son that from now on, whenever he wants to get out of doing a chore, he must go to the list and give you the reason or excuse by number, for example 14 B!

This rather humorous method works very well, because most kids are too embarrassed to look at the list and give you the number and letter of an excuse, so they are likely to just go ahead and do the work. But even if they do come to you with a number and letter, you are still in a good position, because the child either has a good reason or he has already admitted that he is using an excuse! If he has a good reason, you let him get out of doing the chore, but if he uses an excuse, you hold him to it. (It should go without saying that this method is not suitable for use by sarcastic parents— at least not until they have worked out their problem of re- sorting to sarcasm!)

In general—and at any age—excuses are best dealt with by specially designed questions which have the twofold object of "pinning down" the person who uses the excuse and of find- ing out whether there is something *you* could do to help the other person not use the excuse in the future. Suppose, for example, that a husband has been postponing fixing a screen door and says: "Well, I just haven't gotten around to it yet." This excuse is best followed by questions such as:

"Could you tell me the things you still need to do before you fix it?"

"Could you give me a definite date when you know you will be able to do it?" (The date, if given, must be marked on the calendar.)

"Would you feel that I would be nagging you if I re- minded you of it again?" (If the answer is yes, you must ask: "Then please tell me what you feel I should do if I resent its not being done.")

"Is there something I could do to help you fix it earlier?"

These questions must, of course, be made without sarcasm and with a sincere desire to help solve the problem. If the questions do not help, the partners must make some agree- ment involving an automatic rule. In the case above, for ex- ample, the spouses can agree that if the husband has not fixed something within fifteen days of having been given no- tice, the wife is free to call someone else to fix it.

## The pretense of not having a choice

The perceptive reader has already noticed that a large number of excuses involve a common element: the pretense that no other choice was possible than the one which was made. Such excuses implicitly attribute absolute power to other people or to events. Consider the following examples:

"The reason I yelled at my wife was that a customer had given me a bad time in the store." "The reason I yelled at the kids was that I had a headache." "The reason I sassed my mother was that she said no." "I didn't choose him, he chose me." "I didn't drop the vase, it just fell out of my hand." "I know we can't afford it but I simply couldn't resist buying it." "I can't help it; when he starts with those wise-guy remarks I lose all control." "The reason I said all those bad things was that he had insulted me." "It was your constant chatter that made me miss the turn-off on the freeway."

Such examples could be listed ad infinitum. Let us concentrate on some of the most common ones. A frequent excuse for breaking Rule 9 (do not allow discussions to turn into destructive arguments) involves hiding one's own responsibility behind the actions of other people and is often expressed as "It was he (she) who started it." This excuse completely overlooks the fact that no one forces one human being to continue what someone else has started, no one forces you to say something destructive or use an unfair communication technique just because someone else is being destructive. The excuse, "It was he (she) who started it," is actually so primitive that it is used only by children and immature adults.

Exactly because this excuse is used so often by children, it is extremely important to teach them that whatever another person, child or adult, says, their own reply does not have to be destructive. If this is not taught the child, he will fool himself into thinking—sometimes all through his life—that his own destructiveness was forced upon him by other people.

Another form which hiding-behind-other-people-to-justify-one's-own-actions can take is expressed through the phrase, "But everybody else does it." This particular excuse is a special favorite with teen-agers.

One way to deal with excuses attributing absolute power to other people, events, or conditions is to ask questions which will help the other person see the absurdity of the excuse. Consider the following question from a mother.

*Question:* When my son disobeys or breaks a rule together with another child, he will use the excuse, "He made me go there" or "He made me do it." What should my response be?

*Answer:* The best way to deal with such excuses is not to deny their validity but, instead, to ask further questions designed to make the absurdity of the excuse self-evident. First we have to be sure that we are dealing with an excuse. In this case, for example, it is possible (although unlikely) that the other boy is a bully who did threaten to beat up your child if he did not do as he was told. So you start by asking if the other child threatened to do something to him. If the answer is "yes," you are not dealing with an excuse, but with a situation in which the child needs advice on how to handle or avoid the bully.

On the other hand, if your son says: "No, he did not threaten me," you have established that what he said was an excuse, but it is still best to keep asking questions: "Then tell me *how* he made you go," "Do you think it is good to give other people that much power?," and "What do you think you will do about such a situation next time?" Questions like these are much more effective in inducing the child to think than "explaining" or "preaching" about excuses would be. The questions must, of course, be asked with kind concern, interest, and a desire to solve a problem, not sarcastically and not as a way to show the child up.

A large number of excuses stem from the neurotic tendency to think in extremes. In these cases, a conscious or unconscious unwillingness to act constructively is hidden behind the pretense that only two extremes of behavior are possible: "Either I nag him about it or I shut up; what else is there?" "I have to be rough with him; after all, I can't have him walk all over me." "I have to take what he dishes out, because I don't want to start arguments all the time."

The way to deal with this type of excuse is, of course, to ask the person to consider carefully if there might be other solutions than the two extremes. If he is unable to find one, you supply it. In the first example (nagging vs. shutting up) the solution would be reasonable discussion and/or the institution of an automatic rule (automatic rules are discussed in connection with Rule 17). The "excuse-user" may counter with a new excuse, such as "he wouldn't discuss it reasonably" or "rules won't work, I have tried them before," but don't let that deter you. You have many avenues open to probe further, such as "Tell me what happens," "Give me an example," or "For how long did you apply the rules consistently?" And there is always the chance that the person, when pressed for an answer, might realize that he (she) is using excuses and might concentrate on trying to solve the problem instead.

Another large category of excuses involving inevitability is based on generalizing and then applying the generalization to a specific case. These are excuses such as: "Men (women) are that way," "Boys will be boys," "He'll grow out of it," "No wonder, he grew up during the depression." Such excuses serve to keep a problem unsolved by defining it as unavoidable in the first place. Thus, if the problem is going to be solved, the generalization must be challenged and the misconception on which the assumption of inevitability is based corrected.

Most sociological "explanations" are excuses: "The reason he committed the crime was that he came from a poor neighborhood," "The reason he understands (or does not understand) the value of money is that he grew up during the depression," "He vandalized the school because he did not find his classes relevant," "He drinks because he cannot stand the monotony of suburbia." In all these examples and in most sociologically based "explanations" there is a pretense of inevitability which completely ignores the fact that the majority of poor people don't steal, that people were affected by the depression (or the war, or the hustle and bustle of modern life) quite differently, that many students voice their dissent constructively, that many people living in suburbia do not drink, etc.

A most insidious yet widespread way of pretending that there is no other choice available than the one that is made involves the use of *labeling,* and we will therefore examine this method of manufacturing excuses in more detail.

## Labeling

Some excuses are simply based on giving an activity a label and then using the label to "explain" the activity, the implication being that no other choice was available. For example, if a person frequently "flies off the handle," it is said that he has a "bad temper." If you then ask: "Why does he fly off the handle so easily?" you might get the answer: "Oh, that's because he has such a bad temper!" And the person who answers you may actually think that he has given you an explanation, when all that he has really said is: "He flies off the handle because he tends to fly off the handle."

Similarly, a person who does not do things that he should do is called "lazy." But if you ask someone: "Why doesn't he do those things?" you may get the answer: "Because he is lazy!" Other examples:

"Why does he look down his nose at other people?" "Because he is conceited."

"Why is that child so disobedient?" "Because he is a bad child."

"Why do you avoid people?" "Because I am introverted."

"Why are you so silent?" "Because I am not much of a talker."

A person who looks down his nose at other people is called "conceited." But we do not know anything more about the reasons for his contempt for others if we then use the label "conceited" to "explain" his attitude. A person who does not work or study as he should is often given the label "lazy." But we do not know more about why he doesn't work or study as much as he should if we restate the label as an explanation.

The absurdity and circularity involved in using labels as explanations become apparent with just a little thought. Suppose you see an athlete who is running very fast and you ask: "I wonder how come he can run so fast?" No one would then answer you: "It is because he is a fast runner," the reason being that the label is too close to the terminology used in the question and the lack of explanation is therefore too apparent. You might, however, get the "explanation": "That's because he is a good track-man" and your "informant" may truly feel that he has given you an explanation! Consider the following examples:

"Why do you yawn so often?" "Because I am a yawner."

"Why do you speak with such a mumble?" "Because I am a mumbler."

Again, the reason people are unlikely to give these replies is that the label used in the reply is too much like the label already used in the question. The avoidant or excuse nature of the response is therefore too obvious. However, when the label used in the response *sounds* different from the term used in the question, then people feel (unconsciously) that they can get away with it. One reason why some people are afraid of psychologists is exactly because a well-trained psychologist will spot such labeling excuses immediately and will not use them himself (at least not in his office!).

The excuses which deal with supposedly "inborn" characteristics such as "laziness" or "bad temper" are almost always exactly that: excuses. It is true that general personality *tendencies* do seem to be constitutionally determined and differences in "personality" can be observed in very young babies. However, such tendencies are nonspecific, modifiable, even reversible, and depend heavily on the interaction that develops between the baby and the significant people in his environment. But even if such interaction leads to the tendency becoming pronounced, it does not mean that the person is doomed to a certain pattern of behavior for the rest of his life. Suppose, for example, that a baby shows less frustration tolerance (probably a constitutionally influenced characteristic) than is usual. If his mother is not threatened by his low frustration tolerance, but keeps on dealing with him in a calm, kind, and firm manner, following sound principles of discipline, the low frustration tolerance will probably never develop into a significant problem.* However, poor handling by the mother (irritated reactions, lack of kind firmness, rejections, etc.) may lead to this tendency becoming very pronounced over the years: the child will become a "spoiled brat" and, eventually, a highly immature adult. But he will not be doomed to stay this way. If he is willing to cooperate in psychotherapy, he has a good chance of overcoming this problem by (1) challenging the excuses he has erected to "explain" his immature reactions, (2) getting an insight into the interactions with other people which originally led to the "spoiling" and still keep it going, and (3) by actively practicing self-control and patience in both group therapy and "real life."

As in the case of other types of excuses, labeling is best handled by questions. Suppose, for example, that a husband tries to excuse his immaturity and indulgence in temper outbursts by saying: "I really can't help my bad temper. My

---

*An exception to this would be children suffering from a type of neurological dysfunction.

ancestry is Scottish and Irish and it takes very little to set me off. That's the way I am; I have always been quick-tempered." Such a statement is best followed by questions such as:

"Do you feel your bad temper is racially inherited?" If the answer is "yes," you follow up with a further question: "Do you think there are some Irishmen and Scots that are calm 'by nature'?"

"Do you feel that your bad temper is inherited specifically through your genes?" If the answer is "yes," you follow up with such questions as: "Do you think, then, that we should accept that our children will always be unable to control their temper outbursts?," or "Isn't it unfair, then, for us to get mad at our son for losing control, which is something he simply cannot help if it is inherited?," or "Why is it, then, that scientists have not been able to demonstrate the existence of such inheritance?"

"Do you feel that your outbursts are completely beyond your control?" If the answer is yes, you ask: "In that case, if you really have no control, could you not be dangerous to other people and to yourself?" If the answer is: "No, I have some control over it," you ask: "Do you feel that that control could be extended?" If the answer is "I have tried but I can't control myself," you can ask: "What are the methods that you have used so far?"

"Does the setting or the presence or absence of other people make any difference?" If the answer is: "No, I get just as mad if something goes wrong at work," you can ask: "Do you think, then, that your anger outbursts would be just as uncontrollable in the presence of the President of the United States?" or "Would you yell, then, even if you were alone in the house and something had frustrated you?" (Questions like these are difficult to put without sarcasm; do your best to communicate a sincere interest in challenging the validity of the excuse rather than a desire to show up the other person.)

"Do you feel that there is anything available that could help you gain control?" If the answer is no, you ask: "Why is it, then, that so many reasonable people think that such control can be achieved in psychotherapy?"

"Do you feel that I make this problem worse in any way by irritating you or provoking you?" (If the answer is yes, you ask for specifics. Remember not to defend yourself, but to consider the specific charges as valuable information for your self-development.)

## Honesty used as an excuse

Excuses are sometimes based on a superficial cloak of honesty. A hostile person, for example, will often justify his destructive words and actions by saying that he was only being honest in expressing his feelings: if he had acted any other way he would have been a phony!

As we have shown earlier (Rules 10 and 14), one can well be perfectly honest about one's feelings without being destructive. Thus, there could never be any dishonesty involved in being tactful and considerate. If you are so angry or hostile that you do not "feel like" being tactful and considerate, you can say so in so many words, but you still have no cause to act out in a destructive manner.

The fear of being phony is widespread today, partly because of the current fads in psychology that emphasize "authenticity." Authenticity supposedly refers to a person "being what he is and nothing else." This would all be well and good if a person actually *were* something. But the fact is that every human being has different "parts" or "sides" to his personality. Even when we make allowance for some general and presumably stable, constitutional, inherited, or environmentally influenced personality traits, the fact remains that the same person can be good and bad, kind and inconsiderate, brave and cowardly, honest and dishonest, confident and insecure, open and defensive, etc., all depending upon what sides or parts of his personality he chooses—consciously or unconsciously—to support permanently or at the moment. No one can therefore "be himself." He can only be those parts of himself that he chooses to express. Thus, a person's identity does not lie in what he "is" but in what he, for conscious and unconscious reasons, chooses to be.

If authenticity were the goal, it would be desirable to kill a person if you felt like killing him. It would, as a matter of fact, be hypocritical to let him live, it would "go against your feelings." Authenticity, however, is an unrealistic goal, a vain attempt to fool oneself that one·"is" something rather than something else and that all feelings should be expressed, no matter who gets hurt in the process.

As we have pointed out before, being honest about one's

feelings is important if intimacy between partners is to be achieved. However, honesty is not to be used as an excuse for expressing negative feelings destructively.

A man who finds it difficult to show affection to his wife cannot reasonably say: "I would be a phony if I tried to be something I am not." There is no phoniness in his doing what he should do and at the same time being honest about the way he feels. If it makes him feel embarrassed to give his wife a hug, he can always say so while hugging her. The very admission of a feeling of embarrassment, for example, will often dispel its inhibitive effect. If you say "It embarrasses me to say this, but . . . (. . . I love you, . . . I think about you a lot, . . . You are a wonderful person)," you are going to feel less embarrassed than you otherwise would.

A father who finds difficulty in praising his son cannot hide under the cloak of being phony if he did. There are many opportunities every day for genuine praise, and even if the father does not "feel like" praising, his basic motivation for doing so would still be genuinely positive.

Excuses can be clever and difficult to deal with. As a matter of fact, several of the suggestions and rules given in this book, *if taken separately and out of context*, can be used as excuses. For example, Rule 10 (be honest about your feelings) could be used as an excuse by someone who wants (consciously or unconsciously) to pour out his hostility under a cloak of honesty. But this could happen only if the same person broke Rule 14 (be tactful and courteous). In other words, following all the rules in this book would make hiding behind excuses extremely difficult, if not impossible.*

Finally a word of warning: Never use the fact that another person has used an excuse as an excuse for your own reaction. Some people, especially dirty fighters, take the fact that another person hides behind an excuse as an excuse for

---

*The very presentation of this book to another person *could* communicate: "You are a lousy and destructive communicator; I will try to cure you!," but only if the other person reads such a message into the presentation. And if he does, the matter can still be discussed amiably and constructively by following these rules.

Giving this book to another person could also communicate: "Let's try to improve our communication by both of us following these rules." When an action is constructive and the conscious motive positive, it may sometimes be useful to consider (one's own) unconscious motives, but it would not be reasonable to let them stand in the way of the constructive action.

unleashing the anger they have inside (as in "Who wouldn't get angry having to listen to excuses like that!") or as an excuse for using excuses themselves (as in "If you can do it, why can't I?"). Such dirty tactics are to be scorned. An excuse can always be met with a reasonable statement pointing out reality and showing understanding of the other person's feelings.

# 17. "I HAVE TOLD YOU KIDS A THOUSAND TIMES."

## Rule 17: Do not nag, yell, or whine!

Nagging is common. It is at least as widespread as the common cold. However, while the common cold seldom leads to tragedy, nagging can make the lives of all members of a family miserable. At least it is an annoyance, something that sours the emotional atmosphere at home. But if it becomes chronic it can make family life unbearable. As a matter of fact, nagging can turn daily living into a ceaseless torture from which anything, no matter how destructive, can provide a welcome escape.

Nagging is a destructive and unfair communication technique and could therefore have been discussed under a subheading of Rule 11 (do not use unfair communication techniques). However, nagging (and yelling and whining) is such a large subject and it is so important an obstacle when it comes to teaching values to a child that I have decided to discuss it under a rule of its own.

Yelling* and whining are psychologically similar to nag-

---

*The word "yelling" is here used in the way many children use it, namely in the sense of "repetitive scolding" or "verbal temper tantrums." I do not refer only to the raising of voice volume which, in itself, is not destructive except in cases where the partner is especially sensitive or "allergic" to it.

ging and are often, in the vernacular, synonyms for nagging. Therefore, although I will mostly use the word "nagging" in the discussion below, everything I say about it goes for yelling and whining and all other repetitive demands, requests, and admonitions as well.

In our discussion of destructive arguments (Rule 9) we mentioned that people say "I don't want to argue" and yet find themselves drawn into arguments. The same is true of nagging: everyone says he dislikes nagging and yet a great number of people engage in it. I have never in my life heard a person say: "I enjoy nagging," but in doing psychotherapy with two family members in the office at the same time I have often seen people jump at the slightest opportunity to nag.

It would, in fact, be a good principle to follow, that if you cannot get something accomplished without nagging (and if this book does not help you stop nagging), then you should seek professional psychological help. This is important not only because nagging sours, embitters, and poisons the family atmosphere: it also creates more problems than it is consciously intended to solve, as we shall show below.

There is an important difference between nagging and *frequent reminders*. A child, especially, will have to have frequent reminders, because no child is born with a ready-made, built-in sense of responsibility. A sense of responsibility is something that a child has to learn in daily living. Furthermore, a sense of responsibility is something that is difficult to learn (witness the millions of adults who do not seem to have acquired it). A child's inner controls over impulses are still weak and he depends to a great extent on controls from the outside, primarily from his parents. His attention span is rather short if he is not interested and he tends to get carried away with whatever occupies his attention at the moment, so that he forgets his duties. In other words, the vast majority of children, certainly preschoolers and children in the primary grades, need and must have frequent reminders if they are to learn a sense of responsibility.

The first question asked by parents in this connection is: "How do I know whether I am nagging or giving frequent reminders?" One difference is immediately observable, at least by a listener: a reminder, no matter how frequent, remains friendly and there is no tone of impatience or anger.

Nagging can often be diagnosed from the tone alone. There is, however, a more basic difference. Frequent reminders lead to learning, especially when combined with automatic rules based on a reward-punishment system. Nagging produces no learning in a constructive sense; on the contrary, it often forms part of a neurotic interaction in which the child becomes even less likely to accede to your demands than he would have been without the nagging.

Your child (or adult partner, for that matter) is the most sensitive indicator of whether or not you are nagging. When the child starts to become irritated and you feel irritation yourself, then you can be fairly sure that you are getting into a nagging pattern and that you have to change your approach. Impatient answers, vague postponements ("I'll do it later"), chronic excuses ("I didn't get around to it"), and whining or angry attacks (actually counterattacks) such as, "Why do you always pick on me?" or "Why can't you leave me alone?," are signs of a nagging pattern having developed. Formally we can define nagging as repeated impatient or angry requests or demands which do not lead to any constructive learning but rather are upsetting to the person who is the object of the requests as well as to the one who issues them. Nagging often involves destructive ways of communicating, such as exaggeration ("Why can you never do as I say?"), playing the numbers game ("I must have told you a thousand times"), humiliation ("What's the matter with you, don't you understand simple instructions?"), and sarcasm ("I guess it would be too much to ask his majesty to clean up the filth in his room!").

The second question parents usually ask when I lecture on this subject is: "What are the causes for reminders turning into nagging?" There can be several causes, but the most frequent are:

1. Parents often have unrealistic expectations concerning the amount of work involved in being a good parent. They may feel that one or two reminders "should" be enough in dealing with the child. When the child does not respond, the parents then get impatient and angry and these feelings are reflected in the words or tone of voice of the "reminders." As a consequence, the child becomes resentful and may—sometimes consciously but usually unconsciously—take out his resentment on the parents by not doing what he is reminded to do. This will lead to the reminders

being even more impatient and angry and thus we have a vicious circle developing.

2. Another frequent cause is that people—children as well as parents—often unconsciously enjoy showing their power. Not doing something you are asked to do is actually a very effective way of showing power and this is a fact a child will perceive very early in life.

3. A third cause involves breaking Rule 4, which states that you should be clear and specific in your communication, and a corollary of the same rule, which states that you should not accept vague communication from others. Suppose the mother says: "I told you many times to empty the wastepaper baskets" and the child answers, "I'll do it later, mom." The answer, "I'll do it later," actually means "I have a lot of power and you'll just have to keep nagging me about it." The interesting thing is that even though the parents should know the meaning of "later" from previous experience, they usually do one of three things, all of which are destructive in their consequences:

a. They may wait until "later," in which case they will fall into a nagging pattern or more firmly entrench an already existing nagging pattern.

b. They may forcibly yank the child away from whatever he is doing, in which case they teach the child nothing (except how to be rude). Through the same action they also make the child resentful and cause him to feel that he has unreasonable parents, thus making it even less likely that he will cooperate in the future. Who wants to cooperate with someone who is unreasonable?

c. The parents may "give-up" and do the chore (or whatever) themselves. As far as long-term destructive consequences are concerned, this is the worst "solution" of all. While nagging and forcible yanking, destructive as they are, at least constitute *attempts* at solving the problem, doing the chore for the child avoids the problem altogether and leaves it unsolved. For the child it means that he gets too much power: if his manipulation of others works, he is likely to use such manipulation of others all his life and will therefore not be likely to experience any deep and lasting emotional relationships. He will probably not be able to have a satisfactory marital relationship unless he undergoes psychotherapy.

"A lazy mother picks up after her children" is an old saying which contains truth and wisdom. It is easier to let children get away with something than it is to teach them self-discipline. However, if we have brought them into the world we also have an obligation to see to it that they get a reasonably good start in life. If they have not been taught inner discipline, they will enter life with a much worse handicap than material poverty or a physical defect could ever give them.

The thing to do, of course, is something that not too many people do: to *insist on clear communication*. When the child says, "I'll do it later," you should say, "Later is too vague a word. Tell me by what time it will be done." If the child refuses to specify a time or gives you an unreasonable time, you will have to set the time yourself. You then specify to the child what will happen as a consequence if the chore is still not done by the specified time and *then you give no further reminders that day*. This leads us to the fourth cause of reminders turning into nagging.

4. Procrastination, with resulting nagging, tends to develop when the child has not been given any rule specifying the consequences, rewards, or punishments connected with the requested action and its postponement (such as: "You can go out and play only when your room is tidy"). Attention from the nagging parent and the feeling of power in not carrying out a request may then become neurotic substitute rewards, thus perpetuating the procrastination-nagging interaction. More on this when we discuss the steps which can be taken to discourage procrastination and eliminate nagging.

If the emotional atmosphere in the home is sound as a result of positive communication between the family members, reminders will seldom develop into nagging. But if the parents have very little patience, if they are easily manipulated by the child's show of power, if communication is not clear, or if the requested behavior is not tied into a reasonable reward-punishment system, then nagging is likely to develop. The children will show the symptoms of the procrastination-nagging pattern by constant whining, squirming, sulking, and attempts at getting out of doing what they are supposed to do. The parent will show the symptoms by nagging and yelling, threatening without following up, or unreasonable action to enforce the demands.

Then, of course, we have the problem of children who nag or whine (the word "whine" is more often used to describe children's nagging). Children usually learn to whine under one or more of three conditions:

1. When a parent does not respond to a request asked in normal voice. There are parents who only react to their children's requests when they become irritated, when the requests have been repeated several times or said whiningly or in a raised voice. In this case the children quickly learn that they have to be irritating (whine) in order to get through.

2. When a parent postpones promised acts without good and specific reasons or when he uses vague language ("maybe, we'll see"), without indicating the specific reasons for the uncertainty.

3. When a parent tends to say "no" automatically without really having a good reason. Such parents often feel weak and powerless and the word "no" gives them an illusion of having power. Usually they either flounder from excuse to excuse in sticking to the original "no," or they let themselves be maneuvered into saying "yes," not because the child has thought of a good point in his favor (in which case the parents should say yes) but because they are tired of the whining. Either way, the effect is that the children are encouraged to nag and whine even more. If the parent sticks to a "no" based on excuses, the child will perceive the unreasonableness involved and will feel indignant and rebellious. If the parent is maneuvered into saying "yes" because he is tired of listening to the whining, the child has achieved an undeserved victory and has actually been *taught* by the parent that nagging and whining are good methods to use with other people. He will then intensify his nagging and whining when confronted by a "no" in the future in order to repeat his victory.

What can you do to prevent such destructive consequences from developing? You may not be able to completely prevent a child from whining, but you can surely see to it that you do not inadvertently teach your child to whine. You must be sure to give immediate friendly attention to any request given in a normal voice. A child who whines should be told in a friendly but firm manner: "I will answer you as soon as you stop whining." You must beware of any tendency on your part to procrastinate or to be vague in your communication. You must learn to consider each request objectively and to say "yes" if there is no good reason for saying "no." If there is some definite reason why you should say "no" (beware of using excuses), you state that reason and then *stick to what you have said*. You should under no circumstances change your mind just to stop the child's whining; that will teach him to whine even more in the future. You change your mind only if someone—you, your child, or another person—comes up with a *reasonable* point which had not occurred to you before and which throws a new light on the situation.

Many parents, being unsure of themselves, are so afraid of "giving in" that they stick to a "no" even when a reasonable point is brought up which they did not think of before. Such stubborn rigidity teaches only unreasonableness and must be abandoned. Never be afraid to change your mind if your child brings up a point you have not thought of. On the contrary, praise your child for good thinking and show that you are a reasonable person by taking the point into account in making your decision. Far from encouraging whining, this will have constructive effects: (1) it will teach your child that you are a reasonable person to deal with and that he does *not* need to whine to solve a problem; he needs, instead, to think of the crucial issues involved; (2) the child will, consequently, trust your judgment better in the future; (3) it will encourage your child to concentrate on trying to *solve* problems rather than on trying to manipulate other people; and (4) it will improve the child's self-concept to realize that you have attached importance to his thoughts.

Even if you have unthinkingly said no, all is not lost, however. You can still honestly admit that you made a mistake and that you have changed your mind. It will still be a good lesson in reasonableness to your child and will increase his respect for you, not decrease it, as you may fear. It is only the angry or resigned "all right already, go ahead and do it so I get some peace" type of reversal that is destructive.

Nagging, although frequent and widespread, is *not* a minor problem. On the contrary, being in itself a symptom of a frequent type of neurotic interaction, nagging can turn into a very serious situation. A neurotic interaction can be defined as a situation in which you try to accomplish *one* end with another person but, in effect, you are accomplishing the *op-*

*posite* end. Let us take an example of a neurotic interaction involving nagging.

A few years ago a mother came to my office for help with a thirteen-year-old boy whom we can call Alan. The mother was very upset and the first thing she said to me upon entering my office was: "Doctor Wahlroos, you just have to do something about my son Alan." She went on to tell me that Alan was a brilliant boy (I tested him later and he was indeed of superior intelligence); yet his marks in school were mostly D's, with a sprinkling of C's and F's. On the behavior or deportment side of his report card he usually had unsatisfactory marks in work habits and cooperation.

Alan's mother complained to me that her son refused to do any studying at home, no matter how much she asked him or reminded him. He always claimed that he had no homework, or that he had done the homework in school, or something equivalent. The first thing he would do when he came home was to sit down in front of the television set and no amount of coaxing or threats could make him do any studying. The mother "found herself" nagging Alan constantly, and she resented being "forced" to be a nagging mother, because she had hated her own mother nagging at her when she was a child. She also resented her husband for not taking a more active role in the disciplining of his son. Alan's father was a salesman who did a great deal of traveling and who had a rather distant relationship with Alan and very little understanding of the problems his wife was facing. His main conscious motivation seemed to be to keep out of all "hassles" and he left Alan's upbringing primarily to his wife, who complained bitterly about having to do everything alone (actually, he had in earlier years made a few clumsy but well-meant attempts at assuming the role of a father with Alan, but each time his wife had criticized him so severely in front of Alan that he had long ago given up trying).

After I had gotten a full history on Alan from the mother, plus an indication of the daily life of the family, I set up an appointment to see him.

Alan turned out to be quite an unusual boy. Ordinarily, the child who goes to see a psychologist will be a little anxious and a little reluctant—sometimes a little suspicious—about what to expect. Consequently, when I meet a child in the waiting room for the first time, he or she is usually rather shy and quiet in the beginning. It takes a little time and some friendly chatting in the office to overcome this shyness and to help "draw out" the child so that he will talk about himself. Not so with Alan! The moment I greeted him in the waiting room he jumped up from his chair and shook my hand vigorously as if I had been a long lost friend. Then he briskly walked ahead of me right into my office and had hardly sat down in his chair before he started pouring out his troubles to me without waiting for any questions! This is what he said (note his tremendous vocabulary and colorful presentation):

"Listen, Doctor Wahlroos," he started, "you have just got to do something about my mother! She is driving me nuts. If I have to listen to her nagging and picking much longer, I'll have to run away from home. I don't know what she told you, but do you realize that my mother will not let me alone for a single minute? She nags me from morning to night and there is absolutely nothing I can do or not do without her bugging me about it.

"When I go to the bathroom to brush my teeth, she yells all the way from the living room: 'Don't forget to brush your teeth!' When I go out from a room and my hand reaches for the light switch, she yells at me: 'Don't forget to turn off the light!' When I go to the kitchen to get something from the refrigerator she screams: 'Don't leave the refrigerator door open!' I am telling you, Doctor Wahlroos, there is nothing I can do in that house without my mother breathing down my neck and hassling me.

"Every day is full of: 'Where have you been? Wash your hands! Blow your nose! Don't run around with Tony, he is no good! Don't do it and never mind why! Why did you buy that record? Do you always have to spend your allowance on trash? Don't get interested in Susie, she isn't your type! Brush your teeth! Make your bed! Change your shirt! You look pale. Let me see your tongue! Stand up straight.' And on and on she drones; it never ends.

"And if she can find nothing else to nag about, then she always starts in on my homework. It has got to such a point that when I come home from school I don't even have time to close the door behind me before she starts at me with 'Alan, don't you think you should do your homework before you do anything else?' And that just makes me so mad that I could crawl out of my skin and I whisper under my breath: 'Listen, you queen of all naggers and faultfinders, I wouldn't give you that satisfaction if it would be the last thing left for me to do on earth!' Doctor Wahlroos, I know I am intelligent, I do want to go to college eventually, I do want to study and get good grades, but I can't let my mother direct every breath I take, and the only way I can really get back at her is by not studying, because she worries much more about that than I do."

The use of poor school performance as a weapon against

parents is common among children, but it is almost always an *unconscious* motivation: the children themselves are not aware of any deliberate attempt to hurt their parents by getting poor grades. It is highly unusual for a child to be consciously aware of using refusal to study as a weapon against the parents, but such was nevertheless the case with Alan.

Let us stop for a moment to look at how this process of using school performance as a weapon works. If the child feels he needs a weapon, if he feels his parents are unfair, that they are hurting him in some way, or that they constantly want to show their power, there are actually very few ways in which he can "fight back." However, most parents nowadays place a great deal of value on studying and academic performance, and a child soon finds out—usually unconsciously but sometimes consciously—that not studying is a very effective way to get back at the parents. It is usually more effective than not doing chores, for example. By doing poorly in school the child can effectively hurt his parents if their values include a good education, but the child also knows that he is hurting himself in the process and, consequently, *he feels no guilt*. By punishing his parents and himself simultaneously the child is left free of guilt and therefore will feel no motivation to do anything about the situation. This is an example of what I call a "neurotic package deal" or "the perfect neurotic solution." The deal is unbeatable, since the punishment of the other person and of oneself is accomplished through the same action (or inaction). Such "double satisfaction" is not something that the child is likely to give up by himself or through his parents pleading with him. Poor school performance is, of course, not always due to a need for punishment and self-punishment. But when such motivation is present (a psychodiagnostic evaluation by a psychologist will usually ascertain the degree to which destructive and/or self-destructive factors play a role), it usually takes a trained professional, a psychologist or psychiatrist, to (1) help the child see the purpose of his action, and (2) help the family remove the need for punishing the parents.

Let us now examine the neurotic interaction in the relationship between Alan and his mother:

The mother *consciously* wanted Alan to be responsible, wanted him to do well in school, study, go to college, and make the most of his high intelligence and potentials. Most immediately, she wanted to stop "having to nag" Alan about so many things, because she hated being a nagging mother. These were her conscious wishes.

Alan's mother's *unconscious* wishes were quite different. In her psychotherapy it became clear that she was secretly afraid of Alan growing up: she wanted to keep him a baby who needed her for everything and over whom she could exercise complete control. In the beginning Alan's mother considered this idea absurd; why would she not want her son to grow up? But as the evidence mounted (her treating him like a baby, his being the youngest and last child, her poor relationship with her husband, her desperate need to feel needed, her dreams in which Alan was still a baby or a little toddler, her deep involvement with Alan which made her secretly fear— and, even more secretly, welcome—his developing into a sexual being) she began considering the idea that she was afraid of Alan's growing up as a possibility, and this willingness to look into hidden motivation led, in itself, to her developing more control over her behavior.

Alan's mother was enveloped in a neurotic interaction with her son. Her behavior before psychotherapy was influenced mainly by her unconscious wishes. Thus, although she consciously wanted to treat him in accordance with his age and did not want to nag him, she in fact nagged him so unmercifully about every single activity of his and, consequently, made him so angry with her, that her approach achieved the opposite goal from what she consciously wanted. Yet, even in the face of complete failure of the approach, even with a strong conscious desire to stop nagging, she felt compelled to nag him further. This could only have been due to an unconscious wish to accomplish the opposite goal (otherwise, why would she not have abandoned her method?).

What Alan wanted *consciously* was identical with what his mother wanted for him. He wanted to do well in school, study and get good grades, go to college, and put his intelligence to constructive use. Most of all, he wanted his mother to stop nagging him (just as she wanted to stop nagging). *Unconsciously,* however, his purpose was different. Through his behavior, lack of studying, flaunting his mother's authority, he accomplished the opposite goal: his mother nagged him even more. We can see, then, that Alan both consciously and unconsciously shared his mother's goals. When both conscious and unconscious goals are shared and the unconscious goals are destructive, we speak of a neurotic interaction.

The situation was solved through psychotherapy with Alan and his mother and occasional consultation with the father. In their therapy both Alan and his mother were asked to look at their actions (and lack of action) in terms of their communicative value. The mother, as we intimated above, had to face the fact that by her indiscriminate nagging she was really telling Alan: "I want to pretend that you are still my little baby who cannot take care of himself at all." This led to the discovery that unconsciously—as is the case with many mothers who do not have a satisfactory marital relationship—she was afraid of her son growing up and this was the main reason she had kept using a method (nagging) which she consciously hated and which actually insured that he would remain immature. The unconscious reasoning was: better have a bad baby than to lose the baby altogether by his growing up.

Alan made similar discoveries in his psychotherapy. He was already aware of using lack of studying as a weapon and this awareness gave him a flying start in therapy. He made the additional important discovery that he himself was afraid of growing up and that deep down his mother's constant nagging actually made him feel secure (plus the fact that it was an antidote to his father's seeming indifference). This is what made him provoke his mother to constant nagging. Through his behavior he was asking his mother to nag, and she complied!

In psychotherapy we found out, then, what at first appeared totally absurd to both Alan and his mother, namely that the two of them were in perfect agreement both consciously and unconsciously. They both consciously wanted Alan to do well and they were both unconsciously afraid of his growing up. When they realized that their wishes and fears were identical, the symptoms stopped: Alan studied and got good grades and his mother stopped the nagging. Contributing to the unusually speedy and lasting success in this case was the fact that Alan's father began playing a much more active role as soon as his wife had reassured him that she would stop her destructive criticisms in front of Alan. Through this cooperative commitment the marriage situation improved, which, in turn, led to less fear on the part of Alan's mother of her son growing up.*

As mentioned, in the more serious "neurotic package deal" situations you usually need professional help to get out of the vicious circle. But what about less serious situations? What can you yourself do about nagging at home without going to the psychologist?

---

*The psychodynamics involved can also be analyzed in purely Oedipal terms, but the communication aspects of this case are the ones I wish to stress in this book.

1. The first and most important measure to take is to institute *automatic rules* covering the subjects over which there is nagging. Automatic rules, usually tied into a reward-punishment system and often implemented by specific schedules concerning chores to be done and tasks to be carried out, can do a great deal to discourage procrastination and eliminate nagging. The consequences resulting from not following the rules must, of course, be spelled out in advance. Nagging will be eliminated because (1) if the rules are followed, there will be no need for nagging, and (2) if the rules are not followed, a specific consequence or punishment has been spelled out in advance, so that there is no need for nagging in either case.

Let us take poor table manners as an example. Dinner time is (or should be) one of the main regular occasions for family togetherness and happy interchange. But mealtimes can be ruined by the unpleasant atmosphere resulting from nagging. Suppose now that Stevie, age seven, won't eat neatly and properly and that his parents constantly nag him about it at the dinner table. Everyone gets upset and no one looks forward to mealtime as a happy occasion. What can mom and dad do about it? The answer is that they can institute an automatic rule: whenever Stevie uses good table manners, he gets dessert; when he uses poor table manners, he gets no dessert, and not one more word is said about table manners.

This particular rule will work, of course, only if Stevie likes dessert! If he is one of the few children who do not, another consequence has to be found (no television that evening, no playing with friends the next day, or other consequences, depending upon the individual child's likes and dislikes). As with all methods, do not expect immediate results. One or two weeks may be sufficient, but sometimes you have to give the method several months to work. Some children will try to see if they can wear you down and will even get worse for a while just to see if they can't get you to give up the method. Remain firm (and kind and compassionate at the same time) and you will do well!

Let us take another example. In countless homes there is a lot of nagging, yelling, and threatening about the children's rooms being picked up. (Fathers have been known to stop at bars on the way home from work to avoid having to face the screaming and hullabaloo involved in this and other discipline matters.) Again, the problem can be settled by automatic rules, such as: "No playing with other children inside or outside the family until your room is straightened out," or "Everything that is not in its proper place will be taken to the garage for a month," or "No television watching until the room is clean," or you can announce that the child's allowance will be paid on a daily basis from now on, but only if the room is clean by a certain time. Again, do not expect the rule to work right away. But remember: meanwhile there has been no nagging, so you are still ahead.

Once when I lectured on the subject of nagging, a lady asked me what to do with her eleven-year-old son. It seems that he was interested in all kinds of projects, model-building, electronics, magic tricks, etc., and he would constantly borrow his mother's scissors or Scotch tape or his father's tools, which were then never returned and often could not be found. The parents found themselves constantly nagging their son about this.

I congratulated the mother on having an inventive and creative son and told her that there was absolutely no need for nagging her son about it. I asked her how her son got the money to buy the models he was building and she said he had an allowance. I then suggested that she go home and serve notice on her son that he has exactly one week to work out this problem. If at the end of the week the problem still persists, she will never again ask him to return anything he has borrowed. She will simply buy a new pair of scissors or a new tool and take the money for it from his allowance.

A few months later I received a letter from the lady. She wrote that she had not even needed to put the rule into effect. Merely serving notice on her son in such a way that he knew she meant what she said had been sufficient. Whatever he borrowed was returned promptly. Best of all, there had been no nagging in the family since the institution of the rule.

The method of instituting automatic rules can also be applied to parents, as shown by the following excerpt from a case history.

One of the families coming to my office for help had a father who used very foul language at home. His eight-year-old son had begun swearing, too, largely in imitation of his father. For this he was punished by the father who had actually—unwittingly—taught his child to swear! The gross unfairness of this led to tremendous feelings of resentment on the part of the boy which resulted in his becoming a terrible behavior problem at home and in school.*

As part of the psychotherapy with this family, I suggested that the boy (who had an allowance) be fined one penny each time he used a bad word and that the father be fined five dollars each time he used one. The kitty was to be kept by the mother and the proceeds were to go to the family's favorite charity (to use the money from fining for a vacation fund, Christmas fund, or future education fund will not work; the money has to go outside the family for the method to be effective). As a result, swearing stopped almost completely in less than a month and the family was able to send a somewhat larger contribution than usual to the Cancer Fund.

The following example illustrates the use of automatic rules to eliminate nagging between husband and wife.

In the case of one of the couples coming to see me for marital counseling, the wife would constantly nag her husband about things that needed to be fixed around the house. The husband would keep postponing them (partly for the unconscious purpose of provoking his wife) and would not allow the wife to call in anyone else to do the repairs, because he wanted to save the money and felt that he could do a better job himself anyway.

I suggested that the two of them make an agreement. When the wife notices something that needs to be fixed, she will give the husband fifteen days in which to do it and both will initial the date on the calendar (this is to prevent memory from playing tricks, such as the husband saying: "But I don't remember your saying anything to me about it, dear"). The agreement was made and in the year during which I saw this couple (who had many other problems), the wife had to call in a repair man only once. The daily nagging which had been constant for many years had come to a complete stop.

Automatic rules can also be used profitably when wishes and opinions clash, as shown by the following example.

---

*The excerpts from case histories used as examples in this book are, of course, oversimplified. There were many other problems in this family which caused resentment on the part of all members, but for purposes of illustration we must content ourselves with picking out only one of these problems, Similarly, the successful outcome in the psychotherapy with this family depended upon a number of therapeutic measures, not only on the institution of one technique.

Another couple were constantly fighting and nagging each other about what to do on weekends. The wife, who felt tied down to the house and the children, wanted to go out for dinner and dancing; the husband, who had to do a lot of entertaining for his business clients, wanted to spend his weekend evenings at home playing cards or reading and listening to his record collection. This conflict had gone on for years. While the couple were working out their other problems in psychotherapy, I suggested that they alternate the responsibility for planning weekends: the wife plans one weekend, the husband the next, etc. (the very fact that neither one of these intelligent people had thought of such a simple solution shows, in itself, that they had a strong need to be in a chronic superficial conflict in order to cover up for more basic conflicts). Not only did this method work beautifully, it also helped their psychotherapy because, with the superficial cause for their bickering removed, they had to face more basic causes (selfishness, quest for power, manipulation of the partner, etc.). As these basic causes were exposed and worked out, we came to the point that the wife often suggested that they stay home, out of genuine consideration for her husband, while he took delight —when "his" weekend came—in surprising his wife with new ideas for what to do and where to go to dine, dance, and have fun!

2. The second step to take when nagging has become—or is threatening to become—a pattern, is to consider whether the nagging is indiscriminate, whether important and unimportant issues are mixed. If so, and if you are the one doing the nagging, you must forget the unimportant matters (as defined by you) and set up rules to cover the important ones. In other words, follow Rule 2. If it is another family member who engages in the nagging, encourage him or her to decide on what is important and to set up some rules designed to eliminate the undesirable behavior which provokes the nagging, and thereby the nagging itself as well.

3. The third step is to analyze the communication involved to be sure that it is clear and specific; no vagueness is to be allowed (Rule 4). Do not accept the answer, "I'll do it later" or "I'll do it when I get around to it." Remember that such an answer is just an invitation for the partner to nag. In the case of a chore, demand firmly to know by what time it is going to be done or set that time yourself, and set a rule as to what will happen if the chore is not done by that time.

But you have to be sure that you, yourself, are following

Rule 4. Many parents use phrases such as "later," or "when I get around to it," or "we'll see" and do not realize that by doing so they are teaching their children to postpone, also! It should go without saying that in order to apply this rule to children successfully, you must follow it yourself. You must be clear in your own communication and you must be specific in what you say to the child about when you will do things. If it is impossible to state a specific time, you must be specific about the conditions that must be fulfilled before the action can take place.

4. The fourth step is to institute regular family conferences, gripe sessions, or periodic reevaluations of rules. If such meetings have been scheduled on a regular and fairly frequent basis, then nagging and whining behavior can usually be met successfully with: "Be sure to remember it or write it down and bring it up at the next family conference."

5. The fifth matter to consider when a nagging pattern has developed is the possibility of the partners being involved in a neurotic interaction. If you notice that the efforts of one partner lead to the opposite result in the other partner, then a neurotic interaction exists. If automatic rules do not help (try them for at least three months!) and family conferences do not help, then professional assistance *must* be sought, because the tendency to engage in neurotic interactions can and does develop into a lifelong pattern that will influence future families and generations. In other words, if you and your child are engaged in a neurotic interaction, the chances are that your child will be prone to get involved in neurotic interactions all through his life and that this tendency will severely affect his later family life once he gets married and has children.

6. Finally, a practical pointer. It often helps to go up to the child and gently *whisper* the request into his ear. The act itself expresses a feeling of intimacy and usually makes the child feel good. In some cases it saves face for him when he has brothers and sisters. Moreover, children enjoy getting "secret messages" and take pleasure in knowing that others are not initiated in what they are going to do. In any case, even if the whispering should not work, you have at least spared your vocal cords from abuse.

# 18. "I WAS JUST KIDDING. CAN'T YOU TAKE A JOKE?"

*Rule 18: Learn when to use humor and when to be serious. Do not subject your partner to destructive teasing.*

A good-natured sense of humor is one of the most wonderful attributes a human being can have. It is usually (although not always) a sign of happiness and security in the person who possesses it. Such a person can, at least momentarily, make other people feel happy and contented and this tends to deepen the satisfaction he himself experiences in life.

Especially the ability to laugh at oneself without bitterness and to see the humorous side of situations without glee is a mark of a truly mature and "actualized" person. A sign of loving intimacy between two people is the ability to laugh at each other's mistakes and weaknesses without ridicule or mocking and without either one losing face.

Humor, if good-natured, is one way to avoid having a discussion turn into a destructive argument. It is an antidote against the use of unfair and destructive communication techniques. A sense of humor is an important emotional resource: the ability to see things from the humorous side will help a person through many adverse situations, and the capacity for healthy, joyous laughter will enrich his relationships with other people. Humor clears the air and brings relief from pent-up tensions and anxieties. But most of all, humor is one of the ingredients which make life exciting, interesting, and enjoyable.

Exclusive reliance on humor, however, must be seen as a personality defect. A person who cannot suffer and cannot be depressed lacks important dimensions in his personality and is thereby never able to develop a deep and lasting intimate relationship with another human being. Nor is such a person likely ever to come to terms with himself and his underlying feelings. Exclusive reliance on humor is a defensive reaction to unbearable anxiety.

The person who seems constantly driven, for example, to tell dirty jokes is probably acting out anxiety-producing sexual conflicts. In developmental terms he is fixated at the pubertal stage of psychosexual development. Compulsive telling of sexual jokes may also be a form of exhibitionism. In any case it is an immature method of warding off the anxiety produced by sexual feelings.

But humor can also be a vicious weapon. Of course, if we define humor to include only good-natured motivation, it could never be used as a weapon. But that is not a useful definition, because many people who use humor destructively are not aware of any destructive motivation. A person who tries to make himself feel superior by making another person appear ridiculous would not be likely to admit to himself or to others that his basic motivation is hostile (unless he is in successful psychotherapy). It would be better, therefore, to say that humor is positive and good-natured or negative and vicious depending purely on when, in what situation, with whom, and with what conscious and unconscious motivation it is employed. Thus, the same humorous comment made to one person may be good-natured, but made to another person, known to be sensitive to its content, it can be vicious. A joking statement made in one situation to another person may be cruel; made under different circumstances it may be good-natured and positive.

Tactfulness and some ability to sense another person's feelings and needs at the moment are prerequisites to the appropriate use of humor. Timing is extremely important. Sometimes a humorous remark at the right time can lift a depression or change a person's outlook from despair to confidence. On the other hand, there is perhaps nothing quite as maddening as a person who insists on joking when you want to be serious. The timing of humor cannot be learned directly. It is an outgrowth of personal development and maturity and of your interest in and concern for other human beings; thus, there are no rules which can be taught for when and when not to use what kind of humor.

In adult interchange, the destructive use of humor can be

most hurtful, just as its constructive use can be very helpful. Sarcasm, ridicule, mockery, and flippancy are clearly destructive under almost any circumstance and when used against any age group. Destructive ways of communicating, however, have their strongest impact on children and therefore should not be used against them under any circumstances. It is inexcusable to make a child the victim of one's destructive humor. Even when a person is himself unaware of the destructive effects of his humor on the child it is still inexcusable if he persists when another family member or the child himself points out the destructive effects. Children, however, use humor destructively against each other in the form of teasing which, if allowed to go unchecked, can lead not only to constant disturbances of the peace at home but also to failure of the children to learn appropriate ways of behaving and reacting to the behavior of other people. We will devote the rest of this section to an examination of teasing, its manifestations and causes, and ways in which it can be handled constructively.

Teasing is not in itself a destructive technique, since it can also be used to show affection. Teasing is positive or negative depending on the response evoked in the other person. It follows from this that only a person who can sense the partner's reaction can afford to tease without fear of negative consequences, because he will know when to stop.

Teasing can be great fun, provided *both* partners enjoy it. When teasing is fun it is because both partners understand that there is no conscious or unconscious attempt to tear down the other person's self-image. Destructive teasing, on the other hand, is designed to tear down self-esteem in the recipient and to make the teaser feel superior at the "teasee's" expense. Teasing can become extremely destructive if one partner's self-concept is so poor that he cannot "take" teasing or if the other partner is so insensitive or lacking in compassion that he does not know when to stop.

The employment of teasing as a destructive interpersonal technique is seen especially clearly in children whose parents have not learned how to deal with sibling rivalry.* Mild teasing and infrequent destructive teasing is a sign of healthy functioning in the family and should not be interfered with.

---

*In writing some parts of this chapter I have been influenced by Edith G. Neisser's excellent book, *Brothers and Sisters* (New York: Harper and Brothers, 1951).

But when one or more family members start considering it a problem it is time to do something about it. And in order to do something to remedy the situation it may be useful to know something about the usual causes. What are the main factors which lead to destructive teasing behavior in children?

1. Teasing may be a symptom of jealousy. In this case the teaser is trying to make the teasee appear unworthy of the advantages which the teaser feels his brother, sister, or playmate possesses.

2. Teasing may be an attempt to show power. A young child, for example, may enjoy getting his older brother (or sister) in trouble by subtly teasing or provoking the latter into destructive action which will then, in turn, bring down the parents' wrath upon the older one. Thus, one child in the family can pull the strings and let the others, grown-ups and children alike, dance like marionettes without the latter even recognizing that they are being manipulated.

3. Teasing may be an alarm signal to the parents that some condition needs correcting. The conditions to be corrected could involve any number of situations.

> In one family a sudden pattern of destructive teasing had developed between the older boy, who was ten, and his younger brother, six. The parents were very puzzled about the fact that this teasing occurred primarily on Saturday mornings when the boys walked over to their grandparents, who lived less than a mile away.
>
> The explanation here was simple. The older boy wanted to be with his friends and play ball on Saturday mornings. He liked his grandparents, but he had simply "outgrown" seeing them as often as every week. Due to poor communication in the home, he had not learned to go his parents and express these feelings in words. Instead, he showed through his behavior what it was that was wrong. When his visits with the grandparents were cut down to once a month (he also saw his grandparents when they visited his house), the problem was solved. The teasing had simply been an alarm signal that something was wrong and needed changing. And as the family learned better communication techniques other problems were similarly taken care of.

I have seen many cases of older children being given too much responsibility for younger ones, especially when parents are absent. In these cases, the older children often try to assert their authority by teasing the younger ones, ordering them around, or using threats. The younger children, in turn, will try to subvert the authority of the older one by teasing him, provoking him, and refusing to obey his commands. In these cases, again, the teasing serves as a signal that some condition needs correcting.

Let us consider a hypothetical example of teasing given by Parke Cummings:*

> Mother is engaged in some sort of housework, and is interrupted by Peggy, aged five, exactly half her brother Tim's age.
> *Peggy:* "Tim's teasing me!"
> *Mother:* "What did he do?"
> *Peggy:* "He took my beach ball."
> *Mother:* "Well, tell him to give it back to you."

> *Peggy:* "He won't give it back to me!"
> *Mother* (calls): "Tim, give Peggy her ball—and stop teasing her!"
> *Tim:* "Aw—OK."

> *Peggy:* "Mother, he is still teasing me!"
> *Mother:* "Didn't he give you back the ball?"
> *Peggy:* "Yes, but now he says my ears are going to drop off."
> *Mother:* "What! Why does he say that?"
> *Peggy:* "Because I don't like to drink milk."
> *Mother:* "Well, you tell him if there's any more nonsensical talk like that, there's going to be trouble."

> *Peggy:* "He's teasing me! He keeps on teasing me!"
> *Mother:* "You send him in here."

> *Mother:* "Now look here, young man, I'm simply not going to stand for any more of this teasing."
> *Tim:* "But gee, I wasn't doing a thing!"
> *Peggy:* "He was too. He was sniffling."
> *Mother:* "Sniffling? What do you mean?"
> *Peggy:* "He was pretending to cry. Like this—(whimpers)."
> *Mother:* "Tim, you stop that!"
> *Tim:* "But gosh, what's the matter with that?"
> *Mother:* "You were doing it just because you knew it was

annoying her. She doesn't like to be made fun of. You used
to cry too, when Ed teased you."
*Tim:* "Gee whiz—"

*Peggy:* "You're gonna get it! You'll see."
*Tim:* "I wasn't doing a thing!"
*Mother:* "All right, *now* what's the trouble?"
*Peggy:* "He was humming."
*Mother:* "What do you mean, humming?"
*Peggy:* "Like this—(internationally known teasing tune; the
words can vary from "Susie wet her panties" to "Jimmy is a
sissy," but the tune is always the same):

*Mother:* "Tim, you stop that!"
*Tim:* "Goodnight! You mean to say a fellow can't hum
around here if he feels like it?"
*Mother:* "That's *just* what I mean—when you're deliberately
doing it because you know she hates it. Now I'm warning
you, if there is any more teasing, you're going to be sent to
your room."

*Tim:* "I did not!"
*Peggy:* "You did!"
*Mother:* "For heaven's sake, what's the trouble *now?*"
*Peggy:* "He was making faces at me!"
*Tim:* "I was NOT!"
*Peggy:* "You were!"
*Mother:* "Tim, I warned you—"
*Tim:* "But I wasn't! I wasn't making any kind of a face at all."
*Peggy:* "Well, you sat right in front of me and kept looking at
me!"
*Mother:* "Tim, what were you doing?"
*Tim:* "I wasn't making faces! I didn't make any kind of a face
at all."
*Peggy:* "Well, he kept looking at me. Everywhere I'd go, he'd
get right in front of me and look at me—like this."
(Stares.)
*Mother:* "Tim, go to your room!"
*Tim:* "What?!"

*Mother:* "I said go to your room."

*Tim:* "Gosh, what *is* this around here anyhow? Can't a guy even *look* at his sister?"

*Mother:* "No!"

This scene illustrates some important points about teasing. It shows that after a teasing pattern has been set up, almost any behavior will accomplish the goal, even merely looking! It also shows the eagerness of one child to report the teasing, so that the other child will get into trouble. Because of this eagerness to get the other child into trouble, we must say that the mother, in this case, made a mistake. As Cummings himself recommends, she should have warned the children that if the teasing continued, *both* would be punished (or the mother could also choose to stay out of the conflict altogether, saying: "I'm sure the two of you can handle the matter reasonably").

The idea of punishing both the teaser and the teasee strikes many parents as unfair. In fact, it is both fair and realistic, as well as effective. The fact is that the teasee often secretly welcomes and subtly provokes the teasing, so that he or she can get the brother or sister into trouble. Punishing both removes this motivation on the part of the teasee to subtly invite teasing from the teaser and it removes the payoff involved in reporting the teasing to the parent. As a result, the teasing either stops or—at the least—assumes minor and less aggravating proportions.

Let us consider another example (it could be taken from any household where the children tease each other):

> Brother stands in the hallway and sister passes him. As she walks by him she gives him a little jab with her elbow, then hastens her steps.
>
> Brother says, "Why you—," runs after her and hits her in the back. Sister starts screaming for her parents and both children indignantly accuse each other of starting the incident.

In this example, as in the vast majority of teasing, the parents will be lost if they attempt to find out who "started" the argument. They will never be able to determine for certain whether the brush with the elbow was accidental (as the sister will claim) or deliberate (as the brother will claim). Nor will they be able to determine whether the brother perhaps gave his sister a "dirty look" when he saw her coming, or sighed, or turned his head contemptuously, or whatever.

The best way to deal with this type of situation is to discuss it in terms of accepting or rejecting invitations (see Rule 9). If the brother gave the sister a dirty look, sighed, or turned his head contemptuously, this is to be considered an invitation: "I invite you to fight with me." The girl has a fully free choice to accept or reject the invitation. She can accept it— as she did—by doing something "back," in which case she is really saying: "Good idea! Let's fight." In this case, she must accept fifty percent of the blame. Or she can decline the invitation by ignoring it and not doing anything "back," in which case she is really saying: "Thank you, not this time."

The same is true of the brother. When his sister gives him the little jab ("brushes against him accidentally," as she would put it), he is free to choose whether he wants to accept the invitation by doing something "back" (in which case he must assume fifty percent of the blame) or whether he wishes to decline it by pretending that it was, indeed, accidental.

If parents follow this reasoning and see the interaction between the children realistically as involving the issuance of invitations that can be accepted or declined, then they will find it eminently fair to either stay out of the conflict or to punish both if punishment is needed. In any case, the children should be taught to look at the interaction in these terms.

There are, of course, true "bully-victim" situations, but they are rare and marked by repeated attempts by the victim to decline the bully's invitations or by an absence of retaliatory action on the part of the victim. In these cases, psychotherapy for the bully (and probably also for the victim) is definitely indicated.

How can teasing be limited? Let us list and summarize the methods we have outlined.

1. Teach the children the realistic view of teasing in terms of invitations which can be accepted or declined.

2. Make attempts to understand the causes underlying the teasing. Eliminate all realistic causes for jealousy and protest.

3. Encourage the children to have separate experiences. Being constantly together can get on people's nerves, as testified

to by polar explorers and men drifting on rafts over the ocean.

4. Punish both for engaging in a teasing relationship. Or let it go altogether. Some teasing *must* be permitted. Teasing is also a way of showing closeness and affection, and if you attempt to eliminate it completely, you are depriving your children of an important experience, one which is denied "only" children (who must get it from their playmates).

   Under no circumstances should you try to deal with the problem by letting the child taste his own medicine. Children want to look up to their parents and do not want them to stoop down to their own level, except when the joking or teasing is entirely good natured and makes the child feel happy rather than angry.

5. Do not *force* children to share their possessions.

6. Avoid comparing one child with another.

7. Teach your children to respect the privacy of all family members.

# 19. "WHAT DID YOU SAY?"

## *Rule 19: Learn to listen.*

Throughout our enumeration of rules of communication, the importance of listening has been implied when it has not been stated openly. Listening plays a significant part in following Rule 6 (test your assumptions), Rule 8 (family members are experts on you), Unfair Technique 11-VII (do not interrupt), Rule 14 (be tactful and courteous), and Rule 15 (do not preach or lecture, ask questions instead). However, the subject of listening is so important that it deserves to be singled out for a rule of its own. The crucial importance of listening is especially clear in child raising. I would even go so far as to say that successful child raising cannot be accomplished without following this rule.

The first thing we must keep in mind about listening is that it must be *active* if it is to be effective. Active listening implies an obvious interest in the partner's feelings and opinions as well as an active effort to hear and understand the partner. Anything which remains unclear must be clarified through questions.

We have all run across the type of person who, when you are talking, just appears to be thinking of what he is going to say next. There are others from whose answers it is apparent that they did not take anything you said *into account*, even though they may be able to repeat what you said word for word. Such people see your speech merely as a nuisance, an interference with their own speaking. At the time I am writing this, I have a patient who completely disregards everything I say and just continues with "And then . . . ," as if I existed only as a passive tape recorder. Only last week did we start to make progress when I told the patient that she actually made me feel like a tape recorder! With such people, no meaningful positive communication can evolve until they have learned to listen.

There are even people who do not listen to themselves! If you interrupt them to comment on the last thing they said, they will not remember it! These are people who talk defensively. Many of them fool themselves into thinking that they are forming a relationship with another human being through talking, whereas the reality is that all they do is try to ward off anxiety by talking.

One way to communicate positively and effectively is to imagine listening to yourself as another person might. You will then be better aware of how you "come off" and be able to see to it that you lessen the chances of being misunderstood.

In discussing Rule 12 (let the *effect* of your communication be your guideline) we pointed out that the "sender" must take into account the fact that the "receiver's" perception of the message will be colored by his view of the sender. This view may have been shaped by observation of the sender's past performance, but it may also be based on reputation or on appearance and bearing.

It follows that it behooves the listener to take such factors into conscious account and become aware of how he, himself, may color or distort a message on the basis of these factors. If a sarcastic communication partner tries to change his ways, for example, the listener must beware of his own tendency to read sarcasm into the partner's statements. Otherwise the change will be discouraged and the problem perpetuated.

Even regardless of past or present knowledge, the listener's perception is colored by his own values, motivations, problems, and conflicts. To become an effective listener (thereby satisfying fifty percent of the requirements of a good communicator) you must, therefore, honestly assess the effect your own tendencies can have on what you perceive.

Many of the communications we receive each day are ambiguous and can be interpreted in a multitude of ways. There are people who are so suspicious or so interested (unconsciously) in collecting injustices and rejections that they read the worst possible interpretation into *any* communication. There are others who are so pollyanna-ish that they can see no harm in any communication. Both tendencies are distortions of reality and—although the second may be more pleasant—both border on pathology.

It is especially important to listen for *feelings,* because what the other person feels is often much more important in guiding his actions than what he thinks. The poor tester of emotional reality (see Unfair Technique 11-VI) is therefore—by definition—a poor listener.

However, the so-called "active listening" advocated by some psychologists today seems to me to be of limited usefulness. It is a therapeutic technique (also called reflecting or mirroring) which—when used in moderation—works well with a certain type of "feeling-oriented" patient. It involves rephrasing the other person's statement to get at the feeling behind it and *can* sometimes have some value in "drawing out" a person by indicating acceptance and/or understanding of his feelings. However, it is not to be used indiscriminately or mechanically. Its indiscriminate use would result in destructive communication, as illustrated in the following interchange between a child and his parent who had attended a class on becoming a more competent parent:

> *Child:* "Why don't I ever get to go to Disneyland?"
> *Parent:* "You really feel strongly about it. You feel it would be a lot of fun."

*Child:* "Yes, I sure would like to go. When do we get to go again?"

*Parent:* "It would be very important to you, huh? You'd really like it."

*Child:* "I sure would. When can we go?"

*Parent:* "You like it so much you feel impatient. You would like to go real soon."

*Child:* "God, one can't get any straight answers from you ever since you started going to that stupid 'parent school.' "

*Parent:* "You feel frustrated about my not giving you a definite answer."

*Child:* "Forget it, you are driving me crazy."

Only the first one of the "active listening" (mirroring, reflecting) remarks of this parent could possibly be justified. The rest constitute pure crazy-making and the child knows it. It is an unnatural, artificial, and technique-oriented, nonspontaneous way of communicating. I definitely recommend against its use in the home except

1. as an "opener,"

2. when you sense stronger feelings behind a statement than are actually expressed, or

3. when your child or other communication partner likes the approach and does not get irritated or frustrated by your using it.

The parent in the example above could indicate his (or her) understanding of and empathy with the child's feeling much better by seriously discussing with the child when a trip to Disneyland could be made, listening seriously to his opinions, and asking for or suggesting a solution.

The danger involved in the active listening approach can best be illustrated by an example from Thomas Gordon's book, *Parent Effectiveness Training,** which strongly recommends active listening. The author brings up a situation in which a child is terrified that his father is going to force him to go into the water and recommends that the father allay the child's fear by saying: "You're scared and don't want me to force you into the water." It should be clear that such a statement merely rubs in the child's anxiety. No anxious child would be calmed by such rubbing in. A

*New York: Peter H. Wyden, Inc., 1970.

common-sense parent with even a modicum of compassion or empathy would not treat a terrified child in such a manner. Instead, he would reassure the child by a definite commitment: "Don't worry, son. I will *never force you* to go into the water."

The type of active listening I have in mind does not irritate anyone, does not "rub in," and does not depend on any superficial gimmicks. It is not a matter of technique or method but of attitude: an attitude of compassion, willingness to try to understand, acceptance of feeling, encouraging the partner to work out a solution, and seriously attempting to help in solving the problem if the partner can't do it alone. Such an attitude will "come through" if it is genuine without any superficial techniques or gimmicks.

To be sure, active listening must often include feedback, a check on whether you have correctly understood the partner's feelings, opinions, or demands. Restatements such as, "Let me see if I understood you correctly; you mean that . . . ," are very helpful in communication. But once the understanding is confirmed, it must lead to an active attempt to help, reassure, give a counter-opinion, or suggest a compromise, etc., otherwise there is no give-and-take in the communicative interchange. And without give-and-take you cannot "get through" to your partner.

Parents often complain that they cannot get through to their children. In my experience, these are usually parents who do not let their children come through to them! You cannot effectively communicate with an intimate partner if you do not make a sincere attempt to understand his feelings. Only by listening carefully to his feelings and opinions can you come to understand him well. And only if you understand your partner well will you be able to express your own thoughts in such a manner that he will consider them seriously.

An effective way of teaching children to listen is to ask *them* to give *you* feedback: "Please tell me in your own words what I just said" or "Let's go over it once so we are both sure we understand the same thing; could you please tell me what we agreed on in your own words." Adult partners can, of course, also be asked for feedback, but insecure and "touchy" adults often become defensive if they feel that someone doubts their ability to understand, so with them especial tact has to be exercised.

In different contexts throughout this book I have stressed the importance of asking questions. In concluding the discussion of Rule 19 I would like to stress that the object of asking questions, as well as of listening, should be positive: to understand the other person or help him understand himself, to encourage his thinking out problems on his own, to help him develop his own resources as a human being, and—to actively improve your own listening ability. Of course, questioning can also be used negatively, as when the object is to "snoop," interrogate, or trap another person. Thus, in asking the questions as well as in listening to the answers you must be guided by compassion and by attempts at understanding the other person's feelings rather than by a desire to manipulate him. Since such a desire can be unconscious, you must take any accusation to that effect very seriously; that is, you must *listen* to it with an open mind.

# 20. "I AM FED UP WITH BEING TREATED THAT WAY."

## *Rule 20: Beware of playing destructive games.*

Games are interpersonal transactions involving covert as well as overt communication. While many games are positive and "fun," others are highly destructive and antithetical to emotional health. But the destructiveness of a game is seldom realized by the persons playing it. As a matter of fact, the participants do not even see the interaction as a game and, even when they are in psychotherapy, are often reluctant to come to the realization that they are participating in a game at all. On the contrary, each participant considers himself an innocent victim of the other person's unreasonableness! This is partly because of the unconscious purpose of a destructive game and partly because of the failure to look at the covert communication involved.

Psychologists who see patients suffering from marital discord are familiar with the "innocent victim" syndrome. It is manifested by each spouse coming in and listing the sins and faults of his partner. His own contributions to the creation of the problem are denied, minimized, or expressed in vague terms ("I know I have faults, too, but . . .") which may be difficult to pin down (except by listening to the other spouse).

The person who makes a life style out of being an innocent victim has often—and with good reason—been described as an "injustice collector" or "rejection collector." The process of collecting injustices and rejections is, of course, not confined to intimate relationships, such as between husband and wife, parent and child, and brother and sister. It can—and frequently does—occur between employer and employee, salesman and customer, teacher and student. These partners who get involved in destructive games of providing and collecting injustices are usually unaware of playing any game at all and can therefore not stop playing the game. How could one solve a problem if one is not aware of its existence?

In this section we will, therefore, examine games in terms of their covert as well as their overt communicative aspects. We will start by defining the concept of "game" as it is used in this book.

A positive or constructive game can be defined as a repetitive and rather predictable interaction with consciously or unconsciously set rules, in which the result is that each party feels good (positive, pleased, accepting, even neutral, but not negative) about himself and the other party at the conclusion of the game. Thus, the conscious feeling of both parties must be enjoyment (or acceptance) in order for the game to be classified as positive.

Examples of positive games in daily living would include certain social amenities, friendly rituals and arrangements, affectionate teasing, flirting (only when no party is hurt), guessing games, pleasant surprises, compliments, etc. But—it must be stressed—the games remain positive and nondestructive only if both parties consciously enjoy or accept the interaction. Some people cannot stand certain rituals that seem pleasant to others. In such a case, if Partner A likes guessing games, for example, and insists on playing them even though Partner B hates them, then the game must be defined as destructive.

A negative or destructive game can be defined as a repetitive and rather predictable interaction with *unconsciously* set rules* in which the result is that both parties feel indignant, angry, self-righteous, unfairly treated, and—sometimes —secretly triumphant.

A negative game can be seen as a type of neurotic interaction. In a typical neurotic interaction, the conscious and unconscious wishes of Partner A are identical to the conscious and unconscious wishes of Partner B and an unconscious collusion between the partners to keep a problem going can be said to exist. The conscious feeling in a neurotic interaction is one of frustration, despair, and indignation.

In the game-type of neurotic interaction the unconscious purpose involves setting a trap for the other person (usually by provoking him into being unreasonable). When he walks into the trap, the unconscious purpose (winning, showing power, showing superiority, covering up guilt feelings, hurting the partner, avoiding sexual intercourse, being justified in "giving up," etc.) is accomplished for this one time. The unconscious need is momentarily satisfied, but as the need builds up, the game will be repeated. The *consciously* felt purpose of each game is to be reasonable and to get the other person to stop being unreasonable. Destructive games are often carried on under the conscious purpose of exercising a "self-evident" right. Each participant then sees his own negative reaction as being caused by the other person's unreasonableness. In the game type of neurotic interaction, the feeling of "being right" is usually strong in both parties and each party feels that he or she is an essentially innocent victim of the other person's lack of cooperation.

The achievement of a feeling of indignation plays an extremely important role in neurotic (negative, or destructive) games. The immediate purpose (hurting the partner, avoiding closeness, etc.) is difficult to accomplish unless one's conscience is placated by a feeling of indignation or outrage. Thus, the partner must be underhandedly maneuvered into a position (the trap) of being unreasonable. This is best ac-

---

*Only sadists engage *consciously* in destructive games. A sadist is here defined as a person who consciously enjoys hurting another person even in the absence of anger.

complished through a breach of Rule 10 (be honest about your feelings) and by using underhanded and unfair fighting techniques such as were listed in our discussion of Rule 11, although the breach of other communication rules also plays an important role. When the partner has been maneuvered into a position of being unreasonable, one can feel "justifiably indignant" and go ahead with the destructive payoff: launching a vicious attack, stomping out of the room, getting drunk, avoiding or refusing sex, being unfaithful, running home to mother, etc. Since the entire process of maneuvering is unconscious, neither player is aware of what actually goes on.

Destructive games can sometimes be stopped by both partners being willing to *define* and examine the interaction in question as a game. Many people are, of course, not willing to enter into such an examination, the reason often being that such scrutiny would involve a threat to an already weak self-concept.

When two people are involved in a destructive interaction, the "game nature" of their communication is often apparent to an objective observer. There is often a great deal of pre-occupation with who started it, as if that were an extremely important issue. The implication here is, of course, that the participants are following certain rules and that the rules stress the importance of who starts the game. Since games are repetitive and "moves" are made in a fairly predictable pattern, an outside observer—and sometimes even the participants!—can also observe a tendency which could be expressed as "If you say (do) this, I'll say (do) that, and if you say (do) that, I'll say (do) this," almost as if the statements or actions were cards thrown on the table in a bridge game. Sometimes the fact that the repetitive interaction follows rather rigid rules is implicitly recognized through statements such as "Here we go again!" or "We have been through this same thing a thousand times before!" A clear sign that the participants are engaged in a game is the frequent preoccupation with who should make the last move: "You always have to have the last word, don't you!" or "You never let me have the last word!" This preoccupation in itself shows that the participants (both the accuser and the hugger of the last word) are more interested in playing the game than in achieving a solution to whatever problem is being discussed. Throughout many neurotic games an objective observer can also notice a definite competition between the participants as to who has more reason to feel indignant (as we pointed out above, the feeling of indignation is very useful in a neurotic sense, since it can be used as an excuse for one's own destructive actions or lack of positive action).

In many games, however, the game quality is not readily apparent to the untrained observer. Let us, therefore, take an example of a destructive game, dissect it move by move in the manner often done in chess books, and thus put it under a "mental microscope," so that it can be analyzed fully. To some readers this type of dissection may seem silly. It may seem like a tempest in a teapot. But, as we have pointed out earlier, it is of this type of interaction—involving seemingly minor matters—that chronic unhappiness and dissatisfaction are made. And in order to stop such interactions one needs to understand them fully. Therefore, we will analyze the purpose or effect of each "move" (statement or action) made by the participants in our example, as well as point out which communication rules they are breaking.

Joe and his wife Carol are coming in for psychotherapy combined with marriage counseling. Joe has recently been fired from his job because of irresponsibility (coming in late, putting off important assignments, etc.). His days are primarily spent in watching television and taking naps on the couch in the living room (Joe is also hypochondriacal and prone to getting "headaches," which he feels he can cure best by "resting"). He is slow and lackadaisical about getting another job and he does not help his wife much in running the household. Unconsciously he is uncertain of himself as a man, creates excuses to avoid sex, and much prefers to play the role of a naughty little boy. Without being aware of it, he originally chose Carol because she seemed willing to play the role of mother.

Carol works as a head nurse in a hospital cardiac emergency and intensive care unit. Her job is difficult and stressful and involves long hours. Consciously Carol deeply resents her husband's lackadaisical attitude, yet has not learned to be open and frank in her communication, except when she is having an anger outburst. Instead, she "bottles up" her feelings and periodically explodes. Unconsciously Carol is afraid of sex and sees it as dirty and therefore prefers to play mother to Joe and keep him as her naughty boy. In other words, despite her conscious rage at the way he treats her, she has an unconscious stake in keeping him a little boy. As we mentioned above, Joe, too, unconsciously wants to remain a child who is taken care of by mother; this, then, can be seen as the main neurotic interaction of which the game-type interaction described below is merely a part.

Joe and Carol have a nine-year-old daughter, Janie, with whom they have many problems which we shall not illustrate here.

It is five-thirty on a Friday and Carol arrives home to find her husband watching a TV soap opera "as usual."

| *Overt Communication* | *Analysis of Message Involved* |
|---|---|
| *Carol* (comes in hurriedly): | Hurrying would usually be considered neutral behavior. In this case, however, it could be provocative and could constitute Unfair Technique 11-X (rubbing in), especially if Carol moves with exaggerated "busyness" in a preconscious attempt to emphasize how hard she works and how little time she has in comparison with lazy Joe. |
| *Joe* (sprawled in an easy chair, watching television): | Can be neutral but in this context it is clearly provocative and constitutes a breach of Rule 1 and Unfair Technique 11-X (rubbing in both the fact that he is not doing anything to help and the fact that there is nothing Carol can do about it). |
| *Carol* (cheerfully): "Hi, Joe, I'm home." | Ordinarily positive or neutral, but the cheerfulness is in this case actually a breach of Rule 10, since Carol feels very disappointed when she sees Joe watching television rather than helping with the work in the house. |
| *Joe* (grunts something unintelligible): | Unfair Technique 11-XIV and Rule 14. |
| *Carol* (whining): "Aren't you going to greet me?" | Breach of Rule 17. |
| *Joe* (absentmindedly): "Hi." | Breach of Rule 14. |

| | |
|---|---|
| *Carol:* "Did you get the lamb chops?" | Neutral, but in this context probably part of the setting of a trap. |
| *Joe:* "What was that, honey?" | Breach of Rule 19. |
| *Carol:* "I asked you if you got the lamb chops that I planned for dinner tonight." | Neutral, but in this context probably part of the setting of a trap. |
| *Joe:* "No, gee, honey. I didn't get around to it." | The shortness of the answer, the absence of sincere apology, and the absence of adequate explanation constitute provocation and violate Rule 14. |
| *Carol* (incredulous): "You didn't get around to it?" | Rubbing it in and therefore Unfair Technique 11-X |
| *Joe* (silent, absorbed in the program he is watching): | Unfair Technique 11-XIV and Rule 14. |
| *Carol* (whining again). "Well, aren't you at least going to say you're sorry?" | Breach of Rule 17. Joe asks to be treated like a child and Carol complies. |
| *Joe* (irritated, flaring up): "All right, I'm sorry, I'm sorry, I'm sorry! Let me at least see the end of this show, will you!" | Pretending that Carol's request is unreasonable and that she prevents him from seeing the end of the show. Unfair Technique 11-I and Rule 14. |
| *Carol* (silent): | Breach of Rule 10 and Unfair Technique 11-XIV |

(Ten minutes later.)

| | |
|---|---|
| *Joe:* "Honey, you don't mind if I have a nap before dinner, do you?" | In itself neutral, but seen against the background of the current situation and the relationship between Joe and Carol, the request is a clear provocation. It constitutes a breach of Rule 1 since it communicates in *action:* "I do not want to help you." It also sets a trap for Carol because if she says no, Joe can now or later accuse her of being unreasonable; on the other hand, if she says yes he can later say that she herself agreed to |

| | his request and therefore has nothing to squawk about. |
| --- | --- |
| *Carol* (in a resigned voice): "No, go ahead." | Breach of Rules 1 (resigned voice) and 10. |

Joe takes a nap on the couch. Carol heats up a can of macaroni, to which she adds a cheese sauce of her own invention and other odds and ends. She takes pride in her ability to quickly improvise a good meal from modest ingredients. Joe does not care much for macaroni, while Carol and Janie do. However, when Carol reaches out for the can of macaroni she does not consciously think of the fact that Joe does not like it.

Carol calls Joe to dinner but he is hard to wake up and—when awakened—takes his time in coming to the table.

(During dinner.)

| | |
| --- | --- |
| *Carol:* "What do you think of it?" | Ordinarily neutral or positive (showing interest), but here part of setting a trap, since Carol knows that Joe does not like macaroni. Also a breach of Rule 4. |
| *Joe:* "Think of what?" | Neutral if Joe really does not understand what Carol means. Here probably unconsciously provocative and teasing, a breach of Rule 18 (teasing). |
| *Carol:* "The food, of course." | "Of course" in this connection means "you stupid idiot" and is thus Unfair Technique 11-X. |
| *Joe* (deprecatingly, with a sigh): "It's all right." | Simultaneous breach of Rule 1 (sighing), Unfair Technique 11-X (rubbing in), and breach of Rule 14. Joe is unconsciously escalating the conflict and setting a trap for Carol. |
| *Carol:* "That's real appreciation, thanks." | Carol falls into the trap and uses Unfair Technique 11-XIII (sarcasm). Escalates. |
| *Joe:* "What do you expect? Am I supposed to sit here and drool over lukewarm food?" | Further escalation. Unfair Technique 11-I and 11-XIII and, of course, breach of Rule 14. |

*Carol:* "I suppose it is my fault that you took so long coming to the table."

Unfair Technique 11-I and 11-XIII.

*Joe:* "Anyway, you know I just love macaroni."

Breach of Rule 10, use of Unfair Technique 11-I and 11-XIII.

(Silence.)

*Carol:* "I *asked* you to get the lamb chops."

Trying to induce guilt, rubbing it in. Unfair Technique 11-IX and 11-X.

*Joe* (screaming): "Goddamn it, must I hear about those lamb chops for the rest of my life?"

Escalating. Breach of Rule 5, Unfair Technique 11-I and 11-VIII.

(Silence for the rest of the dinner.)

*Joe* (looks at his watch): "Well, I'd better get ready for that job interview."

In ordinary circumstances, neutral. Here clearly provocative, since Joe has not told Carol about it in advance. Breach of Rule 4.

*Carol:* "What? A job interview? At this time in the evening? I thought we could have a nice evening at home for a change."

Understandable and "normal" reaction, but "I thought" breaks Rule 6 and "for a change" is Unfair Technique 11-XIII.

*Joe:* "All right, it is not exactly a job interview, but you said I should take all the opportunities I could. So I'm going to meet Bob (distant acquaintance) for a drink. He said he might be able to get me a job with his brother's firm."

Breaks Rule 16 (excuses) and Rule 5 (minimizing: Joe knows—and knows that Carol knows—that it is not going to be *one* drink).

*Carol* (silent, looks disappointed):

Breach of Rules 1 and 10 and Unfair Technique 11-XIV.

*Joe:* "Well, don't look so glum now again; it was *you* who said I don't look hard enough for . . ."

Breach of Rules 3 and 7, and Unfair Technique 11-X ("glum now again"), and breach of Rules 14 and 16. Joe's pretense that it was Carol who forced him to make the appointment with Bob can also be seen as a crazy-making Unfair Technique (11-XI) if it is typical.

*Carol:* "All right, all right!" (rushes to get Joe's clothes ready)

Part of setting a trap, as shown by subsequent events.

*Joe* (on his way out): "You don't mind taking out the trash this one time, do you? I'm really in a hurry."

In view of the history and the current context this constitutes extreme provocation and lights the fuse for Carol's later explosion. Breach of Rules 14 and 16.

*Carol* (expressionless, but icy): "OK."

Part of trapping Joe into unreasonable behavior which can later be rubbed in. Carol is accommodating Joe and unconsciously setting him up as the target for a later indignant and explosive outburst. Also a breach of Rules 1 and 10.

*Joe:* "Well, aren't you going to wish me good luck?"

An unconsciously hypocritical attempt to cover up the hostility of the interaction (see Unfair Technique 11-VI).

*Carol* (sighing, indifferent voice): "Good luck."

Breach of Rules 1 and 10 and— through exact and laconic repetition of Joe's words—Unfair Technique 11-XIII.

*Joe:* "Good-bye, honey. Remember I love you."

Again an unconsciously hypocritical attempt to cover up the hostility of the interaction.

*Carol:* "Bye." (Slams the door shut.)

Breach of Rules 1, 10, and 14.

(Two-thirty A.M.)

*Joe* (somewhat tipsy, cheerful): "Hi, honey, I'm back. Why are you up so late? You need your sleep, you know."

Picking up where he left off, by "covering up." The lateness and intoxication communicate: "I don't give a hoot about your feelings," thus a breach of Rule 1.

*Carol* (screaming): "You god-
dam bastard! I hate you, I
spit on you, I wish you'd die
so I would be rid of you"
(etc.).

Unfair Techniques 11-VIII and
11-X.

A violent argument ensues in which Joe is first surprised
over Carol's anger but then starts lashing out at her himself.
The argument ends up with physical fighting, after which
(both having accomplished their unconscious mission and
fallen into each other's traps) Carol runs into the bedroom
crying and Joe goes to sleep on the couch in the living room.

Let us now examine the ways Joe and Carol present the
situation when they come in for their separate appointments
the next Monday. Their statements are given juxtaposed, so
that they can be compared more conveniently. Keep in mind
that each is sincere in his view of the situation and is not
unconsciously trying to color it to his or her advantage.

*Joe:* "Doctor Wahlroos, my
wife did it again! She tells me
to look for work and when I
do and try my darndest, she
gets mad. Frankly, Doctor, if
this doesn't stop, I don't know
if I want to try any longer."

*Carol:* "Doctor Wahlroos, my
husband is driving me crazy. He
does nothing all day and at night
he goes out and gets drunk. He
is getting me to a point where
I think I hate both him and
myself. I am seriously thinking
of divorce."

*Dr. W.:* "Tell me what
happened."

*Dr. W.:* "Tell me what
happened."

*Joe:* "All right. I guess it must
have started with her getting
all bent out of shape just because I forgot to get something
for her from the store. She
never forgets my mistakes, she
keeps bringing them up and
torturing me with them. And
then she got mad about my
going to a job interview, even
though she constantly nags me
about setting one up. And
when I came home a little
later than I expected, she
screamed at me like a maniac.
She even scratched me with

*Carol:* "Well, everything went
fine until he left to go bar-
hopping again. Then I started
thinking about how he treats me.
He never helps with anything
that needs to be done around the
house; I have to take care of
everything. He sleeps all day and
he even makes me take down
the trash after I come home tired
from the hospital. And then he
goes out drinking all night while
I slave for all of us. And when
he comes all drunk and wants
sex, I can't take it any longer. I
fly off the handle and I say and

her claws. Just look!" (Shows a tiny scratch on his hand.) "I give up, I'm not going to try any more."

do things I am ashamed of later. But that is no excuse for him to beat me up!"

Note how Joe carefully (but automatically and unconsciously) leaves out his own provocations in recounting the story. The unconscious purpose is to portray himself as an innocent victim of Carol's unreasonableness and cruelty.

Note similarly that Carol carefully, yet unconsciously, omits the fact that she said "yes" both to Joe's request to take a nap instead of helping her and to his asking her to take down the trash. Carol's unconscious purpose is also to portray herself as an innocent victim.

This is a game which—with different variations—has gone on for a long time in Joe's and Carol's relationship. Before Joe was fired, the game was played less often and less hard, but now it is played frequently and unmercifully. The reason for the intensification is the added insecurity on the part of both of them plus the shared secret fear that Joe is losing his "manhood" (thus the unconscious desire to avoid sex).

What is the game from Joe's viewpoint? The immediate unconscious object is to trap Carol into being unreasonable (and thus achieve justification for avoiding sex). Joe accomplishes this by one inconsideration and provocation after another, each in itself of minor significance (but of major significance to Carol because of her feeling that she gets no support from her husband). Let us list and analyze the inconsiderations and provocations, juxtaposing them to the excuses Joe offers in his therapy. This is done on pages 246-250.

Then, in conclusion, let us give some examples of what Joe and Carol could have done to stop (or facilitate stopping) the game at different points of the interaction:

1. Joe could have shown determination and energy in trying to find a job. This would make Carol less allergic to his television watching and napping. (It would, however, go counter to his strong unconscious need to be a little boy; hence the need for psychotherapy.)

2. Joe and Carol could have agreed that Joe will fix the dinner himself whenever he "forgets" or does not "get around" to carrying out his part of the preparation. As a matter of fact, he could fix (or learn to fix) the dinners as

long as he is out of work (but he should not use this task as an excuse for not looking for a job).

3. Joe, knowing that his television viewing and napping are powerful irritants to Carol, could have decided not to engage in either "activity" in Carol's presence, at least not as long as he is out of work.

4. Carol could have put her foot down at any point and demanded a discussion or "constructive fight" about Joe's provocations (Rule 9). This could have been scheduled immediately or within the next forty-eight hours, depending upon Joe's feelings about it.

5. Even at the time of the final explosion, something could have been done. There was nothing inevitable about it: both parties had a free choice (or would have had it, had they not fooled themselves). Carol could have talked about her anger and fury and presented her demands without total unreasonableness. Joe, on the other hand, was not so tipsy that he could not have shown consideration for and understanding of Carol's feelings (as evidenced by the—unconsciously provocative—words: "You need your sleep, you know"). He could then have promised to mend his ways starting the morning of the same day (being, of course, careful not to start a new game involving broken promises).

| Operations | Excuses | Analysis |
|---|---|---|
| 1. Not buying the lamb chops. | "No human being is perfect, for heaven's sake." | This technique (unconscious) is clever in all its simplicity. If Carol get overtly angry, Joe can accuse her of "making a federal case out of it." If she doesn't get overtly angry, he gets away with another inconsideration. Meanwhile he is building up her unexpressed anger toward the eventual goal of an explosion. All this is done unconsciously, of course. |
| 2. Inattention to Carol and absorption in television. | "I merely asked if I could see the end of the program. Can't a man be allowed to relax a little in the afternoon without his wife getting bent all out of shape?" | This technique adds insult to injury. Joe knows very well how Carol feels about his TV-watching and what an irritation it is to her, especially now when he is not working. This method serves the purpose of building up her anger toward later explosion. At the same time it is an invitation for Carol to pick on Joe. |
| 3. The irritated voice, together with an (actually insulting) apology. | "I apologized, didn't I? What more does she want? Must I be her slave and crawl at her feet? Anyway, she's always reading something into what I say; I can't win." | Through this technique, Joe can attack Carol under the guise of being reasonable and apologizing. At the same time—if he is called on the irritated voice—he can say that she "drove him" to become irritated by her whining. |
| 4. The request to be "allowed" to take a nap. | "She herself said it was OK. What is she squawking about?" | A clever trap. If Carol says "no," Joe will accuse her of being unreasonable. If she says "OK," he will get away with using an irritant even more powerful than looking |

| Operations | Excuses | Analysis |
|---|---|---|
| | | at television. Carol's "bottled-up" anger is being built up further. |
| 5. The deprecating attitude about the food. | "I said it was OK, didn't I? Why did she have to press it?" | Adding more insult to injury. Joe knows that Carol does not like to serve canned food and that she would not deliberately select macaroni with the conscious purpose of irritating him. Unconsciously, however, he also knows that he can get her to mention the lamb chops again if he criticizes the food. He does it in such a way that he can later claim—and himself believe—that she "drove" him to voice his disapproval by pressing the issue. And when she then does bring up the lamb chops, he can accuse her of an unforgiving attitude. |
| 6. The outburst about Carol's mentioning the lamb chops a second time. | "Well, after all, there are limits to how much a man can take! Why can't she ever let go of an issue?" | Carol has fallen into the trap and nagged Joe about the lamb chops a second time. Joe's outburst at this point serves the purpose of making Carol feel guilty for being "unforgiving." Having "established" Carol's unforgiving attitude, Joe can then use this incident to justify his later anger. |
| 7. Mentioning the "job interview" at the last minute. | "It just skipped my mind, that's all! Why make a federal case out of it? Anyway, in the mood she was in we would just have had a | This maneuver was probably at least partly conscious or preconscious. Joe consciously wanted to have his evening out with a minimum of hassle and without having to feel guilty. He knew from previous experience that Carol would get mad. Therefore he postponed telling her |

| Operations | Excuses | Analysis |
|---|---|---|
| | longer argument had I mentioned it earlier!" | about it until the last moment, using "her mood" as an excuse. |
| 8. Calling the evening out a "job interview." | "Well, she did say I should take all opportunities, so what is she mad for, anyway?" | There is no doubt that one part* of Joe feels guilty about not doing enough to help Carol (and himself). He wants to drown out this guilt, partly by convincing himself that his friend *might* be willing and able to get him a job and partly by getting Carol to be unreasonable, so that his "justified anger" will hide his guilt. |

Through the use of these inconsiderations and provocations, each one covered by an excuse, Joe has trapped Carol into losing control and being unreasonable, leaving him with the feeling of being an indignant but essentially innocent victim of her unreasonableness.

Let us now look at the game from Carol's viewpoint. Her unconscious purpose is to trap Joe into continuing his inconsiderations and provocations until she can spring the trap and "let him have it" (by which act she simultaneously falls into *his* trap without realizing it). She does it by letting him go further and further without her openly stating her feelings to him. Let us list and analyze her steps in succession, together with her excuses.

| Operations | Excuses | Analysis |
|---|---|---|
| 1. Demanding that Joe apologize for forgetting the lamb chops. | "Well, the least he could do was to apologize! I must be entitled to *some* consideration, for heaven's sake." | This is a clever technique because it provokes Joe into anger while at the same time supporting Carol's pretense that she *is* being open about her feelings. |

*The reader may wonder what "part" of Joe I am referring to. In psychological terms I am referring to the portion of the superego. In practical, everyday language I mean the following. Most of us, when we do something we shouldn't or when we don't do what we should, are aware of an "inner voice" telling us that our behavior is wrong. It is this part of human personality, "conscience," if you will, that I am referring to.

| Operations | Excuses | Analysis |
|---|---|---|
| 2. "Consenting" to Joe's request to be "allowed" to take a nap. | "It would have just started an argument if I had told him how I felt. I think I am entitled to a little peace when I come home, and at least he is not around to bother me when he is sleeping." | This maneuver encourages Joe to take further advantage and adds to Carol's ammunition ("You have the stomach to go and sleep after doing nothing all day when I have to stand in the kitchen and slave after a hard day's work!"). At the same time it allows Joe to pretend that his nap was really OK since Carol said "yes." |
| 3. Asking what Joe thought about the food. | "I was just trying to have a nice conversation. Why couldn't he have complimented me instead for doing the best under the circumstances?" | From previous experience Carol should know that Joe does feel guilty but won't admit it. Consciously she wanted to hear a compliment on how well she could manage on short notice; she is desperately hungry for some appreciation from Joe. Unconsciously she must have known (again from previous experience) that he would not give her this appreciation by her asking for it. |
| 4. The sarcasm about not getting appreciation ("That's real appreciation, thanks"). | "Well, what am I supposed to say when he has the gall to criticize something that is his fault in the first place?" | Carol is unconsciously using Joe's guilt feelings to get him angry and even more unappreciative than before. |
| 5. Further sarcasm about why the food is cold. | (Same excuse as number 4 above.) | Carol is "rubbing it in" further in playing on Joe's guilt, unconsciously knowing that an unreasonable outburst is not far off now. |

| Operations | Excuses | Analysis |
|---|---|---|
| 6. Mentioning the lamb chops again. | "But it was his fault that we had to eat canned food. Why doesn't he ever admit to anything?" | This is the trigger for Joe's outburst and at the same time another step in provoking him to keep adding to his "sins." Joe's guilt feelings, combined with his anger, provide the power for the triggered explosion, the magnitude of which Carol could have predicted if she had examined previous interactions. (Unconsciously such a prediction must have taken place.) At the same time, Carol plays into Joe's hands by giving him "cause" to call her unwilling to forgive and forget. Unknowingly, she also gives him an excuse for further postponing telling her that he is going out. |
| 7. Agreeing to take down the trash cans. | "Well, he *was* in a hurry; what else could I have done?" | This is the major and final step in the setting of the trap which will be sprung upon Joe's return. Carol's agreement provides an excuse for Joe ("She said it was OK, didn't she?"), but the fact that she did take down the trash will be used in the assault on him when he returns. Carol's *conscious* motivation, as usual, is to "avoid a hassle." |

What is meant by a destructive game should now be clear. Nevertheless, it may be useful to take another example, again involving marital fighting. Our old friend, Mrs. G. (whom we met in discussing Rule 16), and her husband can provide a good illustration.

Mrs. G. complained that her husband was not attentive and nice to her, but through her own examples it could be seen that she was engaged in a game with him which had the purpose of discouraging him from being attentive and nice, so that Mrs. G. could feel indignant and not have to feel guilty about her own destructive behavior. For the husband the game served the purpose of his being able to say: "No matter how hard I try she finds fault with it, so what is the use, I might as well give up." Here is a typical example of how the game would be played:

Mrs. G. complained to me that her husband *never* took her to a restaurant so that she could go out to eat for a change. When I explored this complaint in more detail, it turned out that the husband does ask her out, but whenever he suggests going to a particular restaurant, Mrs. G. says: "Oh, I don't want to go to that one *again;* do we *always* have to go to that one?" On the other hand, if the husband leaves the choice of restaurant up to his wife, she accuses him of not being aggressive and manly and not taking the initiative.

Or, Mrs. G. might say: "I am tired of our *always* going out alone; why couldn't we go out with another couple for a change? You never take me out together with another couple." If the husband then suggests that they go out with the Joneses across the street, she replies: "Why do we *always* have to go with them; couldn't we go out with somebody else some time?" (On the other hand, if the husband had suggested going out with a couple with whom they have not been out with before, Mrs. G. would have put a different card on the table: "Why do we always have to go out with strangers; I think it is much nicer to go with someone that we know well.") If the husband then says: "OK, let's go with the Smiths," Mrs. G. puts out her trump card and says: "Well, by now you have ruined all the fun of going out anyway; I can't go out and have a good time when I have to fight so hard every time for every little thing I ask for." The husband can then draw his trump card and say (or think): "Well, I'll be damned if I ever ask you to go out with me again." Both have "won" the game, in a neurotic sense: they have demonstrated that the other one is unreasonable, feel indignant about the unreasonableness, and feel they have tried all they can and can now give up trying. In terms of emotional health they have both lost the game, because the destructive parts of their personalities have been given free rein.

An untrained observer may feel that Mr. G. is an innocent victim in this game, at least until the finale. A trained observer of neurotic games would see it differently. Mr. G. has played this game many times before (although he does not consciously think of it as a game any more than his wife does). Because of having played it before he knows exactly what cards his wife is going to pull. He could easily attempt to stop the game by presenting his dilemma to his wife. He could, for example, say: "I have been thinking this over and I feel I haven't been taking you out enough lately. I'd like to take you to the——restaurant, but tell me if you would like another one instead. I'd like to go just with you (or with the Joneses, depending on Mr. G.'s preference), but tell me if you have some couple in mind you would rather go with." If Mrs. G. is a hard player, she will still answer something destructive, but at least Mr. G. can then truly say that he tried (although he cannot use the fact that he tried as an excuse for giving up).

Similarly, Mrs. G. can attempt to stop the game by not finding fault with her husband's suggestions or by making specific suggestions herself. If Mr. G. is a hard player, he will then come up with something destructive, such as: "Come to think of it, we'd better not go. You know I have to get up very early to play golf tomorrow," but at least Mrs. G. has tried; she is "clean" for the time being.

Games involving "false pride" are potentially tragic. They are played in many variations, the most common being a sort of waiting game which is played after friends, lovers, or relatives, for that matter, have broken up after a quarrel. In this game each party feels that the other party should "make the first move" (note the actual game terminology involved) toward reconciliation. If both partners are hard players or just stubborn, it is possible that they will live out their lives without ever again having contact with each other! There are many examples of such tragedies in life, tragedies which are actually created by the participants in perfect cooperation.

This book contains many examples of destructive games involving parent and child. Nagging situations, for example, are neurotic interactions which involve definite game components, since one of the objects in nagging and being nagged is to see who will "give in." The following example involves a destructive game in which one party teases and the other nags.

> Mrs. H. has finally "given in" (the phrase itself is an almost certain sign of a neurotic game going on) and taken her twelve-year-old son Freddy to an army surplus store to look at a knife which he has seen advertised. He asks his mother if he can buy the knife and Mrs. H. gives a noncommittal answer: "Hmmm." This is a signal for the boy to start whining and nagging his mother, who replies with excuse after excuse: "It is too expensive" (Freddy: "But I'll pay for it with my own money"), "I think we'll have to ask your father first" ("But you know I talked with him yesterday and he said it would be OK if you thought so, too"), "You'll probably lose it anyway, just as you did with that Swiss army knife last year" ("No, I won't and anyway that would be my money that would be lost, not yours"), and then a trump card: "Anyway, it doesn't look safe to me." At this point Freddy gets desperate and starts being sassy, which is the signal for the mother to play her ace and say: "Since you behave that way, I'm not going to let you buy the knife." Freddy then plays his ace, which may be embarrassing his mother right there in the store, or some other revenge.

Again, to the untrained observer, Freddy may appear as the innocent victim of his mother who, by her vacillation, actually teased him into becoming sassy. In a theoretical sense he might be innocent inasmuch as he was born to a mother who was a neurotic game player and who—unwittingly—taught him to play destructive games with her. However, since the mother also is consciously unaware of any game going on, she too can theoretically be considered an innocent victim. Actually, in practical terms both are equally guilty, so the question of guilt is irrelevant. The fact is that both have played the game many times in different versions. Mrs. H. knows exactly what kind of reaction her vacillation (which she rationalizes as being prudent consideration of all facts) will have on her son. She could have stopped the game by making up her mind beforehand which factors would make her say yes and which would make her say no, so that there would be no need for her to vacillate and thus tease her son into being sassy.

Freddy, on the other hand, has played the game just as many times and knows exactly what tactics his mother uses to get him to be sassy. If he really wanted the knife and had no unconscious motivation to fight with his mother (stemming from neurotic sources such as wanting to show his power, deny incestuous desires, or punish her and himself for something), he would not let himself be provoked into sassy behavior. On the contrary, he would kindly and calmly present his mother with the facts as he saw them. Even the trump card, "It doesn't look safe to me," could be met constructively with a "Mother, please don't get mad at my saying this but if the knife really were unsafe, Dad would have brought up that point yesterday and you would have said 'No' the minute you saw the knife" (all said in a respectful and calm voice).

A twelve-year-old would not talk that way? Nonsense; I know many who do and I have taught many to talk respectfully to their parents (while at the same time being open about their feelings) even when it is questionable that the parents' behavior invites the respect. Freddy is perfectly capable of not sassing his mother, just as she is capable of thinking about issues beforehand and stopping the teasing of her son.

Missing from the written story above are elements which would be obvious if we had a sound-film or video-recording of the incident. These elements include the mother's hesitant voice and her irritating facial expression as she tries to find ways of "wiggling out" of buying the knife. They also include Freddy's whining—and finally insulting—voice as well as his increasingly defiant and contemptuous facial expressions. If the reader could hear and see Freddy as his tone gets more and more sassy and his facial expression angrier and more contemptuous, there would be less of a tendency to see him as an innocent victim. The fact is that he and his mother are involved in playing destructive games, and as long as they do not recognize the games as such they cannot stop them. If such recognition cannot be achieved at home or if it does not lead to a discontinuation of the games, the family has to contact a psychologist for help.

Another common destructive game is based on the fact that people's perceptions as well as their memory is dependent upon their needs. Consider the following question and its answer:

*Question:* A week ago my fourteen-year-old daughter asked me if she could sleep over at a friend's house the next Saturday, which is today. I remember telling her that she could not, because we would have to leave early on Sunday morning to visit some relatives who live out of town. Yesterday she reminded me that I had promised her she could do it! Now she is angry with me for "breaking my promise." What do I do?

*Answer:* The first thing to do is to tell her that you recognize that people sometimes differ not only in their memory of what they have heard, but even in what they hear at the time a statement is made! This holds for all types of perception. Two honest and trustworthy witnesses can, for example, observe the same accident yet see altogether different things as having taken place, even if neither one has any conscious or unconscious stake in presenting the accident in a particular way. When a person has a conscious or unconscious need to see or remember a story a certain way, the possibility of distortion of both perception and memory is, of course, even greater. Thus, you must make it clear that you realize your daughter can be absolutely sure she heard you correctly, just as *you* can be absolutely sure she did *not* hear you correctly. Such distortions, if infrequent, are just a fact of life that must be accepted.

However, if the distortions occur frequently and lead to chronic arguments with each party feeling indignant, there is a strong possibility that they are unconsciously manufactured for neurotic satisfactions (feeling indignant and self-righteous, hiding more basic and threatening feelings, etc.) and thus constitute a neurotic game. There is a simple way to break up this game without seeking psychotherapeutic help. All you need to do if the problem is repetitive is to make an agreement that whenever your daughter wants to aks your permission for something she will write it out and then you will initial it! This will make misunderstandings and distortions virtually impossible. Many people are reluctant to do it, their conscious reason being that it involves distrust (the unconscious reason is usually that they are reluctant to give up the game). Actually, no distrust need be present at all; it is a sound procedure to guard against distortions of memory, as is commonly recognized in business and in law without any implication of distrust.

As to the question of what to do for the moment, I would

ask the girl if she can think of a reasonable solution as to how she could come along on the trip Sunday without inconveniencing her hosts. If she can arrange it satisfactorily, why not let her sleep over at her girlfriend's? If she is unable to arrange it, you express your understanding and compassion for her dilemma, but tell her at the same time that she must accept reality.

There are occasions when you need to say to a child: "Tough luck, that's the way things are. If you can find a way of solving the problem to your satisfaction, fine, and I will help you work something out. But if you can't find one and I can't either, then that's it!" (Be sure, however, that your tone is not cold, indifferent, or rejecting when you point out reality to a child.)

As should be obvious from the examples given, it is impossible to play neurotic games if the partners involved abandon the illusion of being an innocent victim and follow the rules of constructive communication. Even if just one partner does this, neurotic games will be almost impossible to play. The most important rule of communication in preventing or stopping neurotic games is Rule 10: be honest about your feelings. Games cannot be played when all cards lie face up on the table. Other important rules in this connection are Rules 11 (do not use unfair communication techniques), 6 (test all your assumptions verbally), 8 (recognize that your family members are experts on your behavior), 9 (do not let discussions turn into destructive arguments), 14 (be tactful and considerate), and, of course, the one we have just discussed: beware of playing destructive games!

# PART 2

## Communication and Emotional Health

In applying the rules given in the first part of this book the immediate goal is to improve communication in the family. But improving communication will also result in enhancing a quality which I have called emotional health; this is the ultimate purpose in improving communication. The second part of this book is therefore intended to describe emotional health and how it is influenced by verbal and especially non-verbal communication.

People sometimes ask me why I use the term "emotionally healthy" instead of the simpler word "normal." As I pointed out briefly in discussing the necessity for being clear and specific in one's communication (Rule 4), the reason is that the word "normal" has too many meanings. "Normal" behavior is, for example, not always what we would like our children to engage in, as Parke Cummings* illustrates so well in the following examples:

An eleven-year-old boy puts in a total of 45 hours cleaning out the garage, pulling weeds, mowing the lawn, and running errands in order to earn the money for a new tennis racket, which he eventually buys. *Abnormal* behavior: The boy practices diligently with his tennis racket and, in due time, becomes an accomplished tennis player. *Normal* behavior: Two days after getting the tennis racket, he removes all the strings and converts them into a line for a "telephone" system. A short time later, he makes the frame of the racket over into a giant slingshot.

A three-year-old girl is presented with a new pail, shovel, and sifter for her sandbox. *Abnormal* behavior: The child takes the toys to her sandbox and plays with them day after day. *Normal* behavior: The child plays with the toys for five

*Copyright © 1951 by Henry Schuman, Inc. Reprinted from *I'm Telling You Kids for the Last Time* by Parke Cummings by permission of Abelard-Schuman Limited, an Intext publisher.

minutes, after which she heaves them into a weed patch. She then makes several trips to the house and proceeds to make sand pies with the following implements: one solid silver spoon, her father's best crystal cocktail shaker, her mother's favorite roasting pan.

Cummings' tongue-in-cheek examples make an excellent point: normal (frequent) behavior is not always normal (desirable) behavior. The word "normal" simply has too many meanings:

1. It may mean regular, conventional, that which is to be expected, something that frequently occurs.

2. It may refer to healthy functioning as opposed to ill health.

3. It may refer to correspondence with a moral code and thus be a synonym for "proper" or "accepted."

As the dictionary will show, there are many other meanings of the word normal, but the three given above are the ones most often confused, the result being ineffective communication. Let us take some examples:

Tooth decay is normal in sense 1 above (it is very frequent), but it is abnormal in sense 2 (it is an unhealthy condition). As far as sense 3 is concerned, it is neither moral nor immoral to suffer from tooth decay.

As another example let us take masturbation. Masturbation is normal in sense 1 (it occurs very frequently, almost everybody has engaged in it during some time of his life), but it is usually considered abnormal in sense 3 (many people see it as improper and even as immoral). As far as sense 2 is concerned, it is neither healthy nor unhealthy to masturbate.

As our third example we could take Albert Schweitzer. He most certainly was an extremely abnormal man in sense 1 (very few people attain his stature as human beings). But in sense 2, and especially sense 3, he was not only normal but "supernormal!"

It should now be clear that we would only achieve confusion in our communication by attempting to use the word "normal." Therefore we will use the term "emotionally healthy" instead and define the characteristics to which the term refers.

Emotional health is a *relative* concept; it exists in degrees. No one, not even an Albert Schweitzer, can attain perfect emotional health; everyone has some shortcomings and drawbacks. Similarly, no one is so disturbed emotionally that there are not some indications of emotional health which can be encouraged and supported. Between Albert Schweitzer on the one hand and a raving maniac or a psychopathic killer on the other there are all shades and degrees of emotional health and ill health. The same is true when it comes to physical health: between the decathlon champion in his best form and the person lying on his deathbed there is an extremely wide range of degrees of health.

It may be best to conceive of emotional health as an ideal state which can only be approached. Our goal then should not be the actual attainment of this state but rather daily attempts to approach it. Keeping this in mind, let us begin to describe emotional health.

# 1. THE STUDENT WHO DOES NOT STUDY, THE HUSBAND WHO SHOWS NO AFFECTION . . .

## *Characteristic I: Helping oneself and others.*

The first characteristic of emotional health is the most important; all others can be seen as corollaries or derivations: AN EMOTIONALLY HEALTHY PERSON IS ONE WHO DOES NOT, FOR SOME CONSCIOUS OR UNCONSCIOUS REASON, HURT HIMSELF OR OTHERS THROUGH HIS ACTIONS OR WORDS; ON THE CONTRARY, HE HELPS HIMSELF AND OTHERS THROUGH HIS ACTIONS AND WORDS.

As Karl Menninger has pointed out in his excellent book, *Man Against Himself,* all of us have an unconscious tendency to hurt ourselves to some extent, to do things that hurt us in the long run, and neglect to do things that would help us or work *for* us in the long run. We have all had the experience, for example, of forgetting an important appointment or postponing doing something we know would best be done now. Sometimes the consequences of this self-hurting behavior are minor, sometimes they can be most serious.

Even such a minor example of hurting yourself as biting your fingernails could sometimes have grave consequences. It could, for example, lead to your missing out on getting the job you want, if the interviewer notices your nails and knows of an equally competent candidate who does not bite his nails!

Other obvious examples of people who hurt themselves are: the student who does not study enough, the driver who is not careful, the husband who does not show his wife enough affection, the alcoholic, the drug addict. The list is endless.

When this self-destructive (or other-destructive) tendency becomes particularly strong in a person, we start to call it emotional disturbance. I think I can safely say that there is only one basic symptom that all of my patients have in common and that is the fact that they in some way hurt themselves or others through their behavior or words or their lack of certain behavior or communications. But often they do not see this tendency in themselves and find it easier to see themselves as innocent victims of the unreasonableness or cruelty of their family members (or bosses or teachers or roommates).

As an example of someone whose tendency to hurt herself was clear and who nevertheless was unable to see the tendency, let me mention a patient, Mrs. C., who recently finished her psychotherapy. When Mrs. C. first came to see me and had given me her long list of complaints (which mostly concerned the unacceptable behavior of the other family members), I asked her whether she could see any way in which she was unwittingly hurting herself and others through her behavior. Her immediate answer was: "No, doctor, that's why I am here! I want to know what I am doing that is wrong, because I can't see it myself." Yet, even by the time I asked this question (in the last half of the second hour), she herself had already—without being aware of it—given several examples of what she was doing to make matters worse between herself and her husband and children. Here are some of the ways in which she was hurting herself and others:

1. Mrs. C. broke several of our Rules of Communication, especially Rule 2 (define what is important and stress it; define what is unimportant and ignore it): she kept finding fault with the actions and words of her husband and children. At those times when she could not find fault with the present behavior, she had a tendency to use Unfair Technique 11-IX: she kept bringing up what her husband and the children had done in the past to hurt her. (She hurt herself through this faultfinding and lack of forgiveness, since it made her husband and children angry with her and thus set the stage for them to engage in further hurtful behavior against her.)

2. She claimed she wanted her husband to take a firmer hand in raising the children, to "act like a father" to them, but when he did make attempts to assume this role, she disagreed with his actions in front of the children and said that he was too strict with them.

3. Mrs. C. was well aware of how particular her husband was about the new furniture they had saved up for; yet she said nothing when the children would scuff it and scratch it through their wild playing.

4. In other ways, however, Mrs. C. overcontrolled her children and spied on them, especially when they reached their early teens. The children resented the overprotective attitude and the snoopiness, and reacted by trying to hide their activities and feelings from her, which in turn led Mrs. C. to become even snoopier and more concerned than ever.

5. Mrs. C. was an over-eater to the point of endangering her health. In this way, in addition to hurting herself she endangered her relationship with her husband who—partly because of her obesity—had begun to find her sexually unattractive. She also hurt her children through her overeating by giving them a poor example of self-discipline.

6. A seemingly minor but rather peculiar way in which Mrs. C. hurt herself and her husband was her low sales resistance! She bought almost everything featured as "special" in the market where she shopped, whether she needed it or not; her home was loaded with encyclopedias since she was such an easy mark for salesmen; she bought pots and pans, brushes, candy, cosmetics, and memberships in record clubs and book clubs. Through these activities she kept her husband busy trying to get out of the contracts she had signed

for, the self-improvement courses, the book clubs, the pay-for-your-funeral-in-advance plans, etc., etc.

Yet Mrs. C.'s words were: "I want to know what I am doing wrong!" To tell her would have been of no avail: it was *she* who had told me these things herself. What was needed was for me first to confront her with the destructive nature of her actions, keeping in mind that her husband and her children also contributed to the destructiveness through their behavior. Secondly, Mrs. C. needed to be encouraged to examine the communicative value of her actions: what was she actually telling her family members through what she did? Furthermore, she needed to look into the basic purposes behind her actions: what needs did they serve for herself and how could these needs be satisfied in a healthier manner? Through this exploration she came to view herself realistically and gained control over the destructive parts of her behavior. When she left psychotherapy she had lost one-third of her weight. But equally important was the fact that she had satisfactory and rewarding relationships with her husband and children. Toward the salesmen, by the way, she had gained the strength to say "no" courteously but firmly.

Many people have the mistaken idea that outpatient psychotherapy is only for people who have major and spectacular symptoms. This is simply not true. The people with major and spectacular symptoms are more often seen in hospitals than on an outpatient basis. The people seen in psychotherapy have "everyday" problems such as Mrs. C. had. These are the people who have realized that they are not doomed to live always in this manner: on the contrary, there is a good chance that the problems can be solved with the assistance of a competent psychologist or psychiatrist (in many cases it is sufficient for the parties concerned to learn constructive principles of communication and apply them in daily living). Other people often do not realize that help is available or they decide to live with their problems (which is all right, as long as children are not involved).

As we pointed out in the introduction to this book, most psychopathology is "everyday" in nature. You do not need to have "major" problems in order to have an unhappy life. Marriages, for example, are seldom unhappy because of major catastrophic events. Rather, they are unhappy because of such seemingly minor matters as, for example, the fact that the spouses communicate poorly or destructively with one another. The unhappiness, the daily torture, may be a result of chronic faultfinding ("picking") by one party and corresponding provocations by the other. The wife may provoke by chronically not putting the milk into the refrigerator and the faultfinding husband falls into the trap by walking into the kitchen and yelling about it. The husband provokes by not putting in a much-needed screen door and the wife falls into the trap by nagging him about it. You can argue as angrily and as viciously about a potato chip on the carpet as you can about sexual infidelity or about whether or not to move to Australia! Life can be made unhappy through sarcastic comments or "merely" a lack of affectionate gestures. These are the matters which lead to divorce, emotional disturbance, and behavior problems in children; so-called major catastrophic events usually do not have that much power.

The tragedy is that there are thousands, nay millions, of people who hurt themselves and their loved ones through such everyday behavior. And the most tragic thing about it is that most of these people do not know and do not realize that such a way of living is not inevitable: help is available in the form of psychotherapy.

From where does this tendency to hurt oneself or others stem?

It probably stems from one or both of two sources: a deficient development of self-discipline and an unconscious *urge* to hurt oneself or others.

A deficient development of self-discipline will result in the individual being unable to adequately control his destructive impulses. Likewise, he will not be able to marshal his constructive impulses into effective efforts to help himself and others. Consequently, one way we can see to it that our children do not hurt themselves or others is by ensuring—through firm, kind, and reasonable discipline—that they will develop a healthy system of self-directed impulse control.

But what about the *urge* to hurt oneself or others? From where does it stem? Actually, it is possible that it is partly an inherited urge. Freud thought so in his later years and referred to this urge as the Thanatos- or death-instinct. But it seems impossible as yet to prove or disprove his theory. A fact that appears to speak for the theory of a universally inherited death instinct is the commonly agreed upon observation that all human beings seem able to hate, while not all seem able to love.* This fact could, of course, be used to support the theory of a familially inherited love instinct. But it could also—and more reasonably—be used in support of the thesis that the ability to love is a "higher" function, more dependent on learning and more specifically "human" than the ability to hate. Be that as it may, we do know that both hatred and love can be encouraged by environmental factors.

It seems easier to explain the desire to hurt *others* (as defense or revenge or, simply, as a reaction to frustration of needs) than it does to explain the desire to hurt *oneself*. However, we do know for certain that some of the desire to hurt oneself stems from unresolved conflicts, destructive wishes, and negative feelings and fantasies which were repressed in childhood and for which the person feels a need to punish himself.

The best antidote against repression is talking about one's feelings! It follows, then, that we have to see to it that our children's feelings and conflicts are not repressed but *communicated*, talked about, discussed, and brought into the open. We have to create an atmosphere in the home where the child feels free to talk about his feelings, problems, and worries.

Note well that I say: TALK about the conflicts and worries. Many people have the mistaken idea that psychologists want children to run around wild and "express themselves" and their feelings through destructive and uncontrolled behavior. There are a few psychologists who subscribe to this view (for example the Summerhill-enthusiasts), but the vast majority of psychologists see unchecked destructive behavior on the part of the child as hurtful both to him and to his environment.

Hostility in some form or other is one of the most common ingredients of emotional illness. It is also the chief impediment to good communication, as we have seen in Part I of this book. Not recognizing or understanding the emotional impact of hostile expression, be it in words or deeds or in lack of words or deeds, leads to countless tragedies in human living. It therefore behooves each one of us to recognize, come to terms with, and control the hostility within us

*"Love" here is defined as the feeling that someone else's happiness and well-being are as important as or more important than one's own and a demonstrable willingness to act upon this feeling.

so that we do not hurt ourselves or others through our actions or lack of action. It similarly behooves us to behave in such a manner as not to give realistic cause for others to give vent to their hostility. Anger must be expressed, not "bottled up" (Rule 10), but it must be done with respect for the feelings of the other human being (Rule 14).

It is important in this connection to differentiate between anger and hatred. Anger is a healthy emotion when it is felt as a reaction to an appropriate stimulus and when it is expressed with reasonable respect for the other person's feelings. However, in moments of intense anger, or as a result of prolonged, chronic anger, an element of hatred may enter. Hatred is a feeling of conscious enjoyment of another person's misery or misfortune, a wish for him to be unhappy or hurt in some way. When hatred is acted upon against another human being, we speak of sadism. Hatred and sadism are signs of emotional disturbance.

The control of hostile-aggressive-hateful-destructive impulses is perhaps the most important task that has ever faced mankind. The achievement of such control would, in effect, mean that earth would be transformed into a paradise where no hostile acts are committed by one human being against another and where, consequently, the dangers that remain arise from extra-human and nonwillful human factors.

Characteristic I is comprehensive; we could end the definition here. All other characteristics are merely partial ways of looking at emotional health. We could say that Characteristic I shows the whole elephant and that the other characteristics merely highlight different parts of the elephant's body. This also means that the selection of the other characteristics is arbitrary: there would be an almost infinite number of ways of describing the different parts of the elephant. As a matter of fact, most psychology books are concerned with describing the elephant and its parts in different ways. In my list I have included those ways of looking at emotional health which have proved most important in my work with patients and which, at the same time, have the greatest degree of relevance with respect to the subject of communication.

Although countless people are leading lives which could best be described as living deaths and which thus constitute a type of long-term self-destruction, the most conspicuous act of self-destruction occurs in the act of suicide or in the attempt to commit suicide. In concluding our discussion of Characteristic I it is therefore important that we give the answer to a frequently asked question.

*Question:* How seriously should you take a person's threat to commit suicide?

*Answer:* Very seriously. You must do everything in your power to get him (her) to see a psychologist or a psychiatrist. Even though a suicidal threat may be a way of gaining attention and even though it may have been preceded by several such threats, it is a most serious indication of emotional disturbance (many suicides are, in fact, preceded by numerous "idle" threats) and a human being's life is in danger. Incidentally, the suicide rate among children and teen-agers is going up. Take very seriously any statements such as, "There is no use in living" or "I wish I were dead"; contact a psychologist or a psychiatrist immediately unless it is very clear that the statements are made in jest and that the person making the statements is not depressed or unhappy.

The majority of suicides resulting in deaths are "accidents."* To understand this fact, we have to recognize that a suicide attempt is a communicative act, a desperate declaration of unhappiness and a call for help. A suicide attempt is also a hostile act, since it communicates—whether the person is aware of it or not—messages such as, "If you had not failed me, I would not have done this," "You will be sorry when I am gone," or "It was your cruelty that killed me." Notes expressing the opposite ("You had nothing to do with this decision," "This will be best for all of you," "I will no longer stand in your way," "You are better off free," etc.) are unconsciously designed to make the partner feel maximum guilt. Because suicide attempts are communicative acts, unconsciously designed to lead to some result (shocking the partner into changing his behavior, punishing the partner, obtaining help, etc.), they are also, as a rule, unconsciously designed in such a way that they are not likely to result in death. But due to accidents such as the husband's not coming home at the usual time, or the friend's telephone line being busy, or

---

*Exceptions are the suicides committed by people suffering from painful terminal illnesses, such as cancer. These suicides carry no communicative message other than the conscious wish to be spared further suffering; are seriously meant on all levels of consciousness, and they are, therefore, in no way accidents.

the action of the pills taken being too fast, etc., the suicide may, indeed, be completed. Therefore, since there is the definite danger that even the first clumsy suicide attempt may lead to death, all threats, hints, or allusions involving self-destruction must be taken very seriously.

It should go without saying that daring another person to go ahead and commit suicide is tantamount to a murder attempt.

# 2. SUPPOSE SOMEONE STEPS ON YOUR TOES . . .

## Characteristic II: Freedom of choice.

The second characteristic of emotional health could be stated as follows: AN EMOTIONALLY HEALTHY PERSON HAS A SENSE OF FREEDOM OF CHOICE. His choices may be limited by external agents, but not by any internal agents other than a code of ethics which is incorruptible and not subject to rationalizations. What I am referring to here is, of course, a *subjectively felt* freedom. I do not wish to get into the ageless philosophical discussion of whether or not "free will" exists or to what extent, if any, it is possible for a human being to have a "truly free" choice. However, it is unquestionably possible for a person to have a subjective sense of freedom of choice, and it is this feeling to which I refer here.

If someone points a pistol at me, my freedom of choice is drastically reduced but, although I will feel anxious and afraid at the moment, I will not become an emotionally disturbed person as a result of this external and temporary limitation of my choices. There are people, however, who in a manner of speaking are chronically pointing a gun at themselves and who limit their own freedom of choice through fears, inhibitions, or a lack of inhibitions. People who are emotionally disturbed usually have less of a subjectively free choice.

Let us take the extreme example of a handwashing compulsion. This used to be a relatively common neurotic symptom; it is not encountered often today. It is clear, however, that the person who suffers from a handwashing compulsion really cannot choose when to wash his hands and when not to. He must wash his hands when he feels the urge; otherwise he will be overwhelmed by a nameless, terrifying anxiety. You and I can choose when we want to wash our hands; a compulsive handwasher cannot.

Let us take a less extreme example, one that can be observed more readily. Suppose someone steps on your toes. You have a clear choice of how to react to the situation. You may smile reassuringly at the "offender" to communicate that no harm was done; you may accept an apology by saying "That's all right" or, if you want to rub it in, you can say, "Next time please watch where you're going." Or if you feel that the action was inexcusably careless, you may react by showing your anger. There are, however, people—we have all encountered them—who have no choice or, rather, who *feel* they have no choice, in the matter: they fly into a rage when someone steps on their toes. They may feel sorry about it afterwards or they may think of rationalizations to "explain" their behavior, such as: "That was just my Irish temper," or "Well, who wouldn't have been angry," or "I am not going to stand there and let people walk all over me." Nevertheless, the fact remains that these people have no subjective sense of being able to choose how to react; they are powerless in the grip of an inner force! These people are slaves to a part of themselves which they do not understand and over which they feel no control. It is one of the tasks of psychotherapy to free these people from such "inner slavery."

Compulsive eaters often have the same feeling of helplessness in the face of the urge; they eat whether they are hungry or not. The classic phobias are examples of this type of limitation on choice which is imposed by "inner" forces. A person who, because of fears and anxieties or inhibitions, "cannot" speak to an audience, fly in an airplane, or ride an elevator is a slave to a part of himself. The same is true of someone who "cannot" become close emotionally to another person or "cannot" ask a girl for a date.

There is only one exception to what we have said. Inner

limitations which are based on a genuine religious conviction or a code of ethics which is incorruptible are not unhealthy. These are "limitations" which serve the *first* characteristic of emotional health: they *help* the person and the ones with whom he comes into contact. It must be remembered, however, that some people use religious tenets and moral considerations as an excuse for their actions or lack of action. Closer examination will reveal whether these considerations are excuses or not, because in the case of excuses we are going to find inconsistencies (Rule 16).

Genuine religious or ethical "limitations" on choice actually free the person in his daily life. Instead of having to waste time fretting over what is "right" or "wrong" he *knows* what is right and acts accordingly. Only when a situation arises in which a fellow human being will be hurt no matter what he does, only then will he be in a conflict. However, he will usually be able to solve this conflict through prayer and consultation with a clergyman or other person of trusted ethical integrity and through an honest fight against the interference of rationalizations and excuses.

Moral and ethical dilemmas cannot and should not be solved by psychologists and psychiatrists. Beware of workers in the mental health field who are self-appointed experts on morals, justice, and national and international politics. Abhorrence of *any* type of dictatorial limitation of individual freedom must, of course, be seen as a characteristic of emotional health, since dictatorship in any form is degrading to a human being. But the self-appointed experts on morals and politics are often hypocrites who cry out against one type of dictatorship while defending or being silent on the subject of another. The fact is, of course, that a psychologist or psychiatrist is no more qualified than you or your next-door neighbor to give advice on ethical or political matters.

In this connection it may be well to point out the difference between psychotherapy and brainwashing, since the latter procedure does involve the "therapist" telling the "patient" what is right and what is wrong.

I have known several cases of people who in desperate need of psychological help have been afraid to come in for psychotherapy, thinking that they will be brainwashed in some way or another. In actuality, however, psychotherapy and brainwashing (as the latter is practiced in present-day totalitarian states) have diametrically opposite goals.

In psychotherapy one of the most important goals is to help widen and increase the choices available to a person. We psychotherapists try to remove those factors (except ethical ones) which limit a person's choices; we try to remove fears, anxieties, and conflicts, so that the person can choose freely whether he wants to fly in an airplane, wash his hands, sing in front of an audience, or show affection to his wife. We want him to be able to choose freely which career he wants to undertake, what party he wants to vote for, or what purpose he wants to see in his life. The communication from the therapist to the patient is: "I will not help you choose because then you will become dependent upon me and you will not be free. I will, however, help you get rid of the obstacles you have unconsciously put in the way of your free choice."

In brainwashing, on the other hand, the goal is the opposite. The goal in brainwashing is to eliminate all significant choices from the subject. He is told what to do, what to say, what to think, and what opinions to hold. He is told where to live, where to work, what party to belong to, whom to love, and whom to hate. When all of his choices are removed (often through torture and/or induced drug addiction, as in the case of Cardinal Mindszenty), then he is no longer a threat to the dictatorship. The communication from the interrogator-brainwasher is: "I have absolute command over your life or death. If you abandon your choices and do and think and feel as I tell you to, you will survive."

How can we help our children develop a sense of freedom of choice? Actually, there are several ways:

1. Ensure—through firm, kind, reasonable, and consistent discipline—that the child develops a healthy system of inner-directed impulse-control. Such self-discipline will essentially remove the danger of his becoming a slave of his own impulses.

2. Create an atmosphere of open, sincere, and intimate communication. Through good communication the problems involving fears and anxieties which can restrict choices so severely have a good chance of being solved in the home without professional intervention.

3. Present choice as a privilege which increases with emotional maturity, with "growing up." The parents must show the child that his choices will increase each year as he gets older. They must also show him that by behaving in a

reliable and trustworthy manner he will be able to increase his choices in spite of his chronological age.

4. Point out the availability of choices. Encouraging a child to experiment with different solutions to problems will have the effect of helping the child realize that there is not just one way of doing something but many. Some parents make the mistake of insisting that their children do things the parents' way. The result will be either that the children will become as rigid as their parents, being afraid of trying out new ways, or that they will go into overt or covert rebellion against their parents. Both outcomes must be considered undesirable, although the rebellion is to be preferred in terms of emotional health, as long as it is not destructive.

5. Increase the child's knowledge of the world. Common sense will tell us that the more you know, the wider your choice is. The higher your grades are in school and the further you go in your education, the more choices you will have in what you want to do with your life.

# 3. "IF YOU LOVED ME, YOU WOULD . . ."

## Characteristic III: Inner security.

An emotionally healthy person feels a high degree of inner security and thus places minimum reliance on defense mechanisms.

A person of optimal emotional health does not hide feelings from himself either through conscious suppression or through unconscious defense mechanisms. He is able to face himself and to accept his shortcomings as well as his assets. He has a feeling of self-respect and self-worth which is originally based on how his parents or parent-substitutes viewed him and treated him but which, as the person grows up, becomes more and more independent of outside confirmation and is directly related to an honest and realistic self-appraisal. In other words, the emotionally healthy person has a positive self-concept.

A positive self-concept can develop only in the presence of basic inner security which, in turn, is dependent upon the early experience of the infant or child interacting with his mother or with the person who has taken over mother-functions. It is not enough that the mother *feel* love for the baby. The love must be *communicated* to the infant through body contact and caresses, holding, cuddling, playing, soothing, and calm handling. If the love which the mother feels is not communicated through loving, tender, and calm behavior, the baby will develop a basic anxiety or basic insecurity which may affect his whole later life adversely. As a matter of fact, if the deprivation of adequately communicated love is extreme, he will either develop a physical disease called hospitalism and literally wither away and die or he will become mentally ill! This will happen even though physical and medical care is otherwise excellent.

Babies are amazingly attuned to the mother's emotional state. If the mother is nervous, high-strung, and impatient, the baby will tend to respond by being fussy and by crying a lot, which is likely to make the mother more nervous and tense than before. Thus, vicious circles can be set up very early in life. Pediatricians know from long experience that calm and emotionally healthy mothers beget calm and emotionally healthy children.* From this it follows that any mother-to-be who is nervous and high-strung should seek psychotherapeutic help before having her child, rather than counting on the child to calm her down (as many a nervous woman does, to her later regret).

Children are also keenly attuned to the relationship between their parents. They soon find out that their total security depends upon these two people and any threat to their parents is a serious threat to themselves. Chronic destructive arguments between parents will, therefore, make the child anxious and insecure, especially if unfair techniques are used such as the atom bomb (threatening to leave or divorce) or

---

*Some babies do appear to be born cranky. If this is not based on neurological dysfunction but rather on a generally inherited tendency, the child will eventually respond to the mother's calm handling.

silence. Although children will often pretend to ignore parents' fights, they are actually very much aware of them. Many a nightmare has been caused by vicious parental fighting.

To reiterate: it is not enough to *feel* love and affection for a child; the love and affection must also be *communicated* in daily living and must permeate the home atmosphere. Angry feelings are to be expressed openly and sincerely and without resort to any destructive techniques. To *communicate* love and affection involves spending time with the child, showing interest in his activities, attaching importance to his statements and opinions, and disciplining him firmly but kindly and fairly. In other words: treat a child as the unique individual he is and realize that, although his problems may seem minor to you, they are major to him.

If the parent does not, *through his actions*, communicate to the child that he or she loves him and sees him as a person of worth and importance, the child's feeling of security will be adversely affected. The same is true if the parent gives *too much* importance to the child (to the exclusion of other important factors in the parent's life: marriage relationship, friends, work, religion, etc.). If the child is the only source of happiness or satisfaction for the parent, the child will become anxious because he is given a power he cannot handle: the power to entirely determine his parent's happiness. Thus, when the child is given too little importance as well as when he is given too much importance, anxiety will be engendered and either a clinging dependence or a destructive and defiant independence will be fostered in the child. The anxiety will then have to be warded off through defense mechanisms which may become permanent ways of handling feelings.

The parent must also make clear to the child that he accepts *all* of the child's feelings (*feelings*, not actions!). If the parent does not make this clear, the child will not be able to accept himself as a person and will, instead, rely heavily on defense mechanisms to ward off such unacceptable feelings and thoughts and the accompanying anxiety. The problems and disturbing feelings the child experiences will then not be communicated and consequently may lead to emotional disturbance and to the occurrence of symptoms.

An emotionally healthy person, then, is one who relies minimally on defense mechanisms. Such a person feels secure and experiences a minimum of anxiety. Especially if he has developed insight into himself and his motivations (see Characteristic VII), he is likely to have developed a sense of good-natured humor which will enable him to enjoy life more and to meet even life's more trying moments with equanimity.

However, suppose a person is insecure and has established a reliance on pathological defenses, such as projection or denial of feeling. What can be done to diminish such a reliance?

Much can be done by honest introspection, a conscious willingness to see and examine drawbacks and unpleasant facts about oneself. This process is, as we have pointed out before, very much aided by listening nondefensively to what others have to say about us. If these measures fail, psychotherapeutic help must be sought.

In terms of prevention, it is important to reiterate that *the inner security on which nondefensiveness rests is a direct result of the love a person has experienced as an infant and child*. The younger the human being, the more important this love seems to be for future development. The love does not need to be communicated in words: in some languages, as a matter of fact, it sounds rather incestuous to say "I love you" to a child! The love must be communicated through tenderness, bodily contact, a clearly communicated wish to be with the child, and a clearly communicated attitude that the child is important not only as a human being but as a *very special* human being. The love must also be communicated through firmness and through clearly showing the child that you will help him control his impulses when he is not able or willing to do so himself. This control must be exercised with reasonableness and fairness, however, and the object must be the gradual abandonment of external control and its replacement by the development of inner discipline; otherwise love cannot be communicated through firmness and control.

The parent must—through his (her) behavior—communicate to the child: "I love to be with you" (but not *"only* with you," that is too much for the child, as we mentioned earlier). If the child does not receive this message, his needs for security are not fulfilled and he cannot develop the inner security necessary for emotional maturity.

The concept of inner security is often confused with other concepts; it will therefore be useful for us to make certain distinctions which will clarify what is meant by inner security. First, it must be pointed out that, although inner security implies a relative absence of anxiety (or nonhurtful and nonlimiting handling of the anxiety through defense mechanisms), it does not imply an absence of fear. Fear is a "healthy" emotion necessary to the survival of the organism. Without fear operating as a motivator we could not cross a street safely or, indeed, engage in any activity without running a high risk of immediate injury or death. Fear enables us to take prudent precautions and mobilizes us, psychologically and physiologically, to meet and ward off a demonstrable or probable danger. Anxiety, however, is a fear which is not engendered by a demonstrable or probable danger. Anxiety is a fear without a reasonable outside referent. When an individual is in a state of anxiety he feels helpless because there is no way for him to ward off the danger or to protect himself against the source of the danger. When an individual experiences fear, he takes measures to protect himself as effectively as possible (unless anxiety is added to the fear, in which case some degree of panic ensues and the individual's efforts to protect himself become ineffective or haphazard).

Thus, inner security should not be confused with an absence of fear. A relative absence of fear indicates the presence of pathological or semipathological conditions, such as immaturity, lack of judgment, tendency toward self-destruction, poor reality testing, etc. The presence of fear (without added anxiety) in the face of a demonstrable or probable danger indicates healthy functioning on the part of the human organism.

Nor should inner security be confused with "being relaxed." Inner security is always something positive and desirable, whereas relaxation may or may not be positive. This is something which many people do not realize. Many see relaxation (the absence of tension) as some kind of heavenly state which accompanies emotional health. However, the emotional health involved in relaxation depends entirely on the factors involved in each situation. As a matter of fact, being relaxed can sometimes be outright dangerous, as can be seen from the following true anecdote.

When I was an advanced graduate student in clinical psychology I attended weekly case seminars at a neuropsychiatric center close to my university. In these seminars the procedure was as follows. The presenting psychiatrist would go over the patient's history and symptomatology with the class, then the patient would be asked to come into the room and we had an opportunity to ask him or her questions. After the patient had left, we would then discuss diagnosis, treatment procedures, and prognosis. The seminars were a valuable part of our training and it often happened that they also turned out to be of benefit to the patients interviewed, since the psychotherapist whose patient was presented often received helpful ideas concerning diagnosis and treatment from the discussions.

During one of these seminars we were presented the case of a catatonic patient, a middle-aged man who had not spoken a word for two years! As a matter of fact, his jaws were sometimes so tightly clenched that he had to be fed intravenously! I will, however, leave out this patient's history and other factors involved in his illness and only concentrate on what happened in our "interview" with him.

The presenting psychiatrist was a resident in his early thirties, slightly obese, with a round friendly face and casual manner. He was jovial, outgoing, perfectly relaxed, and he smoked a cutty-pipe to boot! When he had presented the patient's history, he asked the attendants to bring him in.

The patient was rolled in in a wheelchair (having refused for over a year to walk anywhere else than to the bathroom) in which he sat straight as a pin, lean and haggard-looking, with his face expressing extreme tension and rigidity. In every respect he seemed to be the complete opposite of the psychiatrist. He stared fixedly straight ahead, his lips were pressed tightly together, and one could see the jaw muscles working spasmodically in his tightly drawn cheeks. He made no response as the psychiatrist, in a most friendly and warm manner, told him that we were a group of young doctors who were interested in seeing if we could participate in being of help. The psychiatrist asked the patient to relax and take it easy, but the patient kept staring rigidly forward and did not appear even to hear what the psychiatrist said.

As if to accentuate his own relaxation, the psychiatrist placed his feet on his desk and leaned backward in his chair, pushing it to a position of balance on its two rear legs and rocking it gently to and fro while he puffed on his pipe in perfect comfort. He kept reassuring the patient that there was nothing to be afraid of, that the best thing was to relax, feel comfortable, and engage in some friendly talk. As he kept on talking in his soft, soothing voice, the patient suddenly, fast as lightning, turned to the psychiatrist, his finger shot out to point at him, and he screamed "BOOOOO." The startled psychiatrist, who had been balancing his chair on its rear legs, toppled over and crashed to the floor; only his legs could be seen kicking the air behind the desk. Curtain!

It was a most embarrassing situation. The patient was

whisked away, but when the psychiatrist had had time to recover from the shock and we started discussing the case, we all agreed that the patient had communicated an important lesson to the psychiatrist, namely that it is not always desirable to be relaxed; as a matter of fact, it can be hurtful, and there was a bump on the back of the psychiatrist's head to prove it!*

In the Anglo-Saxon world, especially in the United States, there is such a frantic quest for "relaxation" that people even say good-bye to each other by giving the advice, "Take it easy!" Such advice, given as a good-bye in other languages, would not only seem utterly ridiculous to the participants, it could even be seen as an insult ("You are a nervous kind of person and I must advise you to calm down so you don't get into any trouble through your hastiness!").

It is clear that this frantic, desperate quest for relaxation is in itself productive of tension of the "unhealthy" kind (anxiety, dissatisfaction, agitated boredom). In order to counteract it, each individual has to realize that both tension and relaxation are desirable or undesirable only in terms of the effect they have on the individual. Both can be dangerous and both can be wonderful ingredients in a satisfying life.

Certainly, "constructive tension" or "healthy tension" is one of the most wonderful feelings a human being can experi-

---

*Of course, it was a mistake on the part of the psychiatrist to try to persuade the patient that he should relax. "Why don't you relax" is useless advice and avoids dealing with the problem causing the tension. The psychiatrist should instead have seized upon the clear fact that there must have been some definite reason for the patient to refuse to talk and that reason most probably had to do with some danger which the patient envisaged as a possible result of communicating verbally with other people. Since the patient most probably would still not have responded, the psychiatrist and the class could have begun discussing possible dangers from the patient's viewpoint while he was present. Probably the patient would not have responded to this either, but at least there would have been an attempt made to understand how he felt, rather than trying to convince him that he should feel otherwise.

However, mistakes sometimes have their good points, too. It could be argued that at least the psychiatrist succeeded in what no one had been able to do for two years: he had elicited a definite communicative response from the patient! We students felt that it was a further mistake to whisk the patient away at the very point when he had come out of his shell, but it has to be kept in mind that the presenting psychiatrist was an inexperienced resident who had not yet developed the skills necessary to turn any situation with a patient to advantage in terms of communication.

ence. It is the main ingredient in enthusiasm, in zest, in striving to excel. In the arts, in the sciences, in sports, in the joys of achievement in any field, there is constructive tension. We could even see it as the very essence of being alive, being human, being able to choose. Constructive tension, then, can be seen as the opposite of simply existing or vegetating. Without it, life would be void of excitement and wonder, there would be no urge to explore and to create, the "spark" would be extinguished.

Enthusiasm, joy, excitement, and other forms of constructive tension, however, can only be experienced by people to the degree to which they feel basically secure. If there is a basic insecurity within a person, any tension is likely to be experienced instead as anxiety—as destructive tension. Therefore, a certain degree of inner security is required for a person really to be able to experience the enthusiasm and the joys of life.

There is also another important, related consequence stemming from a feeling of basic security: instead of being squandered in anxiety and in attempts to defend against anxiety, a person's energies can be directed toward constructive endeavor and toward realizing his creative potentials. The result of a person's "living up to" his positive or creative potentials is what is meant by such terms as self-realization and self-actualization.

Each person is born with certain potential *spans*. Intelligence, for example, is inherited as a wide potential span. By this we mean that there is a limit below which a certain person will not perform on intellectual tasks, no matter how poor his educational opportunities and no matter how unfavorable his intellectual environment. There is also an upper limit beyond which the same person cannot perform, no matter how favorable his intellectual environment is. The span between the lower limit and the upper limit appears to be very wide in each person, but it is there and each person differs from everyone else in terms of where his "lower limit" and "upper limit" are with respect to a certain intellectual function. The closer a person functions to his upper limit, the more self-realized or self-actualized he can be said to be with respect to that function.

Intelligence is, of course, only an example (although a good one, because it can be measured rather accurately). The ability to feel and communicate love to another human being would be another example. Both the use of a person's intelligence and his ability to feel and communicate love can be severely interfered with by psychopathology. On the other hand, the healthier a person is emotionally, the more able he is to actualize his positive potentials in all areas.

How do you find out what your potentials are? You do it by testing yourself in different situations. Most people who are not prone to use excuses and rationalizations have a fairly good idea of what their potentials are, although it certainly happens that a person may discover potentials of a magnitude he never dreamed he possessed. This is not an infrequent discovery in psychotherapy.

Most people do not live up to their potentials and, of course, we cannot all be Leonardo da Vincis (as a matter of fact, even Leonardo had some significant interference with the realization of his potentials, especially in the area of interpersonal relationships). But by becoming aware of those factors, internal or external, which stand in the way of our realizing our potentials, we can combat the obstacles more effectively. In the case of our children, we can try our best to provide them with an environment which is stimulating and encouraging. By keeping our communication with our children open and by following the rules of communication outlined in Part I of this book, we can minimize the chances of emotional factors interfering with the development of our children's potentials.

The development of the self-concept is of crucial importance in determining the degree of self-actualization. The extent to which a person sees himself as capable is obviously going to exert a major influence on the extent to which he invests energy in trying. In fact, the nature of the self-concept is of such basic importance in actualizing one's potentials that the definition of Characteristic III could just as well have been: AN EMOTIONALLY HEALTHY PERSON HAS A POSITIVE SELF-CONCEPT.

When we do not live up to our potentials, it is usually because we ourselves unconsciously put obstacles in our way. This is mainly due to the nature of the self-concept, but when the self-limitations become too severe we define them in terms of psychopathology; that is to say, we suspect the operation of negative or destructive potentials.

The degree to which negative potentials (hatred, anxiety, defensiveness) are realized in any individual depends—as in the case of positive potentials—heavily upon what his early childhood experiences have been (to what extent and how he has been neglected or attacked, what defenses have been effective in warding off anxiety, what interactions he has had with parent figures, etc.). Although other influences certainly are of importance (later experiences, the parents' value systems and how they are communicated, adequacy and fairness of discipline, etc.), there is no doubt that the more significant a person's negative experiences have been as a child, the greater is the likelihood of his developing his negative rather than his positive potentials.

The task of the parent, then, is to see to it that hatred in the child is not mobilized, that he is not made to feel insecure, and that he does not need to employ defenses to a pathological degree. The task of the adult individual is to fight the destructive potentials in himself or to channel ("sublimate") them into constructive endeavors. To be able to wage the fight successfully, the individual must gain knowledge of the existence of the destructive "forces," their history, and the way they operate to hurt him or to limit him in his development. In other words, he must develop *self-understanding*. This can be done through honest introspection aided by listening to other people's comments about oneself openly and without defensiveness. When destructive potentials persist in being realized, however, there is a need for psychotherapy. Most of the communication of the psychotherapist is designed to help the patient fight against the realization of destructive potentials.

Emotional insecurity is at the root of several psychological disturbances. In rather pure form it can be seen in the "love-tester." The love-tester is a person who openly or through implication communicates: "If you loved me (or had any consideration for me as a human being) you would. . . ." The tragedy in the love-tester's life is that other people are likely to constantly fail the tests because of the stringent conditions for passing. The love-tester says, in effect: "You pass if you do exactly what I want you to do (or say exactly what I want you to say), but you fail if you do (or say) anything else." This, of course, means that the likelihood for failing is infinitely greater than the likelihood for passing, especially since the love-tester usually feels that the partner should know what he has to do or say to pass without being told. The following case illustrates a typical love-tester:

Nancy was twenty-six years old and unmarried when she entered psychotherapy. She was an attractive woman, but her appearance was marred by the fact that she appeared cold, rejecting, conceited, aloof, and interested only in herself. She spoke in a voice which was either whining-complaining or shrill-angry. She had no close relationships except with her divorced parents and even those relationships were based on hate-love rather than on love. She constantly saw evidence of rejection in how her parents treated her: they did not call her often enough, they did not ask her how she was, they phrased what they said in such a way that she was hurt, they were nicer to her sister, etc. Nancy did have short-lived relationships with men, but the latter could never please her. She had no close girl friends because no one could pass her tests. For example, if she did something for another girl, she would be very uneasy unless the girl very soon did something equivalent or more for her. If the girl did not "pay her back," Nancy would be so angry and feel so rejected and "used" that she would terminate the relationship.

Nancy worked as a secretary but she could not stay long at any one place of employment because her employers and co-workers did not treat her well enough. The employers would give her too much work compared with other girls or they would give her too little work, thus implying that they did not have confidence in her ability. The employers would smile in a friendly manner to other girls and either ignore Nancy or just give her a perfunctory nod. The other girls would not invite Nancy to lunch as often as she invited them, would be friendlier to each other than to her, would use her by asking her to help, and would reject her by not asking her to help.

Nancy's approach to me was the same. I did not keep the kinds of magazines that she liked in my waiting room, I did not empty the ash trays before she came in, I did not notice her new hairdo, I did not say she was prettier than her sister when she showed me the latter's photograph. If I wanted Nancy to come in more often, it was just to milk more money of her; if I agreed to see her less often it was because I wanted to get rid of her. If I made a comment to her during the session it showed that I wanted to interfere with her thought processes; if I did not make a comment it was clear that I did not care whether she got well or not.

Nancy's insecurities stemmed far back into her childhood. Her mother was a borderline psychotic who constantly threatened to commit suicide and had actually made several abortive attempts, some of which Nancy had witnessed. Her

father had teased Nancy unmercifully about sending her away
to a mental hospital, sometimes going so far as to actually
start dialing the number on the telephone. In Nancy's childhood there had been no one stable and dependable on whose
love she would have been able to count. By the time Nancy's
sister was born (when Nancy was eight years old), however,
the parents were divorced and the sister grew up in a less
unstable atmosphere. The mother, with whom the girls lived
after the divorce, sought help in psychotherapy and, consequently, did a better job of raising the sister than she had
done with Nancy. The latter was by now an angry, demanding, sassy child and the mother found it very difficult to show
her love. The sister was quiet, easily satisfied, and loving.
Consequently, she was scolded much less than Nancy, who
took this to mean that her sister was favored over her. This
made her even angrier and more alert to what the mother did
for the sister as opposed to what she did for her. The vicious
circle was in full swing.

In psychotherapy Nancy had to be confronted with what
she was doing; she had to be told that she was engaging in
love-tests and herself come to see them as love-tests. She also
had to develop an understanding of why she engaged in the
love-tests. Finally, in group psychotherapy, she had to learn
a give-and-take approach in her interactions with other human
beings. She had to face the fact that her conceited, contemptuous, aloof attitude invited rejections by other people and
that the very voice in which she spoke "turned them off."
Nancy was encouraged to work on her voice at home with a
tape recorder. At first she was shocked at how she sounded,
but the shock itself provided her with motivation to work on
it, and gradually her voice became mellower and less whining.

The next step for Nancy was to learn to act *as if* she were
compassionate, tolerant, and interested in others. She had to
learn to act as if her self-concept was positive. At first she
felt that this was a terrible thing to do since it was not honest
and she felt like a phony. But the group members pointed
out to her that the basic motivation for doing it was genuine,
since she wanted to improve herself as a human being. After
considerable resistance to the idea, Nancy did begin to act as
if she were the kind of person she secretly desired to be and
gradually other people began responding to her positively and
approvingly as if she were indeed such a person. This made
Nancy really feel like being kind to them "in return," and
thus her friendly approach became more and more genuine
and less phony in her own eyes. Finally, after a rather stormy
courtship in which some of the old love-testing returned, she

married and the marriage has so far been quite successful. Psychotherapy had a profound effect on Nancy: she changed from a narcissist interested only in her own welfare and feelings and viewing other people solely in terms of how useful they were to her, to a person who was genuinely interested in other people and their feelings and took pleasure in helping them without paying close attention to what they did for her in return.

Finally, some questions and answers on the subject of inner security versus anxiety.

*Question:* My four-and-a-half-year-old boy, having attended classes for three weeks, dislikes going to nursery school. In the mornings he cries, throws temper tantrums, and claims that he does not feel well. What can I do about this problem?

*Answer:* In order to answer this question, the psychologist must know the reasons (conscious and unconscious) why the boy is sent to nursery school *and* the reasons why he dislikes it. The main message expressed in the boy's action-communication is clear: "Something is wrong." But the specific meaning is not clear and there are many possibilities as to what that could be. For example:

1. The act of sending him to nursery school could communicate to him: "I am rejecting you because you are bad and I don't want you around me." If this is the interpretation the boy reads into the act, it is likely to be based on earlier experiences the boy interpreted as rejections.

2. The boy may not have had enough experience in extraparental relationships and may be worried about whether or not to trust other people. Consequently, he may be afraid of what will happen to him in the absence of both parents.

3. The boy may consciously and/or unconsciously feel angry toward his mother and may even have (repressed) death-wishes toward her. Overcompensating for these, he may be worried about what will happen to *her* in his absence.

4. Perhaps the boy fears that his mother will concentrate all her attention on someone else in the family, such as a younger brother or sister.

5. Perhaps the boy is afraid of being left or abandoned, because of some unfortunate experiences in the past.

6. It might also be wise to consider the personality of the nursery school teacher and her approach to the child. This would not detract from the boy's need for help with his own insecurity, but it is possible that the teacher is not dealing adequately with the problem. If such is the case, the problem will be more difficult to solve and, thus, in addition to getting help for the child, the parents should also consider getting another teacher for the child.

Not being able to adjust satisfactorily to nursery school within a week at the age of four is a sign that basic security is lacking and professional psychological help should be sought by the family.

What about the case in which you are faced with a child who was not given enough love in his early infancy and childhood? Such a situation could have resulted either from your own past and present limitations and problems or through the child being adopted after having experienced a period of emotional deprivation. A mother once asked the following question.

*Question:* Is it possible to "make up" in later childhood a lack of communicated affection in the first years?

*Answer:* To a significant extent it is possible, although perhaps not completely. However, the following considerations will have to be kept in mind:

1. An emotionally deprived child will need to have *more* evidence of love communicated to him than a child who was given much affection in his early years.

2. Such a child will be less receptive to evidence of being loved and will not respond as readily to it. He may even respond negatively to it, either because of guilt feelings over his own felt "badness" or because he wants to test— sometimes continually—whether his parents' love is genuine and lasting or superficial and "breakable."

3. Such a child will probably be more difficult to show love to, because of his constant tests of your patience. He may be irritable, or constantly "into something," or may have a low frustration tolerance. Due to his early deprivation he may unconsciously feel that the world "owes him something" and that he does not have to earn any love. But the old saying holds true: the most unlovable child is the one most in need of love. Remember, however, that love is shown not only through tender affection but

also through kind and firm discipline, not only through giving and providing but also through reasonable demands of performance and imposition of necessary frustrations.

4. If there are other children in the family than the one who was emotionally deprived, they may resent the extra attention and time given him by the parents. The parents must not let such reactions stand in the way of letting the child get what he needs. The best way to handle such a situation is to have a private talk with each of the other children, explaining the problem openly and asking for each child's support and cooperation in carrying out the program of helping the deprived child. Most children respond very well to such a private and confidential request for help and feel important over having obtained the parents' confidence and trust in such an undertaking.

5. Finally, it is important to keep in mind that such a child almost always will need psychotherapy in addition to the efforts on the part of the other family members. The latter, too, will often need counseling or—especially if they themselves caused the emotional deprivation—psychotherapy.

It is perhaps never possible to *completely* make up for loss of love in infancy, but a patient, understanding, and lovingly firm parent can certainly do a lot to help an originally deprived child live a satisfying and emotionally healthy life.

*Question:* If a child demands more attention than you think is normal, how do you handle it?

*Answer:* By giving him a lot of affectionate attention and showing sincere interest in him when he is *not* asking for your attention. Your response to his direct demands for attention must be courteous and warm but also realistic and firm, so that he is not able to manipulate you into "dancing to his tune."

*Question:* How do you help a child overcome a bed-wetting problem?

*Answer:* There is probably a hereditary predisposition in bed-wetting, but this has not been proved. It could also, in some cases, be a family "tradition" or expectation which is being communicated from generation to generation rather than anything physiological. Seldom is there any demonstrable physical or physiological problem involved. In the vast majority of bed-wetters the symptom must be seen as a sign of emotional insecurity.

Bed-wetting is seldom the only symptom a child has. Bed-wetters are often characterized by one or more of the following: whining, moody, irritable, restless, fidgety, excitable, disobedient, stubborn, oversensitive, touchy, or self-conscious. Almost always other members of the family will also show an emotional problem. Therefore, it should not be enough to cure the bed-wetting symptom: the family should treat the *causes* underlying the symptom, and in this effort a psychologist can be of help.

Some of the common psychological causes for bed-wetting are:

1. The child may have an unconscious wish to regress to an earlier stage of development: he wants to be a baby again, with all the pleasures connected with such a state of being. He communicates this wish through his behavior, which imitates that of a baby. This happens especially often in the cases of children who are faced with the birth of a sibling and whose parents have not handled the situation properly. Feelings of rivalry and jealousy toward a younger sibling are often expressed through bed-wetting.

2. As is the case with so many symptoms, bed-wetting may be caused by anxieties, worries, fears. (The reasons why one symptom rather than another is "chosen" to express anxiety are not well understood.)

3. The mother may be overprotective. Some mothers go too easy in toilet training or postpone it too long, considering the baby too small or delicate to be trained. The excuse is designed to hide the real reason: the mother unconsciously wants to keep her child dependent upon her for as long as possible!

4. The opposite may also happen: some mothers are overambitious and go at the training so hard that they get the child to hate the idea of going to the bathroom. These children often unconsciously rebel by using bed-wetting as a weapon against the parent(s). Sometimes the rebellion is not directed at harsh toilet training per se but against some other unreasonableness on the part of the parent, such as unduly harsh or unfair discipline, nagging, demands concerning food, etc.

Toilet training should start only when the bladder begins to hold for a couple of hours at a time. For most babies this does not happen until they are about fourteen or fifteen months old, but some are later and some earlier than this. Boys, on the average, are slower than girls to become dry. Only when the child has reached his third birthday and still wets the bed can we speak of a bed-wetting problem.

When the existence of a bed-wetting problem has been established, a prudent parent will consult the pediatrician to rule out the possibility (although unlikely) that there is something physically wrong. Then the family should consult a psychologist in order to have an evaluation of the emotional health of the family.

Under no circumstances should the parents punish, scold, or shame the child for wetting the bed. However, telling the child that he can't help it at all is also bad policy, since it makes him feel hopeless. The best approaches are:

1. Work on the emotional health of all members of the family and see the bed-wetting as a secondary issue, a symptom which will disappear when the causes are removed. If you stop making bed-wetting an issue, the child will feel calmer and more secure and this, in itself, will eventually be of help in his gaining control of his bladder. In other words, concentrate on making the child's life agreeable, calm, and satisfying.

2. The child should be encouraged to get up at night to urinate if he feels the need. In order to make this agreeable, his room should be kept warm and there should be a night light in the bathroom and/or corridor.

3. Incentive systems often work. Some pediatricians recommend the use of star charts (the child is given a gold star for each dry night); when the child is old enough to be interested in money he can be given a penny or a nickel for each dry night.

4. Bladder training during the day is sometimes helpful. The training should be introduced as a game in which the child should try to break his own record. He is to hold off going to the bathroom as long as possible and is then asked to urinate in a measuring container. The amount he was able to hold is written down. When the child is able to hold twelve to fourteen ounces, the likelihood of his overcoming the bed-wetting may be increased.

5. If the child gets to be eight or nine and still wets the bed, and you are sure you have done everything to alleviate emotional problems (including psychotherapy—which, provided the family members are cooperative, almost always helps!), then and only then should you consider getting one of the conditioning devices obtainable in the market (you can also make one yourself and save a lot of money—all it requires is some netting rigged up to a bell and a dry-cell battery). But this should be done only if the child himself wants to try it; do not force this method on a child.

*Question:* What about the teen-ager who overeats? Will anxious parents make the situation worse? What are some of the causes of overeating and what can be done to overcome it?

*Answer:* Yes, anxious parents can make the problem worse by nagging. However, parents must treat the problem as a serious one with which the child needs all the help he can get and make it clear to the child that you will provide that help, first at home, and if that does not work, by seeking professional help from a physician and a psychologist.

There is, in all probability, a slight constitutional tendency toward overweight in many cases of obesity, but that does not contradict the fact that the overwhelming majority of reasons for overeating are psychological in nature. There are a multitude of possible psychological reasons for overeating and only some of the most common ones will be listed here (endocrinological factors have, of course, been left out; they rarely play a significant role in obesity, but a physician should nevertheless be consulted since it *could* be a case of underactive thyroid, for example, or a brain injury in which certain centers in the hypothalamus are involved).

1. Overeating can be a way of pleasing someone, usually a parent who wants a child who is a "good eater." In the case of such parents, food assumes an unconscious symbolic value: it comes to stand for acceptance, security, love. The two immediately following reasons for overeating are often direct consequences of this basic reason.

2. Overeating may be a temporary way of allaying anxiety or of consoling oneself.

3. Overeating may be one way of communicating: "I have been deprived."

4. Overeating can be used as a weapon against others (parents or spouse).

5. Overeating can be a way of showing power ("see what you can do about it").

6. Overeating may be a way of punishing onself.

7. In the case of teen-agers and adults, overeating can express a fear of being attractive to the opposite sex.

8. Overeating can express a fear of being weak and insignificant (with the concomitant wish to be big, important, and conspicuous).

9. Overweight can be used to hide a personality defect: "The reason people don't love me is my weight, not the fact that I am selfish (or hostile or clinging or conceited, etc.)!"

The best way to treat obesity at any age (after endocrinological or other medical factors have been ruled out) is the simple technique I call the "chart method." I have recommended it to many of my patients with excellent results. This is how it works. The patient buys chart paper and draws a graph with weight calibrated on the vertical axis and weeks divided into days on the horizontal axis. He weighs himself and enters the weight on the chart. Now he draws a line from this point through one pound less the next week through one pound less the following week, etc., until the line (we can refer to it as the "course" to be followed) is down to the target point (the desired weight). From this point on, he draws a horizontal line. Thus, if the patient wishes to lose twenty pounds, for example, it will take him exactly twenty weeks to do so.

The patient decides to forget about making any decisions with regard to dieting and to let the chart take over these decisions one day at a time. All he needs to do is to weigh himself each morning when he gets up and plot the weight onto the chart. If the resulting curve is *above* the "course," the patient must diet *that day only;* he must keep a slight feeling of hunger until the next day. The next day, if the curve is still above the course, he must also keep the slight feeling of hunger. He must keep dieting until the curve shows that he is on or below the "course." On such a day he forgets about dieting and eats what and as much as he pleases. In this way, his weight is slowly (sometimes with considerable "swings," partly due to differences in fluid retention) brought down to the desired level.

This chart method works very well when the psychological reasons for eating are not overwhelmingly strong. The reason the method works so well is that it eliminates the worst drawbacks of all other dieting systems:

1. Other dieting systems create anxieties and doubts about having enough "will power" to see them through. With this technique, no other will power is needed than to diet for one single day.

2. Other dieting techniques often require the dieter to abandon his favorite foods and may give him a feeling that he will never again be able to eat himself to satiation. When using the chart technique the dieter *knows* that there will be many days when he can eat himself sated and savor his favorite foods, even if they be chocolate or cake.

3. The chart technique is so slow that the body does not rebel. It slowly adjusts itself to the decreasing weight and all the medical dangers of the crash techniques are therefore avoided.

There are instances when the chart technique does not work. In those cases psychotherapy must be initiated.

# 4. THE WORD "NO" CAN EXPRESS LOVE!

## Characteristic IV: Postponement of need-gratification.

The fourth characteristic of emotional health can be stated as follows: an emotionally healthy person is able to postpone need-gratification.

Of the many characteristics which distinguish human beings from animals, the ability to postpone need-gratification is one of the most important. Without this ability, culture or civilization as we know it could never have evolved. Education, on which culture rests, would have been limited to certain fighting, hunting, and food-gathering skills.

Much of the raising of each individual child involves helping him develop the ability to postpone his immediate needs. Thus, the educative process starts in babyhood and will continue throughout his productive life, barring interference from external or internal sources. A certain degree of postponement of immediate needs must have been learned already before the child goes to school. The schoolchild, in order to be able to achieve even a modest degree of success, must be able to postpone his immediate pleasures, work for long-term goals, and wait for the fruits of his labors.

The more an individual can learn to postpone his immediate pleasures for future goals, the more he will achieve in his personal development of his potentials and the better he will do in those areas of life which he considers important.

How can we teach this characteristic to children? There are five important points for the parent to keep in mind:

1. Postponement of need-gratification is best taught *by example*. If we, as parents, give in to immediate pleasures, this fact in itself communicates to the child that immediate pleasures are very important to gratify (Rule 1). We cannot then reasonably expect our children to learn to sacrifice for future goals.

Parents tend to be most inconsistent in this respect. They often see work as a *necessary evil* with which to buy pleasure. Father comes home cursing about all the work he has had and plops himself down in front of a television set to watch a Western or a football game. Mother complains about having had to clean the house and talks about the pleasures of her social club. In this manner, even though neither parent may be talking directly to the child, both parents communicate: "Work is horrible, pleasure is wonderful, work can never be pleasure." This teaching is reinforced by the attitudes of other children (work is bad, playing is great) and the child learns that he should not work, he should "have fun," and that the two are incompatible. When he then shows that he has learned what he has been taught—by not doing his homework, for example—the parents behave in a most indignant and upset manner! When he finds excuses to get out of doing chores, the parents get angry and start nagging him. Yet, much of the antiwork attitude is something that the child has learned from the parent. The parents' expectation that the child on his own should unlearn everything he has been taught and eagerly throw himself into his homework and cheerfully perform his chores without reminders, is most unrealistic.

The enjoyment of work and of meeting challenges and solving problems, as well as the satisfaction in efficiently handling necessary routine tasks, must be taught *by example*.

2. Parents can make work a pleasure by working together with the child beginning at an early age (provided the parents are praisers and not faultfinders). There are numerous opportunities in a home to show that not only the attainment of a goal but the very process of pursuing it can be most pleasurable. The work involved in painting, cooking, sewing, and building can be just as much fun—sometimes even more fun—than the attainment of the finished product. Even the so-called drudgeries (cleaning, picking up) will usually be taken in their stride by children if they have not been taught to complain about them by their parents.

3. The parents must—largely through their own behavior—teach the child that what a person wants for himself is not the only important thing in life. There are other considerations of equal or greater importance: contributing to the happiness of another human being, for example, working for a "higher" principle, or gaining the satisfaction involved in doing what one considers one's duty (this last "old-fashioned" satisfaction will be in danger of dying out if not revived soon).

4. Parents must realize that loving a child does not mean only giving: it also means withholding. To give a child a piece of candy when he asks for it could mean love, but it could also mean rejection ("I don't care enough about your welfare to say 'no' when a 'no' would be best for you"). Such rejections are often hidden behind flimsy excuses such as "It is not good for a child to be frustrated." The truth is that it is very good for children to be frustrated when such frustration teaches them the realities and necessities of everyday life. Frustration is harmful only when it occurs as a consequence of an arbitrary show of

power on the part of the parents ("You will get it when *I* say so and not before"). When satisfaction or frustration of desires depends simply on the mood of the parent, the child will learn nothing else than that his parent is an unreasonable and unfair person.

5. Parents must keep in mind that the concept of time is different for a child than it is for an adult. As we mentioned earlier, time, although measurable by mechanical devices, is a psychological function. On the whole, time is shorter for an adult than for a child, probably because time can be measured psychologically only by comparison to time already experienced. If you think back to your childhood summers, you can readily remember how long they seemed. You can also remember how difficult it was to wait for Christmas: it seemed like an eternity until it finally arrived. Now it seems that summer has hardly started before it is gone. And Christmas comes so fast that you find it difficult to get everything done in time. The older you get, the shorter time seems to become ("the faster it flies").

This fact must be taken into consideration when tasks or chores are set for the child (preferably with his participation). In order to experience work itself as pleasurable, he must be able to complete it in a time which *he* considers reasonable. One half hour for your child may well be psychologically equivalent to two hours or more for you: an important fact to keep in mind when tasks are set. (The same applies to rewards and punishments.) Unreasonably long postponement of need-gratification can backfire and make the child hate the idea of postponement altogether. Thus, the postponement of a pleasure must be reasonable and must take into account the child's particular conception of time.

The importance of learning to postpone the gratification of impulses cannot be overestimated. No one can be truly independent if he is not self-directed. If he is a slave of his impulses, he may *seem* to be independent on the surface but, not being capable of choosing, he actually remains as much of a slave as if he were a black man on a cotton plantation two centuries ago. He may try to hide his slavery under the cloak of being "spontaneous," "honest about his feelings," "doing his thing," or "being a real person," but to those who know him he communicates through his actions: "I am a slave of my impulses, I do not have a choice" (note the interrelationship of this characteristic with Characteristic II; all of these characteristics are, in a sense, just different ways of looking at the same "thing": emotional health).

The ability to postpone need-gratification should never be confused with lack of spontaneity. On the contrary, a person who automatically chooses the alternatives which work for his and others' long-term interests is going to be spontaneous in the most constructive sense of the word. To be spontaneous means to be able to give free rein to *constructive* impulses the gratification of which will benefit rather than hurt the person in the long run.

A corollary to the ability to postpone need-gratification is the ability to take frustrations in one's stride and not be discouraged by them. A child must be taught to see certain frustrations as a part of life which must be accepted, otherwise he will become one of those unfortunate, chronically dissatisfied people who live out their lives with constant and daily complaints about things they can't change. The ability to carry on and not lose courage despite frustrations is a definite sign of emotional health.

Parents are supposed to be more mature than children. Yet I have seen a large number of parents who "fly off the handle" at the slightest little frustration or instance of misbehavior on the part of the child. And these parents wonder why their children are immature! If a child has a parent who cannot "keep his cool" in the face of repeated minor frustrations and who overreacts to provocation, the child will learn that the way to handle one's feelings of frustration is to blow up, scream, and yell or to nag and whine. Before a parent can insist on impulse control in the child, he must thus see to it that he has his own impulses under reasonable control. This does not mean that he has to let the child get away with his provocations. It merely means that rules can be set, warnings issued, and punishments given with kind firmness rather than with hysterics.

# 5. "HOW COULD SHE MAKE SUCH A BIG DEAL OUT OF NOTHING?"

## Characteristic V: Ability to evaluate emotional reality.

An emotionally healthy person is able to evaluate emotional reality; he is attuned to feelings in himself and others.

Psychologists use the term "intellectual reality testing" to refer to the ability of a person to reason and to logically conceive of his environment: his ability to perceive reality in a logical, analytical, intelligent way. Intelligence, however, is unrelated to emotional health. A person can be an imbecile and be emotionally healthy or emotionally disturbed; he can be a genius and be emotionally healthy or disturbed.

There is, however, another type of reality testing which we shall call "emotional reality testing." Emotional reality testing refers to the ability of a person to perceive feelings in himself and others, sense the needs, wishes, and hopes of the people with whom he comes in contact, judge the "emotional atmosphere," and, not least, correctly interpret the emotional communication value in behavior and speech.

Intellectual and emotional reality testing are completely unrelated and are present in every person to varying degrees. A mentally retarded person can have a high or low degree of emotional reality testing and the same is true with a highly intelligent person. Let us take an example of a person with a brilliant intellect who had a very low degree of emotional reality testing.

Some years ago I had a space scientist, Dr. N., in treatment. He was one of the most logical, analytically and mathematically minded persons who could be imagined. He thought in strictly logical terms and his whole life centered around intellectual problem solving. His mind was constantly preoccupied with calculations, formulas, and equations. As a matter of fact, Dr. N.'s exclusive preoccupation with logical aspects of reality was one of the reasons he came to see me in the first place: it had created havoc with his relationship with the rest of his family. His wife, especially, was unhappy in the marriage and had been pushing him to seek professional help for a long time before he actually came in. She herself had taken the first step and entered psychotherapy (with another psychotherapist). The incident which follows is illustrative of Dr. N.'s interaction with his wife.

One Monday morning in June when Dr. N. came to my office for his regular appointment, he told me the following story. In the course of his fifteen years of marriage he had very seldom taken his wife out to dinner, perhaps once a year at the most. And on the few occasions when he *had* made a date to go out with her, he had found—by an amazing coincidence!—that he had so much work at his office that he was compelled to come home late on that particular day. This, he claimed, happened by chance and he even tried to prove to me that it *could* happen by chance by using statistical methods of assessing probability! He was absolutely convinced that there was no unconscious message or purpose behind his coming home late on those particular occasions.

Having recently been pressed by me concerning the reasons behind his taking his wife out so seldom, Dr. N. had made a date to take her out for dinner on the previous Friday. And again, by the same incredible coincidence, he had found a lot of work at the office that just had to be done before he could leave. So he called his wife, explained the situation to her, and told her he would just have to be late "this time."

When he finally got into his car to drive home Dr. N. was already over two hours late. At that time he suddenly remembered that this was the very day he had promised to return some power tools he had borrowed from a friend that he kept in the trunk of his car. So he decided to drive to his friend's house first, "since he was late anyway."

The month was June and it was still light when Dr. N. finally arrived home almost three hours later than usual. He parked his car on the street instead of in the garage "in order to save time" and then started to walk toward the front entrance of his house. He noticed that the curtains in the living room, where he knew his wife would be waiting for him, were not drawn: she wanted to be able to see his arrival, so that they could get as early a start as possible.

Now as Dr. N. walked up toward the front door, he remembered that last week he had used a new type of fertilizer on his lawn and he was curious as to its effects. So he stooped down and examined the ground in order to see how the grass was doing. But he spent only fifteen or twenty seconds looking at the ground and then he went to the front door and opened it, expecting to find a happy wife ready to go out for a nice evening.

But when he opened the door, his wife screamed at him: "I hate you, I hate you," then began to cry and could not stop crying. She ran to her bedroom and slammed the door shut and did not respond to his questions as to what was the matter. Dr. N. is mystified about what could possibly have made her so upset, because on the phone earlier in the day she had seemed quite understanding. His wife, by the way, gave him the silent treatment until Sunday night, when she finally told him that it was the fact that he had looked at the lawn that had made her so mad!

Now Dr. N. says to me: "You see what I mean when I say she is unpredictable and completely irrational? How could she make such a big deal out of nothing? *What possible difference did it make if we came to the restaurant fifteen seconds later?*" And he shakes his head in indignant disbelief.

To many people Dr. N.'s puzzlement and indignant reaction would seem very natural. He could not help being late, he had called his wife and told her so, and he only examined the lawn for fifteen to twenty seconds. What difference is there, indeed, whether they arrive a few seconds earlier or later at a restaurant?

The trouble with Dr. N.—and with the people who reason as he does—is that they see only the logical and objective aspects of a situation, whereas the *fact*—regrettable or not—is that the logical aspects are not all that important. Dr. N. got into trouble because he did not consciously understand the *emotional communication value* of his actions and because he did not understand his wife's needs. He used the logical, formal, and objective aspects of his actions to hide or cover up the actual message his behavior transmitted to his wife because of her emotional needs.

By (unconsciously) covering up the emotional communication value of his actions, Dr. N. had cut himself off from emotional reality. He was cut off from the very factual and undeniable reality that his wife was a person in desperate need of emotional response. She had for fifteen years been exposed to his constant insistence on logic and "practical reality," his disdain for birthdays, holidays, and anniversaries ("Christmas is just another day, that's all"), his reluctance to show her tokens of affection ("You know that I love you; that should be enough"), and his total lack of childish enthusiasm ("Why make a big deal of everything; you know I am not the type that gets all excited over trivia"). On the few occasions that they had had a date to go out, his wife would desperately hope that this would be one time he would not come home late, that this would be the beginning of a change.

The day of the incident she had again said to herself: "Perhaps things will be different this time." Her hopes were especially high because her husband had agreed to see Dr. Wahlroos and perhaps he had already changed a little. Maybe this evening would turn out to be the turning point in their relationship for which she had been waiting so long!

Then, during the day, she received the first blow. As always before, her husband called home and said that he will be late, extra late at that! But she made excuses for him and thought: "Well, he really can't help having to work late: we'll still have a nice evening out, even if we get a late start." And she was full of eagerness and anticipation. Finally she heard the car park and went to the window with happy anticipation and looked out. What did she see? There was her husband sauntering up the walk as if he had all the time in the world. And then he *stopped!* He stooped down leisurely to look at the fertilized lawn *as if his wife would be the least important thing in the world!*

What was Dr. N. really communicating to his wife at that moment? The true message of his behavior (based on the reality of his past behavior and her needs) is: "At this particular moment, at least, fertilizer is more important to me than you are!"

Such "reading" of his behavior seemed crazy to Dr. N., as it would to anyone who blocks out emotional reality. Nevertheless, Mrs. N. was *not* crazy and her reaction was perfectly understandable in view of the history of the relationship between her and her husband.

That is not to say that her reaction was healthy, far from it! Just as it was my task to help Dr. N. come to consciously understand emotional reality, it was the task of his wife's therapist* to help her react more reasonably to the irritations she experienced. In this particular instance, for example, she could have *ignored* the message from her husband, if she had kept in mind that he did not consciously intend to hurt her, and she could have done her part in seeing to it that the evening would have turned out successfully anyway, thus

---

*Generally, I like to have both spouses see the same therapist. In this case, however, Dr. N. was—unrealistically—concerned that his wife may have biased her therapist against him.

encouraging her husband to propose further evenings out. Or she could have told him what message she had read into his action, suggested that he bring the issue up in his therapy, and then proceeded to have a good evening out. However, Mrs. N. suffered from many emotional problems herself and did not at this time possess such a degree of emotional stability and understanding. She simply exploded.

It was only through psychotherapy that Dr. N. finally gained an understanding of the unconscious purposes of his behavior and of its emotional impact on others. As a matter of fact, individual psychotherapy was not sufficient in Dr. N.'s case; it was only after he had entered group psychotherapy that he was able to understand, accept—and change! —the emotional communication value of his words and actions. A necessary condition for his solving of this problem was admitting the fact that the unconscious purposes of his actions (and lack of action) entailed a hostility directed against his wife which he had previously felt only vaguely and had never expressed openly.

In the case of Dr. N. it was clear from his history (a letter from his much older sister indicated that he was emotionally deprived as a baby) that his "inability" to perceive emotional reality was actually due to a deep fear of all emotions. Whether there is "emotional retardation" on a biological basis (due to inherited factors or brain anomalies) is not known, but there do seem to be a small number of babies who from the very first months of life are rather unresponsive to cuddling and loving care. Perhaps future research will bring clarification on this point. At the present time, all we can say is that the "inability" is fortunately in most cases due to a deep unconscious unwillingness to see emotional reality and that psychotherapy, therefore, can be of great use in helping a person so afflicted to live a full life with all its joys and all its suffering.

The case of Dr. N. illustrates only one type of deficiency in emotional reality testing: insensitivity to the emotional needs of other people and a resulting inability to correctly interpret the emotional communication value in a behavioral or verbal message. There are a number of other ways of misjudging emotional reality which have to do with distortion, exaggeration, or minimization of perceived messages due to fears, distrust, poor self-concept, etc. The injustice collector, for example, misjudges emotional reality in the sense that he chronically feels unfairly accused or picked on, mistreated or rejected, by other people. In a sense, one could say that he is *over*-sensitive to emotional reality. The fact is that all of us have to take a certain number of minor rejections, unfairnesses, and inconsiderations in daily living at home or at work because of the fact that the people we come into contact with are people and thus imperfect. The emotionally healthy person accepts these minor rejections as an unavoidable aspect of living, knowing that he himself cannot live his life completely without rejecting others in minor ways. He knows that on the membership card to the human race it says in fine print: "You must accept a certain number of rejections from other people without squawking about it; otherwise you will be miserable." The injustice collector, on the other hand, misjudges this reality and believes that he is singled out for special rejection. If he behaves in such a manner as to "retaliate," he may then indeed be singled out for some special rejection and will, as a consequence, feel that his initial estimate of the emotional reality was correct.

Finally, a few words on how we can develop emotional reality testing in children. It can only be done by example, by the parents attaching great importance to feelings as well as to how feelings are expressed, showing compassion, tactfulness, and concern for other people, and trusting their children and behaving in such a way as to earn the children's trust in return. It is also important for parents to teach their children to accept minor rejections, teasing, and unfairness as a part of daily life, reserving their indignation for major attacks which realistically threaten to limit their lives in a significant way. In issuing guidelines as to what constitutes a major attack and what should be overlooked, each set of parents must, of course, follow its own values.

# 6. THE DANGER OF "DOING ONE'S OWN THING"

## Characteristic VI: Deep and lasting emotional relationships.

An emotionally healthy person is able to give of himself fully in deep and lasting emotional relationships.

Why don't we just say: "An emotionally healthy person is a happy person?" The reason is that happiness is not necessarily a desirable characteristic. Professional burglars can be very happy—provided they are not caught! Sadists can achieve great happiness in seeing other people tortured.

The value of happiness is dependent upon the question: of what is the happiness a by-product? If it is due to selfish striving at the expense of others, or the by-product of destructive behavior, or reliance on ultimately harmful drugs, I would consider it undesirable. If it is a by-product of a constructive relationship—between the individual and his God, between the individual and his fellow-men, between the individual and what he sees as his mission in life—then the happiness is desirable.

Unfortunately, one often hears statements such as: "All I want is to be happy" or "All I want for my child is that he be happy." Not only is such communication too vague; the statements in themselves indicate that the person making them is not aware of the equivocal nature of happiness in terms of desirability. All indications are that the members of the Manson "family"* were very happy in murdering their victims, but no parents would wish that kind of happiness for their children!

*A gang of hippies who in 1969 broke into two homes in the Los Angeles area and killed all the occupants.

However, even if we restrict the definition of happiness to something like "a feeling of inner peace and joyful contentment resulting from constructive actions or relationships," it still remains a fact that happiness cannot be pursued directly. It is by its very nature a by-product, a by-product of *the extent to which an individual is able to give of himself fully in deep and lasting emotional relationships*. It is this ability which is a characteristic of emotional health and not the happiness itself. As a matter of fact, it is possible to be emotionally healthy and still be deeply unhappy. A parent whose child suffers from a terminal illness is an example. In a more general sense, any emotionally healthy person would have to feel some significant unhappiness about the suffering of his fellow human beings in the world (Characteristic IX). In this sense, an absence of unhappiness can even be seen as pathological.

Just as some people harbor the misconception that happiness is a sign of emotional health, there are others who think that the emotional health of an individual can be measured by how many friends he has, by how "outgoing" he is. In the United States, especially, there is a great premium on being an "extrovert." The worship of outgoingness is so exaggerated that the term "introversion" often has been used as synonymous with "neurotic," even by professionals! Carl Gustav Jung, the Swiss psychiatrist who first described these orientations toward other people, certainly never meant to say that one of these tendencies is pathological and the other healthy. On the contrary, both are healthy tendencies and only the extremes are unhealthy. The extreme extrovert, that is to say the person who fears being alone, is as "sick" as the extreme introvert who is afraid of being with other people.

The question, then, is not whether a person is an extrovert or an introvert. The question is: to what extent is he able to give of himself in relationships with other human beings and to what extent can he *communicate* this ability through his actions, so that others perceive him as indeed being a giving person? (There are many people who *feel* that they love others and, indeed, all mankind, but who do not manage to convince others through their actions that such is the case. The feeling must be *communicated* and *received as intended* in order to have value in terms of emotional health.)

Involved in such an ability will be factors we have mentioned earlier, such as the skill in testing emotional reality, tactfulness, and the ability to listen actively and to empathize. An emotionally healthy person, in this sense, would be one who sees other people's needs as important and who strives to help others fulfill their needs, provided they are not neurotic needs (the fulfillment of which would be destructive in the long run).

The opposite to an emotionally healthy person, in this same sense, would be the narcissist, the one who sees other people only in terms of whether they could be of use to him or not. To a narcissist, other people possess no intrinsic worth, they exist only as pleasure-providers or obstacle-placers. A narcissist is often an injustice collector, he is unable to live his life without being outraged over the minor injustices, unfairnesses, and rejections which befall us frequently for the simple reason that people are not perfect. He is imbued with the importance of his own minor "rights" and he flaunts these at any opportunity. But a narcissist is actually someone for whom we should feel compassion (even though it can be difficult, in view of his behavior), because a narcissist creates his own tragedy: he can never experience a satisfying emotional relationship with another human being, unless he is willing to see his narcissism as the problem it is and to seek help for it in psychotherapy.

Why do we not simply say that an emotionally healthy person is one who is able to love? Primarily because the term "love" has too many meanings and is too vague. People "love" chewing gum, people "love" a movie star whom they have never seen in person, some people "love" to create trouble, a few even "love" to kill and maim! The mere existence of a positive feeling does not qualify for emotional health: the feeling must be *communicated*. If we define love as the degree to which a person feels that someone else's happiness and well-being is more important than his own and as the concomitant actions through which this feeling is communicated, then we could, indeed, say that the emotionally healthy person is one who is able to love. But how many people use this definition of love?

An emotionally healthy person, being secure and having a positive self-concept (Characteristic III), is not possessive of other people. He respects another person's individuality, independence, and freedom of choice. In intimate relationships, an emotionally healthy person does not cling desperately to his partner; he shows his partner through affection and other actions how strong his feelings are, but he does not *demand* that the partner respond in kind.

This does not mean that an emotionally healthy person "does his own thing" (what an awful expression!) and is unconcerned with what his partner does or says. On the contrary, he will try to bring out the best in his partner and help him develop as a person. He will not, however, treat his partner as if he owned him and he will not attempt to exercise power over him, except to prevent him from doing something clearly destructive.

The ability to form deep and meaningful relationships with others can be taught effectively only in the home by loving parents and it can be taught only *by example*, not by exhortation. Despite all the talk about schools becoming centers for "life adjustment," the fact remains that schools can do little or nothing to help the students develop this characteristic. As a matter of fact, much of the trouble with American education is a direct result of the idea that teachers somehow should become the guardians of the children's emotional health! The orientation of a person with regard to other people is determined largely at home and, therefore, all that the schools can do to help is to spot those instances where emotional health is failing and recommend referral of the family to a psychotherapist.

Many parents unwittingly teach their own children to become narcissists. These parents become outraged when minor rights of their children are infringed on. They protect their children from frustrations and injustices, take their children's side in conflicts against other children and parents or against teachers, police, and other authorities, may verbally preach the importance of sharing, but often get upset if the child is generous in giving another child a toy or doing work for a neighbor for free. These parents are extremely alert to their child "being taken advantage of" and they wish him to "stand up for his rights"; they are afraid that people will "walk all over him." Thus, in wishing to avoid one pathological extreme: the spineless dishrag, they create another: the intolerable spoiled brat who is only concerned with his own advantage and is incapable of a give-and-take interaction with others, because he must constantly count debit and credit to see to it that he does not lose on the deal!

A person closely related to the narcissist is the power-hungry manipulator of other people. He uses logic (methodology) to hide from the emotional reality that the very manipulativeness precludes any development of intimacy or trust between him and the manipulated partner (see Unfair Technique 11-VI). He engages, consciously or unconsciously, in the manipulation primarily for the feeling of power it gives him to see other people dance to his tune. He is the parent who "uses reverse psychology" on his children, the husband who "tests" his wife to see if she will pass or fail, the wife who uses sex as a weapon.

Narcissism, as well as manipulativeness, is most difficult to treat in adulthood and it can seldom be treated successfully in individual therapy alone; in the majority of cases group therapy is necessary. The reason for this is that the very concentration in individual sessions on "I" and "me" and "mine" tends to "feed the neurosis," as the saying goes (actually "compound the personality disorder" would be more accurate). In the therapy group, however, the member is almost forced to help the others; if he doesn't he will stand out like a sore thumb. When he does help them, on the other hand, he will slowly learn to experience a satisfaction he had not thought possible. The very "family" nature of the group provides a climate for unlearning old destructive patterns and learning new ones in their stead. The narcissistic or manipulative member may have to go through a period of communicating a *pretended* interest in and compassion for others, but since the basic motivation ("I want to change in a constructive, helpful, positive direction") is then also communicated, the results will be rewarding and will reinforce the behavior until it becomes genuine in every sense of the word. Similar results can otherwise be produced only in some rare cases of deep personal tragedy and through some religious conversions.

In discussing human relationships with your child, it may be good if you point out to him that no one can like everyone and no one can be liked by everyone. We cannot choose our feelings, but we most certainly can choose what we *do* about our feelings. We can be kind and courteous to people we do not like; we do not need to add to the conflict by showing our dislike and being unkind or rude. Some fanatics will call this hypocritical, but nevertheless it is in that case a most desirable and positive hypocrisy where the basic motivation—to do one's best—is still genuine. Nor do we have to use the fact that some people dislike us as an excuse for destructive action or avoidance on our part. We must realize that we do not have power over other people; we can only do our best, and if they do not respond in kind, we have to satisfy ourselves with the knowledge that we have tried.

In conclusion, let us give the answers to two common questions asked by parents:

*Question:* How do you help an unpopular child who is friendly to others and would love to have their company but who is avoided or tormented by other children?

*Answer:* You must find out what it is about him or his behavior which makes him unpopular. You must observe him in his interactions with other children and see if there is anything he does that irritates or annoys them. Perhaps he is too desperate for company and thus pushes himself on other children, a process which generally backfires. Listen carefully to what other adults (teachers, neighbors, relatives, friends) have to say about your child's behavior and take seriously what they say even if you yourself have not made the same observations. Your child might act quite differently in your absence compared with when you are present. Also listen to what other children have to say about your child and to the words they use when they torment him (if they do not torment him within your hearing, you must ask your child to quote them). Do not be offended by what you hear and do not be defensive about it. The key to what your child is doing can only come from this type of inquiry.

When you have found out what it is that your child is doing to unwittingly discourage the friendship of other children, you must sit down and discuss these findings with him, tactfully but firmly. He will probably deny the validity of your findings, but you must keep firm and tell him that the way others see us is an important fact and can help us in finding out things about ourselves that we don't realize. If several discussions of this nature (preferably including examples of actual behavior) do not change the situation, you must seek professional psychological help, because a child without friends is deeply unhappy and can be handicapped for life by having to live through these future-determining years in loneliness and torment.

*Question:* Is shyness in a child to be considered a serious problem?

*Answer:* That depends upon the degree to which the

child hurts himself or limits himself through his shyness. Shyness based on fear must be considered harmful whereas shyness based on respect and reluctance to force or pretend a close relationship is a positive quality. The child who is too shy to strike up friendships with other children even when they take the initiative is obviously in need of help. The same is true of the child who is too shy to ask the teacher if he can go to the bathroom or for help with something he does not understand. However, the mere fact that a child does not speak until spoken to, or looks down instead of into the other person's eyes, need not be a matter of concern.

# 7. THE NEUROTIC PACKAGE DEAL

## *Characteristic VII: Learning from experience.*

An emotionally healthy person is flexible; he is willing and able to learn from experience.

An emotionally healthy person modifies his behavior when he sees that it works against him, is harmful to others, or does not lead to the set goal. The emotionally healthy individual is flexible, not rigid, except in the case of deeply felt ethical convictions (see Characteristic X). His emphasis is on trying new methods to solve problems rather than on rigidly sticking to methods which have proved destructive or futile.

The attempts on the part of an emotionally healthy person to modify his own behavior are not based only on an intellectual realization that his methods have been ineffective. Rather, his effort to change is based on emotional insights achieved not only by introspection based on conscious thoughts, but by learning something about himself from examination of his past behavior. The fact is that the behavior we engage in can tell us more about our unconscious motivation than any amount of introspection. However, a prerequisite to being able to learn from one's own behavior is nondefensiveness (Characteristic III).

There are many types of problem solving in life, but since this is a book on communication in the family, I will concentrate on the type of rigidity in problem solving which is most likely to lead to problems between family members: the rigidity which characterizes involvement in neurotic interactions. This type of rigidity is in large part due to a fear of examining one's behavior in order to learn something about one's unconscious motivation. It is such a common resultant of this fear that we could add a subheading to Characteristic VII stating: AN EMOTIONALLY HEALTHY PERSON DOES NOT GET INVOLVED IN NEUROTIC INTERACTIONS.

In our discussion of Rule 20 (beware of playing destructive games) we pointed out that destructive games constitute a type of neurotic interaction. A neurotic interaction exists when the participants in a relationship work for one goal but achieve its opposite.

Guilt feelings as well as intellectual considerations usually prevent a person from repeating behavior his past experience has shown to be destructive or ineffective. However, in neurotic interactions there is so much concomitant hurting of oneself (partly by unconsciously provoking the other person to behave destructively) that little guilt is felt. This is what is meant by the "neurotic package deal": both partners are punished by the same action. At the same time the conscious intent is so positive and the underlying motivation so well hidden that intellectual controls tend to be replaced by excuses and rationalizations.

The most usual type of neurotic interaction occurs when two individuals share conscious goals and also share unconscious goals which are diametrically opposite to the conscious ones. We gave an example of this type of interaction and of the neurotic package deal in the discussion of nagging (the case of Alan and his mother, Rule 17), but the principle involved here is so important to the concept of emotional health that I would like to cite further examples.

> Eleanor was a twenty-nine-year-old single woman who was living with her divorced mother. She came to therapy mainly because she was concerned over the fact that she had not met anyone she wanted to marry and she was afraid of becoming an old spinster. Her mother, whom I also saw a few

times, was a very kind, oversolicitious, overprotective parent, a typical "smother-mother" who, needless to say, consciously wanted the very best for her daughter. She sincerely wanted to see the daughter happily married to a good man and she shared Eleanor's worry about her becoming a spinster.

Consciously, in other words, the mother wanted her daughter to be mature, adult, and independent and to establish a good relationship with a man. However, chronically recurring actions are a good indication of unconscious motivation and the mother's behavior in this case indicated that her unconscious wishes were the opposite: she wanted her daughter to remain an immature child!

Behaviorally, the mother treated Eleanor as if the latter had no judgment whatsoever and as if she could never be counted on to take care of herself. Furthermore, the mother persisted in bombarding her daughter with questions which the mother knew from experience would lead to immature behavior outbursts. The mother would then feel justified in her distrust of Eleanor's maturity and judgment: anyone reacting so immaturely must indeed not have very good judgment! For example when Eleanor would come home after shopping in the neighborhood market, the mother would ask her such questions as: "Were there men in the store?," "Did anyone look at you?," "Did anyone try to talk with you?," "Why did you wear the blue dress instead of the red?," and so on without end. The mother's questions in this and other situations (especially on the rare occasions Eleanor had been on a date) exhibited her unconscious fears of the daughter's growing up, being sexually attractive, leaving the home, and marrying, as well as being an indication of her own envious feelings and sexual conflicts. The mother, in other words, unconsciously did not want an adult and mature daughter whose judgment she could trust. On the contrary, by treating Eleanor as if she were an irresponsible person without mature judgment, the mother showed that she unconsciously wanted to keep her daughter on the level of a child. It is of interest in this connection to note that the mother frequently bought clothes for Eleanor and that the dresses she selected for her looked as if they had been made for a huge seven-year-old!

Eleanor, on the other hand, bitterly resented being treated like a child by her mother. But instead of reacting toward the mother's behavior with mature poise and firmness tempered by compassion, she would fly into violent temper tantrums or pouting depressions. If she then received a call from a man, she would "get back at her mother" (!) by saying "I am busy," or "I don't feel well, or "I already have a date." This would lead to further reproaches from the mother and the vicious circle kept turning.

It took months for this young woman to realize in her psychotherapy that she, herself, was scared of growing up and becoming a mature woman. She had many times accused her mother of wanting to keep her a baby, but she had never considered the possibility that she, herself, unconsciously was afraid of sex and of any intimate emotional involvement with a man, and that she therefore felt more comfortable in the mother-daughter relationship which she had had for nearly three decades. Yet, Eleanor's *behavior* communicated strongly that this was the case. On an unconscious level she had the same goal as her mother: to keep on being a baby. Her behavior had served a dual purpose. Consciously her behavior kept her convinced that she was *against* her mother's keeping her a baby: "I am rebelling against it; I wouldn't get so upset about it if I were *for* it, would I?" But on an unconscious level, through the "rebelling" behavior itself, she was really saying: "You are right, mother, I am just an immature little girl who can't control herself."

When Eleanor finally started listening to the language of her own behavior and the information this communicated from her own unconscious regarding her secret fears, she changed radically. She felt compassion for her mother, whose own marriage had been a most unhappy one and she could understand why her mother was so afraid, unconsciously, of losing her daughter. She became much more flexible in her reactions to the mother's provocations and realized the futility of her past immature confirmation of her mother's allegation that she was still a child: she "learned from experience." She began answering her mother's previously infuriating questions with friendly humor and when she found herself getting angry she told her mother so, but in a mature and concerned manner without the old temper tantrums and poutings. As is usual when one partner stops a neurotic interaction unilaterally, the mother got worse for a while and felt that her daughter "did not love her any more." But as the daughter kept treating her mother with love, respect, and consideration, the mother's feelings changed too, and she, in turn, developed respect and admiration for her daughter.

When therapy ended after a year and a half of treatment, Eleanor was engaged to a man who had had a divorce but who had *learned* from his divorce and from his own therapy experience. Every Christmas during the ten years since this took place I have received a letter from Eleanor and her husband and, as far as I can see, they have a most satisfying and rewarding marriage and—even more remarkable in view of the history—they have a good relationship with Eleanor's mother, who turned out to be a perfect grandmother.

Another typical case comes to mind involving a "weak" man and a "strong" wife. Mr. and Mrs. D. had been married for ten years when they came in for marriage counseling (the counseling approach was soon found to be insufficient and was changed to psychotherapy, which was what they needed.) They were referred to in their neighborhood as "the Bickersons" and their bickering had indeed continued unceasingly ever since their courtship. The reason they came in at the time they did was that their children had begun to ignore their father completely and behaving as if the mother were the only parent in the house.

Consciously, Mrs. D. wanted a "strong" husband. She wanted to be able to lean on her husband and depend on him. As a matter of fact, during her psychotherapy it came out that she had initially been attracted to him partly because he had been a sergeant who had seen combat during the war and partly because he had served as an Explorer Boy Scout leader after the war. She had felt that here was a man used to making independent decisions, one who had to be strong, reliable, and full of initiative. But Mrs. D. had been grievously disappointed. After the honeymoon the husband had developed into a milksop, one who never stood up to her or "kept her in check," who spent most of his time fiddling around with electronic gear in the garage or building radio-controlled model airplanes. He left the running of the house and the raising of the children completely up to her.

When I asked Mrs. D. how she and her husband had gained the nickname "the Bickersons," she revealed that her husband did attempt to resist her, but ineffectively. He would try to argue her out of things, but he would stop as soon as she raised her voice or appeared to become upset. He did not want to make waves. According to Mrs. D. he had never suggested a vacation, near bought tickets for a concert, never brought home anything for her, never called if he was going to be late coming home from work, never fixed something in the house without her asking for it, never . . . but the list seemed endless.

As usual, seeing the spouse in the office provided some light for studying the opposite side of the medal. Mr. D. felt that he had been trying for years to be the kind of husband his wife wanted him to be, but she had never given him credit for trying, never uttered one word of appreciation about how hard he worked for the family, never asked him nicely to do anything, never responded with understanding when he did call her to say that he was going to be late coming home, never let him decide anything on his own, never brought him a cup of coffee to the workshop in the garage, never . . . but it seemed as if his list, too, was endless.

Note how fond these spouses were of the word "never." Breaking communication Rule 5 by using "never" and "always" in accusations is a common element in neurotic interactions. The conscious purpose for the employment of these words is usually to make a realistic appraisal of fact (it *really seems* as if it were never or always). The preconscious purpose which usually comes to light upon challenge of the exaggeration is an attempt to make the story sound more convincing or to emphasize the intensity of feeling. The unconscious purpose which emerges in psychotherapy is usually to facilitate the development of a vicious circle. It is accomplished as follows: The wife says her husband never calls home from work. The husband says: "If I don't get credit for the times I have called, what's the use of calling at all?" Whereupon he calls even more seldom, giving rise to more recriminations on the part of his wife, etc. Looking at it from the "other direction," the husband says that his wife never brought him a cup of coffee to the garage. The wife says that she waits hand and foot on the whole family and that if this is the way he feels about it, she is certainly going to stop all further service to him. As she then provides less in the way of "considerate services," the husband feels even less like helping out in the house and withdraws more often and for longer times to his electronic escape-land in the garage.

Consciously the wife wants a "masterful" (her terminology) husband. Her actions show that she unconsciously wants to be the dictator and to make all the decisions. Consciously the husband, too, wants to be masterful. Unconsciously, he would rather not take any more responsibility ever again in his life; he would just like to be a little child who plays with his toys and lets mother take care of everything that needs to be done. The criterion for the existence of a neurotic interaction is met: the conscious purposes of the two spouses are identical and the opposite unconscious purposes of the spouses are also identical!

In psychotherapy, both Mr. and Mrs. D. gradually came to realize these unconscious tendencies and thus were able to gain control over them. Both spouses recognized the rigidity with which they had reacted to each other's provocations and became determined to "learn from experience." Thus, the power involved in the destructive elements of these tendencies was drastically diminished and no longer interfered in their relationship. Mr. D. would still spend some time with his beloved electronic gear, but the time was reasonable and he would take time out to invite his wife for a coffee break in addition to involving the children in his hobby by teaching them electronics. In other words: "I am going to the garage" no longer carried a message of rejection and escape.

Mrs. D., in turn, still made many of the decisions but she felt better about it because in those areas where she felt insecure (disciplining the children and financial management, for example), she could now count on her husband to take action and initiative. When he made what to her seemed like mistakes, she would ignore them if they seemed minor (Rule 2) and bring them up frankly but reasonably if they seemed major (Rule 10).

These are typical examples illustrating the nature of neurotic interactions. In contrast to the tactical or "game" type of neurotic interaction, which is comparatively easy for the partners to recognize and sometimes can be stopped without psychotherapy, the deeper or strategic type of neurotic interaction usually requires professional assistance before it can be stopped. The main reason for this difference is that the unconscious purposes of a game are rather temporary in nature (feeling indignant, winning, showing up the other party as unreasonable, etc.) and thus fairly obvious and observable. The unconscious strategic purposes involved in the deeper type of neurotic interaction, however, seem too absurd or "far out" for the conscious mind to even consider as a serious possibility (in the first example: "I want to stay immature" and "I want my child to stay immature"; in the second example: "I want a child rather than a husband" and "I'd rather be a child than a husband").

How can we help our children stay out of neurotic interactions? The answer is as difficult in practice as it is simple in theory: by the parents not engaging in neurotic interactions with each other or with one or more of the children. The best way to stay out of neurotic interactions, apart from psychotherapy, is again to work on self-understanding and to follow the rules of communication given in this book.

Although the typical neurotic interaction involves two persons, there are many examples of neurotic interactions involving three or more individuals, even large groups (witness labor-management conflicts and international conflicts). In the family, it could work like this:

Al, a recently married junior executive, has strong feelings of insecurity. He doubts his masculinity and constantly feels a need to "build up his muscles" through physical exercises in order to prove to himself that he is not a homosexual. Needing constant proof that he is loved, he feels that his wife neglects him. Yet he feels it would be unmasculine for him to show any other than sexual affection to his wife. Accordingly, the only time he ever shows her any tenderness is in bed.

Al's wife, Bonnie, is what psychologists refer to as a "castrating" woman; that is, without consciously meaning to, she takes every opportunity to put men down, her husband in particular. She sees his constant need for signs of affection as childish and sissified. On the other hand, she resents him for not showing her any affection in daily living. He can only show sexual affection and even that he does not do very well! This latter circumstance provides the content for many of Bonnie's sarcastic communications.

Now Bonnie becomes pregnant and delivers a baby daughter, christened Michelle. Al is ecstatic. Here is proof of his virility: he has shown to himself and others that he is a "man"! Michelle becomes his life, he worships her, he dotes on her (showing affection is no longer unmasculine to him when the object is a child). Bonnie becomes more jealous with every day that passes. She begins to resent Michelle as a rival, unconsciously at first, then more and more consciously. As her resentment is expressed in anger and over-reactions to the daughter's provocations, Al takes Michelle's side, which further increases Bonnie's resentment. The vicious circle is rotating faster and faster.

In psychotherapy we found all three engaged in a neurotic interaction: Al, Bonnie, and Michelle. The girl, five at the time, was "impossible to handle," disobedient and selfish, and actively provoking fights between the parents by such methods as saying to her mother: "You can't do anything to me, because I'll tell Daddy," and then telling Daddy how unfair Mother had been all day.

Consciously, all three wanted a happy home life. Unconsciously, all three needed to punish themselves and felt undeserving of happiness. Al and Bonnie both had had childhoods which engendered these feelings of needing to be punished. Michelle suffered from unconscious guilt over "causing" all the fights and thus had the same need to be punished. Only through psychotherapy (for the parents) were the three able to solve this neurotic folie-à-trois. (It is interesting to note that Al and Bonnie sought psychotherapy only for Michelle when they came in; they saw the whole problem as being caused by the daughter's uncontrolled and disobedient behavior!)

These three examples, together with other examples elsewhere in the book, should suffice to illustrate the phenomenon called "neurotic interaction." Such interactions can occasionally be handled successfully by confronting the participants with the rigidity of their reactions. This is the exception rather than the rule, however, and usually the vicious circle can be broken only by at least one partner understanding the unconscious purposes involved in his participation. A person who has insight into himself, who has learned something about himself and his unconscious motivations by examining the evidence from his past experience, is not likely to engage in neurotic interactions. Often, however, such insight can only be achieved through psychotherapy.

How flexible are children? Parents confronted with children who "just don't seem to learn" often ask themselves—and me—this question. They see their child repeat the same negative or destructive behavior (e.g., whining) or neglect to engage in a certain constructive behavior (e.g., studying), and they sometimes begin to wonder if hereditary or constitutional factors could play a role, since the behavior seems so impervious to environmental manipulation.

However, the fact is that *specific* personality traits or behavior patterns seem to be influenced only to a minor extent by hereditary factors. Repetitive behaviors of a negative or destructive nature are usually engaged in for some purpose and when the purpose is found, the behavior is, indeed, modifiable through environmental influence. Whining, for example, is engaged in because it works. If the parents see to it that it does not work, whining disappears (usually after first getting worse)—the child discards it as an ineffective technique. But the *purpose* of the whining must be found. The purpose may not only be for the child to gain his way. It may be to make the parent upset, to gain his attention, make him care! If so, the whining will *not* disappear merely by seeing to it that the child does not have his way. The parent will also have to give the child attention and love and show interest in the child's accomplishments and ideas when the child is *not* whining. This will, in time, take care of the whining problem.

When a repetitive problem exists, it is probably because of the gain achieved in the interaction with the environment. Remove the gain and fulfill the purpose of the behavior in more constructive ways and the problem will disappear, usually gradually but sometimes immediately and spectacularly.

On the other hand, as any mother knows who has had

more than one child, children do have observably distinct personalities from the day they are born. They differ from each other in such general variables as activity level, control and coordination, amount of crying, response to stimulation, frustration tolerance, and strength of certain needs (such as for sleep, affection, company).

These are, however, quite general characteristics and they are responsive to interaction with the environment. Let us take an oversimplified example. Suppose a mother would like to have a passive, doll-like child, but gets a constitutionally very active baby. The mother may be disappointed, she may become anxious in handling and controlling the baby's activity, or she may "give up." In either case, an interaction between the baby's needs and the mother's needs will result which will be completely different from what it would have been had the baby been constitutionally placid. One cannot, therefore, truthfully say that any resulting problem regarding activity is inherited or constitutional. Nor can one realistically say that such a problem is entirely due to environmental exposure. What one *can* say with confidence is that a problem—or the absence of a problem—is a result of a certain interaction between the needs of the child and the needs of the significant figures in the child's environment.

This has important implications with regard to limiting the parents' feelings of guilt if problems do develop. Although there are a few sadistic parents who take pleasure in seeing a child suffer or who glory in wielding power over a helpless being, the vast majority sincerely wish the best for their children and the fact that problems develop is not entirely due to the parents. The same set of parents may raise three children very successfully but may then experience tremendous problems in raising the fourth. If such is the case, the reason is probably that the fourth child has a different constellation of characteristics and needs and will, therefore, interact very differently with the parents. To this must be added another inescapable fact: each child likes to occupy a unique role in the family (one child will often say no only because another said yes). Thus, it would be unfair to burden the parents with all the blame; parents can justifiably be blamed only if they neglect their responsibility to seek help if significant problems do develop.

Children are actually very flexible and can make healthy adjustments to an amazing variety of situations, provided their needs are met in a healthy manner. The importance of communication in teaching children to develop healthy rather than unhealthy modes of adaptation should be obvious. It is not! We constantly meet with parents who break Rule 1 (actions speak louder than words), for example, and who teach one type of behavior verbally while teaching the opposite behavior through tone of voice or through action or inaction. Thus, in teaching children to take advantage of their flexibility in achieving constructive ends, it is of utmost importance to follow the rules of communication given in Part I of this book.

# 8. BY THE SPARKLE IN HIS EYE . . .

## Characteristic VIII: Enthusiasm.

An emotionally healthy individual takes an interest in constructive and challenging aspects of life; he experiences enthusiasm.

The majority of patients seen in the office of a psychotherapist are people who find it difficult to "work up" enthusiasm for anything. They are either too preoccupied with their personal problems, or too involved in neurotic interactions, or too anxiety-ridden to be able to enjoy the challenges of their work or to pursue an absorbing interest or hobby. Sometimes repeated disappointments in life (often clearly self-engendered) have made them afraid to feel enthusiastic about anything lest the "inevitable" disappointment cause them renewed pain.

Enthusiasm is a type of constructive tension and thus can be seen as one of the antitheses to anxiety (others being self-understanding, love, faith, etc.). An enthusiastic person is either secure within himself or he has found an effective way to deal with or channel his anxieties. Such a person lives an exciting and satisfying life, a "full" life. On the other hand, a person who cannot enthusiastically tackle his work or who cannot make up for necessary "boring" activities by finding or creating interesting activities cannot be said to live a satisfying and emotionally healthy life.

An emotionally healthy person is able to take interest in and invest enthusiasm in people and things around him. This, in turn, will make his life more enjoyable and rewarding and will thus serve to further counteract or channel anxiety. Thus it is that an emotionally healthy person can often be recognized by the sparkle in his eyes indicating his satisfaction and joy in life and by his way of talking which communicates the enthusiasm and excitement he experiences.

Most people who lack enthusiasm nevertheless see it as a desirable characteristic and would like to develop it in themselves. There are, however, certain cynics or intellectualizers who look down on enthusiasm as childish. Such people are to be pitied, because they will live out their lives without ever experiencing life's real joys.

Seeming enthusiasm is sometimes observed in patients suffering from emotional disturbance. In these cases it is usually a defensive, "frantic" type of enthusiasm indicating a desperate desire to escape from or hide one's problems under the cloak of an absorbing interest. In the few cases of emotional disturbance with concomitant "genuine" enthusiasm, a favorable prognosis is the rule.

If enthusiasm serves to hide psychopathology in some form, it is clearly destructive. The same is true if the enthusiasm or absorbing interest serves the purpose of escape from problems or responsibilities. Housewives who devote themselves to clubs and charitable organizations at the expense of their own families are clearly using enthusiasm as an escape. The same holds for men whose enthusiasm for sports or other activities leaves them little time to devote to their wives and children.

Enthusiasm can be encouraged in children partly through example, partly by providing the child with opportunities for success and then praising him enthusiastically when he succeeds, and partly by seeing to it that the child must *earn* most of the luxuries he gets. Children who are "handed everything on a silver platter" will become unappreciative and unenthusiastic. Children who have something to look forward to with eagerness tend to develop enthusiasm as a way of life.

# 9. SHARED HAPPINESS: DOUBLE HAPPINESS

## Characteristic IX: Identification with mankind.

An emotionally healthy person accepts his fellow human beings and identifies with all mankind.

An emotionally healthy person accepts other people with all their peculiarities and problems. He realizes that he does not have the power to change others and he follows the old precept "live and let live." The only exception to this acceptance is violence or the threat to commit violence. In the face of such a threat an emotionally healthy person, because of his desire to help and protect other human beings, feels it to be his duty to contribute to the disarming and control of the destructive individual (unless the latter himself is acting in the defense of someone in need of help).

Sensitivity to and respect for other people's feelings, combined with empathy and compassion and a willingness to help, is characteristic of a person with a strong degree of emotional health. This sensitivity and compassion must be potentially *observable* to others, however. There are many people who feel—or claim to feel—strong love and compassion for others, yet act in such a way as to hurt other people.

An emotionally healthy person is able to say with John Donne (1624): "Any man's death diminishes me, because I am involved in Mankinde. . . ." An emotionally healthy person shares with and tries to alleviate other people's sorrow and suffering; he also shares with and tries to contribute to their joy. Such empathic sharing of feelings is one of the most important qualities of emotional health, because, as the

Swedish proverb states: *"Delad glädje är dubbel glädje, delad sorg är halv sorg"* (literally, "shared happiness is double happiness, shared sorrow is half sorrow").

Acceptance of and empathy for other people *can* coexist with rather severe emotional problems, but this is—as in the case of enthusiasm—exceptional and an indication of favorable prognosis. The lack of acceptance and empathy is perhaps most evident in the narcissists. Successful treatment for narcissistic patients often involves encouraging them to engage in projects which entail help for others, such as volunteering to read for the blind ("talking books"), door to door collecting for charities, teaching Sunday School, etc. By acting "as if" he felt deep concern for others, the narcissist gets the same rewards which accrue to a kind and considerate person and this experience, together with his work in therapy, often gives him motivation to abandon the neurotic pleasures inherent in narcissism.

As with the other characteristics of emotional health, acceptance and empathy can only be taught children through example. To accomplish this end, the parent must realize that he is not likely to have exactly the kind of child he would like to have. The child may be introverted when the parent would rather see him extroverted, he may be below average intelligence, he may be interested in mechanics when the parent would rather see an interest in humanities, etc. The parent must accept the unique personality of his child and must realize that he cannot completely control the development of this personality. The parent can provide a healthy environment for the child's personality to develop in, give him friendly guidance and discipline, teach him sound values, keep the channels of communication open, and provide for expert help if needed, but that is the extent of the parent's ability to influence the child constructively. If the parent realizes this and treats his child with acceptance, compassion, and respect, the child will also become accepting, compassionate, and respectful of the dignity and uniqueness of other human beings.

# 10. THE PURPOSE OF IT ALL

## Characteristic X: Faith.

An emotionally healthy person is committed to a principle higher than himself: he has a faith.

An emotionally healthy individual is guided in his life by values and principles he sees as more important than himself. Because of his feelings of security and self-worth, he also has the courage to take a stand for the ideas and principles in which he believes.

This does not mean *any* ideas, however. Deeply disturbed and emotionally damaged individuals are often attracted to philosophies which in practice involve the destruction of other human beings, such as communism and nazism, for example. Nor does it mean standing up for any minor "rights"; that is simply rudeness. An emotionally healthy person is not attracted to destructive "ideals." He is not drawn to fanatical sects which look down on all nonbelievers and consider them condemned. On the contrary, an emotionally healthy person tends to be attracted to ideals which emphasize the basic dignity of all human beings, respect for life, and the infinite glory of love; in short, ideals which most religions incorporate in their teachings.

As Carl Gustav Jung has shown, there exists in each human being a religious need, a need to believe in a principle beyond and higher than oneself, and this need must be satisfied in order for the individual to live a meaningful life. The religious need appears to be universal; no culture has ever been found where this need does not manifest itself.

Whether or not the need to believe in a higher principle is met through a formalized religion or through a philosophy of life seems to be of secondary importance. The important point seems to be that there must be a purpose to one's life, otherwise all suffering, striving, and efforts to improve are in vain. And if the individual cannot accept a dictated purpose, such as one proclaimed by a formalized religion, then he must *choose* a purpose for his life if he is going to live and not just exist.

This purpose, chosen or dictated, implies a faith in something higher than the individual: a creative principle, love, perhaps God, however visualized or conceptualized. Without such faith no one can be said to be emotionally healthy, because a basic human need has in that case been denied: the need to experience oneself as part of a higher purpose; in other words, the religious need. Faith alone is, of course, no guarantee of emotional health (a devout clergyman can suffer from neurosis as well as anyone else), but conversely, no one can be said to be emotionally healthy if he does not have faith in something higher or more important than himself.

It has become modern and sophisticated to say: I can't believe in the teachings of such and such a faith because it is not logical, it cannot be proved. This argument is, in itself, naively illogical and involves a semantic misconception. Faith, *by definition,* implies that reason, logic, and observable fact are unnecessary if not irrelevant to the belief in question. To a person with a faith, no proof is necessary. If the teachings of a particular faith could be "proved," there would, of course, no longer be any need for faith.

Other people refuse to become involved in a formalized religion because of all the cruelties which have been committed in the name of religion in the past. That this is an excuse can be seen from the following considerations:

1. Such cruelties are no longer being committed (except by isolated fanatical sects).

2. *Anything* can be used for good as well as for evil. This is true of fire, love, a stone, even hatred.* It is also true of religion.

3. The same people who use this argument can often be seen to belong to other groups in whose name cruelty has been committed: business, labor, a political party.

*Certainly the hatred of disease has led to many "good" discoveries.

Certainly one could not say that a person without a faith is automatically emotionally disturbed *in a clinical sense*. That would be just as silly as saying that a person with a deep faith is immune to developing emotional problems. But if we look at the question of faith coldly and practically in terms of everyday psychological reality, we have to recognize that the person with a religious faith tends to have an advantage, especially in the area of inner security. If we compare religious and nonreligious families, all other aspects being equal, we find that, on the whole, the religious families are emotionally healthier and less likely to break up. The cliché, "A family that prays together stays together," is thus not an empty one. The reason for this is not found exclusively in religious taboos on divorce, although they certainly may play a role in inducing the spouses to work on their relationship. The most important reason for the relative stability of religious families is that most religions encourage attitudes of love and compassion, understanding and forgiveness, self-scrutiny and self-improvement, in addition to providing a stable point, a pillar of security as it were, for the believer.

But there are other reasons why a religious position in one's attitude toward life carries an advantage. A person with a deep faith tends to develop the courage to live his faith, act on his ethical convictions, and practice what he preaches. This tends to be recognized by the people around him (not always, of course) who tend to respond in a positive manner and thus reinforce the faith in question. This is particularly so because a true religious faith is accompanied by a feeling of humility, a realization of one's own smallness in comparison with the universe. The very action of working for something higher than oneself encourages a feeling of humility. And yet, at the same time, working for something higher and bigger than oneself also encourages a person to use his potentials to the utmost.

Nietzsche, a deeply religious man despite his violently anti-Christian attitude, has given some of his readers the impression that he was haughty and conceited and that he looked down scoffingly on others. On the contrary, in a deeper sense Nietzsche was truly humble. He said he knows that no one today can be superman. But, he said, everyone can be a *link* in the bridge that leads to superman, to the not yet attained ideal. It was his desire to be such a link, nothing less and nothing more.

For children a faith is especially important. Very soon in his life a child notices that he lives in a dangerous world and that he could lose his parents and his home at any moment. If he has the faith that there is someone more important and more powerful than his parents who still loves him no matter what happens in his life, then his feelings of security and his peace of mind are strengthened and he can face life with greater confidence than a child who lacks this faith. The development of the child's conscience is facilitated by a belief in a religion, since the values communicated by the parents in daily living are confirmed and strengthened by the church or religious system in question. And impulse control based primarily on conscience and bolstered by reasoning is, of course, always more effective than impulse control based on intellect and reasoning alone.

A family whose members share a faith in a higher being or principle becomes a haven of strength and security. A person who has grown up in such a family enters life with inner resources which can help him through the most difficult of hardships. For there may come a time in his life when all external supports fail, and when hope is seemingly lost. In such a crisis, this person is likely to pull through exactly because of the inner strength he developed by growing up in a family characterized by faith.

## Communication and emotional health

Now that we have described the ten interrelated variables involved, we can define a person's emotional health as the degree to which these variables characterize him. As a matter of fact, we could add an eleventh variable and say that a person is emotionally healthy to the degree that he follows rules of positive and constructive communication.

A person can, however, be in reasonable emotional health and still not possess the knowledge necessary for good and constructive communication. He may be unaware of sending contradictory messages, he may not understand the importance of being specific or of testing his assumptions, he may confuse tactfulness with walking on eggs, etc. Thus, two otherwise emotionally healthy individuals can have problems in their relationship because they do not follow the rules of communication outlined in Part I of this book. Communication is always a two-way process and the result of a communicative act depends not only on the sender but also on the receiver. Thus, when two emotionally healthy individuals communicate we are likely, but not certain, to have reasonably good and nondestructive communication, much less so when one partner is emotionally disturbed, and least so when both partners show a significant degree of emotional disturbance. Thus, in the treatment of communication problems the mere teaching of communication rules may be sufficient if the partners are in reasonably good emotional health. To the degree that one or both of the partners are not emotionally healthy, however, the emotional disorder will need to be treated in psychotherapy because the emotional disorder itself is likely to interfere with the individual's ability to follow the rules of communication.

The main emphasis in the field of emotional health should be on preventive measures. Effective prevention will, however, only be possible when children take psychological examinations as regularly as they would go for physical or dental check-ups.

The only other practically feasible method of improving general mental health (at least as far as I can see) is strongly to urge all candidates for marriage or remarriage to take a certain number of hours of counseling, singly and jointly. A course on "constructive communication" could be combined with such counseling.

## Conclusion

This book stresses the importance of communication in creating as well as in solving problems between family members, in impeding as well as in facilitating the attainment of emotional health. We have seen how consciously well-meant messages can communicate hostility and rejection but also how the adoption of certain rules can overcome this problem and thus eliminate some of the causes for the frequent unhappiness in today's families. I have attempted to show how communication influences marriage, child rearing, and the formation of each individual's personality. Finally, I have tried to give examples of situations in which psychotherapeutic intervention is needed.

I would like to reemphasize an important point and end with an appeal to the reader. Use this book for self-improvement and as a guide to relating to your family members in an emotionally healthy way. But do not use it as a club with which to inflict hurt on someone who breaks its rules and precepts. That is likely to backfire and, besides, it would violate the spirit of the book and show that you are throwing stones in a glass house. If your partner in communication breaks some of the rules, discuss this with him in a spirit of compassion as well as concern. If you do, and if you try conscientiously to apply what you have learned, you are likely to experience increased happiness and contentment in your family life.

# INDEX

## Other SIGNET Titles of Special Interest to Parents

☐ **PREPARATION FOR CHILDBIRTH, A LAMAZE GUIDE by Donna and Roger Ewy.** Here is the book to instruct prospective parents in the Lamaze techniques for easier childbirth, complete with diagrams and photographs outlining each sequence from labor through delivery. "Excellent . . . provides the necessary tools for a self-controlled, shared childbirth experience."—The Bookmark        (#E6615—$1.75)

☐ **PREGNANCY, BIRTH AND FAMILY PLANNING by Alan F. Guttmacher, M.D.** This great classic has been expanded, updated and revised to include an entirely new section on family planning. The one necessary total guide for expectant parents in the 1970's. "Dr. Alan F. Guttmacher is the Dr. Spock of unborn children."—The New York Times
(#J7097—$1.95)

☐ **YOU AND YOUR BABY: A Guide to Pregnancy, Birth and the First Year by Dr. Frederick W. Rutherford.** A practical handbook for new parents that tells them everything they need to know about pregnancy, preparation for the baby as well as the emotional and physical development of the average infant in his first year.        (#J6974—$1.95)

☐ **PLEASE BREAST FEED YOUR BABY by Alice Gerard.** A fascinating look at the latest scientific findings on the benefits of breast-feeding for both mother and child and a simple, helpful guide to make nursing easy and successful.
(#Y6666—$1.25)

☐ **LIFE BEFORE BIRTH by Ashley Montagu.** Vital information for the mother-to-be to increase her chances of bearing a normal, healthy baby. Introduction by Dr. Alan F. Guttmacher.        (#Y6590—$1.25)

**THE NEW AMERICAN LIBRARY, INC.,**
P.O. Box 999, Bergenfield, New Jersey 07621

Please send me the SIGNET BOOKS I have checked above. I am enclosing $_____(check or money order—no currency or C.O.D.'s). Please include the list price plus 25¢ a copy to cover handling and mailing costs. (Prices and numbers are subject to change without notice.)

Name_____

Address_____

City_____State_____Zip Code_____
Allow at least 3 weeks for delivery

## More SIGNET Books of Interest